Engineering MLOps

Rapidly build, test, and manage production-ready machine learning life cycles at scale

Emmanuel Raj

BIRMINGHAM—MUMBAI

Engineering MLOps

Copyright © 2021 Packt Publishing

Group Product Manager: Kunal Parikh

Publishing Product Manager: Aditi Gour

Senior Editor: Mohammed Yusuf Imaratwale

Content Development Editor: Nazia Shaikh

Technical Editor: Arjun Varma

Copy Editor: Safis Editing

Project Coordinator: Aishwarya Mohan

Proofreader: Safis Editing

Indexer: Priyanka Dhadke

Production Designer: Joshua Misquitta

First published: April 2021

Production reference: 1160421

Published by Packt Publishing Ltd.

Livery Place

35 Livery Street

Birmingham

B3 2PB, UK.

ISBN 978-1-80056-288-2

www.packt.com

Contributors

About the author

Emmanuel Raj is a Finland-based Senior Machine Learning Engineer with 6+ years of industry experience. He is also a Machine Learning Engineer at TietoEvry and a Member of the European AI Alliance at the European Commission. He is passionate about democratizing AI and bringing research and academia to industry. He holds a Master of Engineering degree in Big Data Analytics from Arcada University of Applied Sciences. He has a keen interest in R&D in technologies such as Edge AI, Blockchain, NLP, MLOps, and Robotics. He believes *the best way to learn is to teach*, he is passionate about sharing and learning new technologies with others.

About the reviewers

Magnus Westerlund (DSc) is a principal lecturer in information technology and director of the master's degree programme in big data analytics at Arcada University of Applied Sciences in Helsinki, Finland. He has a background in telecoms and information management and earned his doctoral degree in information systems at Åbo Akademi University, Finland. Magnus has published research in the fields of analytics, IT security, cyber regulation, and distributed ledger technology. His current research topics are smart contract-based distributed security for IoT edge applications and the assessment of intelligent systems. He participates as a technical expert in the Z-inspection® network, which works for a Mindful Use of AI (#MUAI).

Stephen Oladele is the co-founder of AgServer, a peer-to-peer knowledge-sharing platform for smallholder farmers in Africa. He also assists in building data science talents at TheGradientBoost, a staffing and recruiting company. He has consulted as a data scientist for companies and individuals, helping them go from business ideas to execution with notable projects in computer vision, business analytics, and NLP (document analysis), using cloud machine learning services such as those in Google Cloud Platform and Microsoft Azure. In his spare time, he loves volunteering. He runs nonprofit organizations helping underrepresented groups in Africa get into AI and technology. He has volunteered with Google and AWS for projects in the past.

Emerson Bertolo is a data scientist and software developer who has created mission-critical software and dealt with big data applications for more than 12 years. In 2016, Bertolo deep-dived into machine learning and deep learning projects by creating AI models using TensorFlow, PyTorch, MXNet, Keras, and Python libraries to bring those models into reality for tech companies from LawTech to security and defense. By merging Agile concepts into data science, Bertolo has been seeking the best blend between Agile software engineering and machine learning research to build time-to-market AI applications. His approach has been *build to learn, validate results, research and identify uncertainties, rebuild, and learn again*!

Table of Contents

3

Code Meets Data

4

Machine Learning Pipelines

5
Model Evaluation and Packaging

Section 2: Deploying Machine Learning Models at Scale

6
Key Principles for Deploying Your ML System

10
Essentials of Production Release

Section 3: Monitoring Machine Learning Models in Production

11
Key Principles for Monitoring Your ML System

12

Model Serving and Monitoring

13

Governing the ML System for Continual Learning

Other Books You May Enjoy

Index

Preface

MLOps is a systematic approach to building, deploying, and monitoring machine learning (ML) solutions. It is an engineering discipline that can be applied to various industries and use cases. This book presents comprehensive insights into MLOps coupled with real-world examples to help you to write programs, train robust and scalable ML models, and build ML pipelines to train and deploy models securely in production.

You will begin by familiarizing yourself with MLOps workflow and start writing programs to train ML models. You'll then move on to explore options for serializing and packaging ML models post-training to deploy them in production to facilitate machine learning inference. Next, you will learn about monitoring ML models and system performance using an explainable monitoring framework. Finally, you'll apply the knowledge you've gained to build real-world projects.

By the end of this ML book, you'll have a 360-degree view of MLOps and be ready to implement MLOps in your organization.

Who this book is for

This MLOps book is for data scientists, software engineers, DevOps engineers, machine learning engineers, and business and technology leaders who want to build, deploy, and maintain ML systems in production using MLOps principles and techniques. Basic knowledge of machine learning is necessary to get started with this book.

What this book covers

Chapter 1, Fundamentals of MLOps Workflow, gives an overview of the changing software development landscape by highlighting how traditional software development is changing to facilitate machine learning. We will highlight some daily problems within organizations with the traditional approach, showcasing why a change in thinking and implementation is needed. Proceeding that an introduction to the importance of systematic machine learning will be given, followed by some concepts of machine learning and DevOps and fusing them into MLOps. The chapter ends with a proposal for a generic workflow to approach almost any machine learning problem.

Chapter 2, Characterizing Your Machine Learning Problem, offers you a broad perspective on possible types of ML solutions for production. You will learn how to categorize solutions, create a roadmap for developing and deploying a solution, and procure the necessary data, tools, or infrastructure to get started with developing an ML solution taking a systematic approach.

Chapter 3, Code Meets Data, starts the implementation of our hands-on business use case of developing a machine learning solution. We discuss effective methods of source code management for machine learning, data processing for the business use case, and formulate a data governance strategy and pipeline for machine learning training and deployment.

Chapter 4, Machine Learning Pipelines, takes a deep dive into building machine learning pipelines for solutions. We look into key aspects of feature engineering, algorithm selection, hyperparameter optimization, and other aspects of a robust machine learning pipeline.

Chapter 5, Model Evaluation and Packaging, takes a deep dive into options for serializing and packaging machine learning models post-training to deploy them at runtime to facilitate machine learning inference, model interoperability, and end-to-end model traceability. You'll get a broad perspective on the options available and state-of-the-art developments to package and serve machine learning models to production for efficient, robust, and scalable services.

Chapter 6, Key Principles for Deploying Your ML System, introduces the concepts of continuous integration and deployment in production for various settings. You will learn how to choose the right options, tools, and infrastructure to facilitate the deployment of a machine learning solution. You will get insights into machine learning inference options and deployment targets, and get an introduction to CI/CD pipelines for machine learning.

Chapter 7, Building Robust CI and CD Pipelines, covers different CI/CD pipeline components such as triggers, releases, jobs, and so on. It will also equip you with knowledge on curating your own custom CI/CD pipelines for ML solutions. We will build a CI/CD pipeline for an ML solution for a business use case. The pipelines we build will be traceable end to end as they will serve as middleware for model deployment and monitoring.

Chapter 8, APIs and Microservice Management, goes into the principles of API and microservice design for ML inference. A learn by doing approach will be encouraged. We will go through a hands-on implementation of designing and developing an API and microservice for an ML model using tools such as FastAPI and Docker. You will learn key principles, challenges, and tips to designing a robust and scalable microservice and API for test and production environments.

Chapter 9, Testing and Securing Your ML Solution, introduces the core principles of performing tests in the test environment to test the robustness and scalability of the microservice or API we have previously developed. We will perform hands-on load testing for a deployed ML solution. This chapter provides a checklist of tests to be done before taking the microservice to production release.

Chapter 10, Essentials of Production Release, explains how to deploy ML services to production with a robust and scalable approach using the CI/CD pipelines designed earlier. We will focus on deploying, monitoring, and managing the service in production. Key learnings will be deployment in serverless and server environments using tools such as Python, Docker, and Kubernetes.

Chapter 11, Key Principles for Monitoring Your ML System, looks at key principles and aspects of monitoring ML systems in production for robust, secure, and scalable performance. As a key takeaway, readers will get a concrete explainable monitoring framework and checklist to set up and configure a monitoring framework for their ML solution in production.

Chapter 12, Model Serving and Monitoring, explains serving models to users and defining metrics for an ML solution, especially in the aspects of algorithm efficiency, accuracy, and production performance. We will deep dive into hands-on implementation and real-life examples on monitoring data drift, model drift, and application performance.

Chapter 13, Governing the ML System for Continual Learning, reflects on the need for continual learning in machine learning solutions. We will look into what is needed to successfully govern an ML system for business efficacy. Using the Explainable Monitoring framework, we will devise a strategy to govern and we will delve into the hands-on implementation for error handling and configuring alerts and actions. This chapter will equip you with critical skills to automate and govern your MLOps.

To get the most out of this book

You should have access to a Microsoft Azure subscription and basic DevOps-based software used to build CI/CD pipelines. A personal computer or laptop with a Linux or macOS is a plus.

Software/hardware covered in the book	OS requirements
Python	Linux, macOS, or Windows
Git	Linux, macOS, or Windows
Docker	Linux, macOS, or Windows
Kubernetes	Linux, macOS, or Windows
Microsoft Azure	Linux, macOS, or Windows
Azure ML Service	Linux, macOS, or Windows
MLFlow	Linux, macOS, or Windows
Azure DevOps	Linux, macOS, or Windows
Fast API	Linux, macOS, or Windows
Locust.io	Linux, macOS, or Windows

If you are using the digital version of this book, we advise you to type the code yourself or access the code via the GitHub repository (link available in the next section). Doing so will help you avoid any potential errors related to the copying and pasting of code.

Download the example code files

You can download the example code files for this book from GitHub at https://github.com/PacktPublishing/EngineeringMLOps. In case there's an update to the code, it will be updated on the existing GitHub repository. We also have other code bundles from our rich catalog of books and videos available at https://github.com/PacktPublishing/. Check them out!

Download the color images

We also provide a PDF file that has color images of the screenshots/diagrams used in this book. You can download it here: https://static.packt-cdn.com/downloads/9781800562882_ColorImages.pdf.

Conventions used

There are a number of text conventions used throughout this book.

Code in text: Indicates code words in text, database table names, folder names, filenames, file extensions, pathnames, dummy URLs, user input, and Twitter handles. Here is an example: "The preprocessed dataset is imported using the .get_by_name() function."

A block of code is set as follows:

```
uri = workspace.get_mlflow_tracking_uri( )
mlflow.set_tracking_uri(uri)
```

When we wish to draw your attention to a particular part of a code block, the relevant lines or items are set in bold:

```
# Importing pre-processed dataset
dataset = Dataset.get_by_name (workspace, name='processed_
weather_data_portofTurku')
```

Any command-line input or output is written as follows:

```
python3 test_inference.py
```

Bold: Indicates a new term, an important word, or words that you see onscreen. For example, words in menus or dialog boxes appear in the text like this. Here is an example: "Go to the **Compute** option and click the **Create** button to explore compute options available on the cloud."

> **Tips or important notes**
> Appear like this.

Get in touch

Feedback from our readers is always welcome.

General feedback: If you have questions about any aspect of this book, mention the book title in the subject of your message and email us at customercare@packtpub.com.

Errata: Although we have taken every care to ensure the accuracy of our content, mistakes do happen. If you have found a mistake in this book, we would be grateful if you would report this to us. Please visit www.packtpub.com/support/errata, selecting your book, clicking on the Errata Submission Form link, and entering the details.

Piracy: If you come across any illegal copies of our works in any form on the Internet, we would be grateful if you would provide us with the location address or website name. Please contact us at copyright@packt.com with a link to the material.

If you are interested in becoming an author: If there is a topic that you have expertise in and you are interested in either writing or contributing to a book, please visit authors.packtpub.com.

Reviews

Please leave a review. Once you have read and used this book, why not leave a review on the site that you purchased it from? Potential readers can then see and use your unbiased opinion to make purchase decisions, we at Packt can understand what you think about our products, and our authors can see your feedback on their book. Thank you!

For more information about Packt, please visit packt.com.

Section 1: Framework for Building Machine Learning Models

This part will equip readers with the foundation of MLOps and workflows to characterize their ML problems to provide a clear roadmap for building robust and scalable ML pipelines. This will be done in a learn-by-doing approach via practical implementation using proposed methods and tools (Azure Machine Learning services or MLflow).

This section comprises the following chapters:

- *Chapter 1, Fundamentals of MLOps WorkFlow*
- *Chapter 2, Characterizing Your Machine Learning Problem*
- *Chapter 3, Code Meets Data*
- *Chapter 4, Machine Learning Pipelines*
- *Chapter 5, Model Evaluation and Packaging*

1
Fundamentals of an MLOps Workflow

Machine learning (**ML**) is maturing from research to applied business solutions. However, the grim reality is that only 2% of companies using ML have successfully deployed a model in production to enhance their business processes, reported by DeepLearning.AI (`https://info.deeplearning.ai/the-batch-companies-slipping-on-ai-goals-self-training-for-better-vision-muppets-and-models-china-vs-us-only-the-best-examples-proliferating-patents`). What makes it so hard? And what do we need to do to improve the situation?

To get a solid understanding of this problem and its solution, in this chapter, we will delve into the evolution and intersection of software development and ML. We'll begin by reflecting on some of the trends in traditional software development, starting from the waterfall model to agile to DevOps practices, and how these are evolving to industrialize ML-centric applications. You will be introduced to a systematic approach to operationalizing AI using **Machine Learning Operations** (**MLOps**). By the end of this chapter, you will have a solid understanding of MLOps and you will be equipped to implement a generic MLOps workflow that can be used to build, deploy, and monitor a wide range of ML applications.

In this chapter, we're going to cover the following main topics:

- The evolution of infrastructure and software development
- Traditional software development challenges
- Trends of ML adoption in software development
- Understanding MLOps
- Concepts and workflow of MLOps

The evolution of infrastructure and software development

With the genesis of the modern internet age (around 1995), we witnessed a rise in software applications, ranging from operating systems such as Windows 95 to the Linux operating system and websites such as Google and Amazon, which have been serving the world (online) for over two decades. This has resulted in a culture of continuously improving services by collecting, storing, and processing a massive amount of data from user interactions. Such developments have been shaping the evolution of IT infrastructure and software development.

Transformation in IT infrastructure has picked up pace since the start of this millennium. Since then, businesses have increasingly adopted cloud computing as it opens up new possibilities for businesses to outsource IT infrastructure maintenance while provisioning necessary IT resources such as storage and computation resources and services required to run and scale their operations.

Cloud computing offers on-demand provisioning and the availability of IT resources such as data storage and computing resources without the need for active management by the user of the IT resources. For example, businesses provisioning computation and storage resources do not have to manage these resources directly and are not responsible for keeping them running – the maintenance is outsourced to the cloud service provider.

Businesses using cloud computing can reap benefits as there's no need to buy and maintain IT resources; it enables them to have less in-house expertise for IT resource maintenance and this allows businesses to optimize costs and resources. Cloud computing enables scaling on demand and users pay as per the usage of resources. As a result, we have seen companies adopting cloud computing as part of their businesses and IT infrastructures.

Cloud computing became popular in the industry from 2006 onward when Sun Microsystems launched Sun Grid in March 2006. It is a hardware and data resource sharing service. This service was acquired by Oracle and was later named Sun Cloud. Parallelly, in the same year (2006), another cloud computing service was launched by Amazon called Elastic Compute Cloud. This enabled new possibilities for businesses to provision computation, storage, and scaling capabilities on demand. Since then, the transformation across industries has been organic toward adopting cloud computing.

In the last decade, many companies on a global and regional scale have catalyzed the cloud transformation, with companies such as Google, IBM, Microsoft, UpCloud, Alibaba, and others heavily investing in the research and development of cloud services. As a result, a shift from localized computing (companies having their own servers and data centers) to on-demand computing has taken place due to the availability of robust and scalable cloud services. Now businesses and organizations are able to provision resources on-demand on the cloud to satisfy their data processing needs.

With these developments, we have witnessed **Moore's law** in operation, which states that the number of transistors on a microchip doubles every 2 years – though the cost of computers has halved, this has been true so far. Subsequently, some trends are developing as follows.

The rise of machine learning and deep learning

Over the last decade, we have witnessed the adoption of ML in everyday life applications. Not only for esoteric applications such as **Dota** or **AlphaGo**, but ML has also made its way to pretty standard applications such as machine translation, image processing, and voice recognition.

This adoption is powered by developments in infrastructure, especially in terms of the utilization of computation power. It has unlocked the potential of deep learning and ML.. We can observe deep learning breakthroughs correlated with computation developments in *Figure 1.1* (sourced from OpenAI: `https://openai.com/blog/ai-and-compute`):

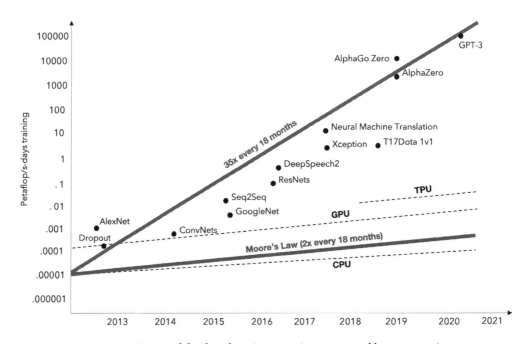

Figure 1.1 – Demand for deep learning over time supported by computation

These breakthroughs in deep learning are enabled by the exponential growth in computing, which increases around 35 times every 18 months. Looking ahead in time, with such demands we may hit roadblocks in terms of scaling up central computing for CPUs, GPUs, or TPUs. This has forced us to look at alternatives such as **distributed learning** where computation for data processing is distributed across multiple computation nodes. We have seen some breakthroughs in distributed learning, such as federated learning and edge computing approaches. Distributed learning has shown promise to serve the growing demands of deep learning.

The end of Moore's law

Prior to 2012, AI results closely tracked Moore's law, with compute doubling every 2 years. Post-2012, compute has been doubling every 3.4 months (sourced from AI Index 2019 – https://hai.stanford.edu/research/ai-index-2019). We can observe from *Figure 1.1* that demand for deep learning and **high-performance computing** (**HPC**) has been increasing exponentially with around 35x growth in computing every 18 months whereas Moore's law is seen to be outpaced (2x every 18 months). Moore's law is still applicable to the case of CPUs (single-core performance) but not to new hardware architectures such as GPUs and TPUs. This makes Moore's law obsolete and outpaced in contrast to current demands and trends.

AI-centric applications

Applications are becoming AI-centric – we see that across multiple industries. Virtually every application is starting to use AI, and these applications are running separately on distributed workloads such as **HPC**, **microservices**, and **big data**, as shown in *Figure 1.2*:

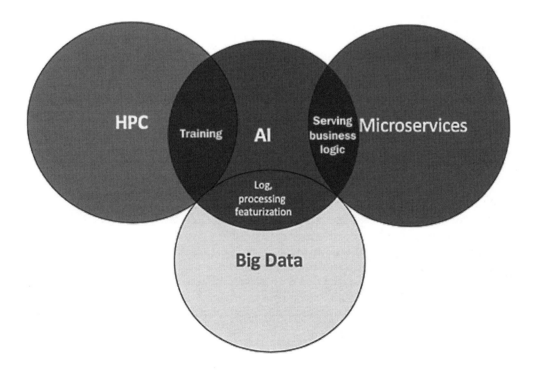

Figure 1.2 – Applications running on distributed workloads

By combining HPC and AI, we can enable the benefits of computation needed to train deep learning and ML models. With the overlapping of big data and AI, we can leverage extracting required data at scale for AI model training, and with the overlap of microservices and AI we can serve the AI models for inference to enhance business operations and impact. This way, distributed applications have become the new norm. Developing AI-centric applications at scale requires a synergy of distributed applications (HPC, microservices, and big data) and for this, a new way of developing software is required.

Software development evolution

Software development has evolved hand in hand with infrastructural developments to facilitate the efficient development of applications using the infrastructure. Traditionally, software development started with the waterfall method of development where development is done linearly by gathering requirements to design and develop. The waterfall model has many limitations, which led to the evolution of software development over the years in the form of Agile methodologies and the DevOps method, as shown in *Figure 1.3*:

Figure 1.3 – Software development evolution

The waterfall method

The **waterfall method** was used to develop software from the onset of the internet age (~1995). It is a non-iterative way of developing software. It is delivered in a unidirectional way. Every stage is pre-organized and executed one after another, starting from requirements gathering to software design, development, and testing. The waterfall method is feasible and suitable when requirements are well-defined, specific, and do not change over time. Hence this is not suitable for dynamic projects where requirements change and evolve as per user demands. In such cases, where there is continuous modification, the waterfall method cannot be used to develop software. These are the major disadvantages of waterfall development methods:

- The entire set of requirements has to be given before starting the development; modifying them during or after the project development is not possible.

- There are fewer chances to create or implement reusable components.

- Testing can only be done after the development is finished. Testing is not intended to be iterable; it is not possible to go back and fix anything once it is done. Moreover, customer acceptance tests often introduced changes, resulting in a delay in delivery and high costs. This way of development and testing can have a negative impact on the project delivery timeline and costs.

- Most of the time, users of the system are provisioned with a system based on the developer's understanding, which is not user-centric and can come short of meeting their needs.

The Agile method

The **Agile method** facilitates an iterative and progressive approach to software development. Unlike the waterfall method, Agile approaches are precise and user-centric. The method is bidirectional and often involves end users or customers in the development and testing process so they have the opportunity to test, give feedback, and suggest improvements throughout the project development process and phases. Agile has several advantages over the waterfall method:

- Requirements are defined before starting the development, but they can be modified at any time.

- It is possible to create or implement reusable components.

- The solution or project can be modular by segregating the project into different modules that are delivered periodically.

- The users or customers can co-create by testing and evaluating developed solution modules periodically to ensure the business needs are satisfied. Such a user-centric process ensures quality outcomes focused on meeting customer and business needs.

The following diagram shows the difference between **Waterfall** and **Agile** methodologies:

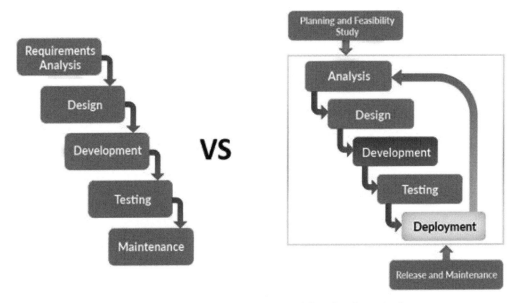

Figure 1.4 – Difference between waterfall and agile methods

The DevOps method

The **DevOps method** extends agile development practices by further streamlining the movement of software change through the *build*, *test*, *deploy*, and *delivery* stages. DevOps empowers cross-functional teams with the autonomy to execute their software applications driven by continuous integration, continuous deployment, and continuous delivery. It encourages collaboration, integration, and automation among software developers and IT operators to improve the efficiency, speed, and quality of delivering customer-centric software. DevOps provides a streamlined software development framework for designing, testing, deploying, and monitoring systems in production. DevOps has made it possible to ship software to production in minutes and to keep it running reliably.

Traditional software development challenges

In the previous section, we observed the shift in traditional software development from the waterfall model to agile and DevOps practices. Agile and DevOps practices have enabled companies to ship software reliably. DevOps has made it possible to ship software to production in minutes and to keep it running reliably. This approach has been so successful that many companies are already adopting it, so why can't we keep doing the same thing for ML applications?

The leading cause is that there's a fundamental difference between ML development and traditional software development: *Machine learning is not just code; it is code plus data*. A ML model is created by applying an algorithm (via code) to fit the data to result in a ML model, as shown in *Figure 1.5*:

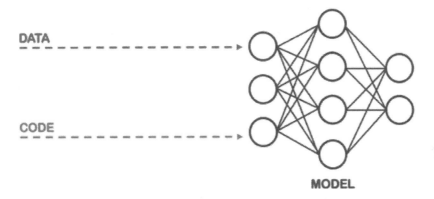

Figure 1.5 – Machine learning = data + code

While code is meticulously crafted in the development environment, data comes from multiple sources for training, testing, and inference. It is robust and changing over time in terms of volume, velocity, veracity, and variety. To keep up with evolving data, code evolves over time. For perspective, their relationship can be observed as if code and data live in separate planes that share the time dimension but are independent in all other aspects. The challenge of an ML development process is to create a bridge between these two planes in a controlled way:

Figure 1.6 – Data and code progression over time

Data and code, with the progression of time, end up going in two directions with one objective of building and maintaining a robust and scalable ML system. This disconnect causes several challenges that need to be solved by anyone trying to put a ML model in production. It comes with challenges such as slow, brittle, fragmented, and inconsistent deployment, and a lack of reproducibility and traceability.

To overcome these challenges, MLOps offers a systematic approach by bridging data and code together over the progression of time. This is the solution to challenges posed by traditional software development methods with regard to ML applications. Using the MLOps method, data and code progress over time in one direction with one objective of building and maintaining a robust and scalable ML system:

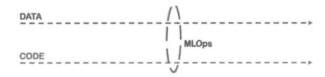

Figure 1.7 – MLOps – data and code progressing together

MLOps facilitates ML model development, deployment, and monitoring in a streamlined and systematic approach. It empowers data science and IT teams to collaborate, validate, and govern their operations. All the operations executed by the teams are recorded or audited, end-to-end traceable, and repeatable. In the coming sections, we will learn how MLOps enables data science and IT teams to build and maintain robust and scalable ML systems.

Trends of ML adoption in software development

Before we delve into the workings of the MLOps method and workflow, it is beneficial to understand the big picture and trends as to where and how MLOps is disrupting the world. As many applications are becoming AI-centric, software development is evolving to facilitate ML. ML will increasingly become part of software development, mainly due to the following reasons:

- **Investments**: In 2019, investments in global private AI clocked over $70 billion, with start-up investments related to AI over $37 billion, M&A $34 billion, IPOs $5 billion, and minority stake valued at around $2 billion. The forecast for AI globally shows fast growth in market value as AI reached $9.5 billion in 2018 and is anticipated to reach a market value of $118 billion by 2025. It has been assessed that growth in economic activity resulting from AI until 2030 will be of high value and significance. Currently, the US attracts ~50% of global VC funding, China ~39%, and 11% goes to Europe.

- **Big data**: Data is exponentially growing in volume, velocity, veracity, and variety. For instance, observations suggest data growing in volume at 61% per annum in Europe, and it is anticipated that four times more data will be created by 2025 than exists today. Data is a requisite raw material for developing AI.

- **Infrastructural developments and adoption**: Moore's law has been closely tracked and observed to have been realized prior to 2012. Post-2012, compute has been doubling every 3.4 months.

- **Increasing research and development**: AI research has been prospering in quality and quantity. A prominent growth of 300% is observed in the volume of peer-reviewed AI papers from 1998 to 2018, summing up to 9% of published conference papers and 3% of peer-reviewed journal publications.

- **Industry**: Based on a surveyed report, 47% of large companies have reported having adopted AI in at least one function or business unit. In 2019, it went up to 58% and is expected to increase.

Information

These points have been sourced from policy and investment recommendations for trustworthy AI – European commission (`https://ec.europa.eu/digital-single-market/en/news/policy-and-investment-recommendations-trustworthy-artificial-intelligence`) and AI Index 2019 (`https://hai.stanford.edu/research/ai-index-2019`).

All these developments indicate a strong push toward the industrialization of AI, and this is possible by bridging industry and research. MLOps will play a key role in the industrialization of AI. If you invest in learning this method, it will give you a headstart in your company or team and you could be a catalyst for operationalizing ML and industrializing AI.

So far, we have learned about some challenges and developments in IT, software development, and AI. Next, we will delve into understanding MLOps conceptually and learn in detail about a generic MLOps workflow that can be used commonly for any use case. These fundamentals will help you get a firm grasp of MLOps.

Understanding MLOps

Software development is interdisciplinary and is evolving to facilitate ML. MLOps is an emerging method to fuse ML with software development by integrating multiple domains as MLOps combines ML, DevOps, and data engineering, which aims to build, deploy, and maintain ML systems in production reliably and efficiently. Thus, MLOps can be expounded by this intersection.

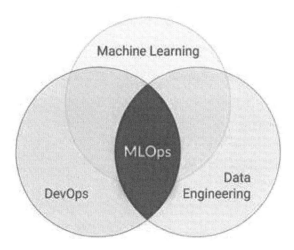

Figure 1.8 – MLOps intersection

To make this intersection (MLOps) operational, I have designed a modular framework by following the systematic *design science method proposed by Wieringa* (`https://doi.org/10.1007/978-3-662-43839-8`) to develop a workflow to bring these three together (Data Engineering, Machine Learning, and *DevOps*). Design science goes with the application of design to problems and context. Design science is the design and investigation of artifacts in a context. The artifact in this case is the MLOps workflow, which is designed iteratively by interacting with problem contexts (industry use cases for the application of AI):

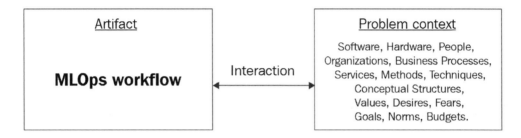

Figure 1.9 – Design science workflow

In a structured and iterative approach, the implementation of two cycles (the design cycle and the empirical cycle) was done for qualitative and quantitative analysis for MLOps workflow design through iterations. As a result of these cycles, an MLOps workflow is developed and validated by applying it to multiple problem contexts, that is, tens of ML use cases (for example, anomaly detection, real-time trading, predictive maintenance, recommender systems, virtual assistants, and so on) across multiple industries (for example, finance, manufacturing, healthcare, retail, the automotive industry, energy, and so on). I have applied and validated this MLOps workflow successfully in various projects across multiple industries to operationalize ML. In the next section, we will go through the concepts of the MLOps workflow designed as a result of the design science process.

Concepts and workflow of MLOps

In this section, we will learn about a generic MLOps workflow; it is the result of many design cycle iterations as discussed in the previous section. It brings together data engineering, ML, and DevOps in a streamlined fashion. *Figure 1.10* is a generic MLOps workflow; it is modular and flexible and can be used to build proofs of concept or to operationalize ML solutions in any business or industry:

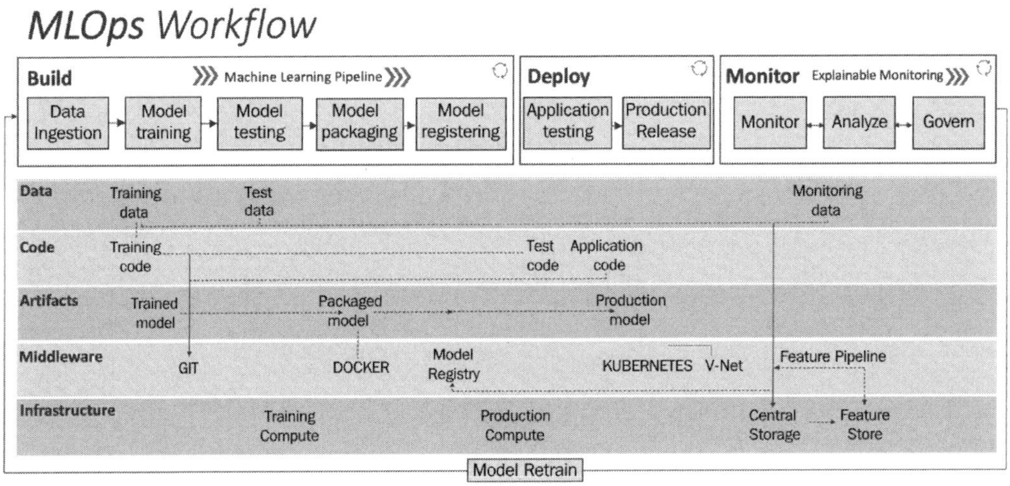

Figure 1.10 – MLOps workflow

This workflow is segmented into two modules:

- **MLOps pipeline** (build, deploy, and monitor) – the upper layer
- **Drivers**: Data, code, artifacts, middleware, and infrastructure – mid and lower layers

The upper layer is the MLOps pipeline (build, deploy, and monitor), which is enabled by drivers such as data, code, artifacts, middleware, and infrastructure. The MLOps pipeline is powered by an array of services, drivers, middleware, and infrastructure, and it crafts ML-driven solutions. By using this pipeline, a business or individual(s) can do quick prototyping, testing, and validating and deploy the model(s) to production at scale frugally and efficiently.

To understand the workings and implementation of the MLOps workflow, we will look at the implementation of each layer and step using a figurative business use case.

Discussing a use case

In this use case, we are to operationalize (prototyping and deploying for production) an image classification service to classify cats and dogs in a pet park in Barcelona, Spain. The service will identify cats and dogs in real time from the inference data coming from a CCTV camera installed in the pet park.

The pet park provide you access to the data and infrastructure needed to operationalize the service:

- **Data**: The pet park has given you access to their data lake containing 100,000 labeled images of cats and dogs, which we will use for training the model.

- **Infrastructure**: Public cloud (IaaS).

This use case resembles a real-life use case for operationalizing ML and is used to explain the workings and implementation of the MLOps workflow. Remember to look for an explanation for the implementation of this use case at every segment and step of the MLOps workflow. Now, let's look at the workings of every layer and step in detail.

The MLOps pipeline

The MLOps pipeline is the upper layer, which performs operations such as build, deploy, and monitor, which work modularly in sync with each other. Let's look into each module's functionality.

Build

The build module has the core ML pipeline, and this is purely for training, packaging, and versioning the ML models. It is powered by the required compute (for example, the CPU or GPU on the cloud or distributed computing) resources to run the ML training and pipeline:

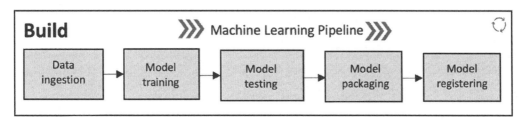

Figure 1.11 – MLOps – build pipeline

The pipeline works from left to right. Let's look at the functionality of each step in detail:

- **Data ingestion**: This step is a trigger step for the ML pipeline. It deals with the volume, velocity, veracity, and variety of data by extracting data from various data sources (for example, databases, data warehouses, or data lakes) and ingesting the required data for the model training step. Robust data pipelines connected to multiple data sources enable it to perform **extract, transform, and load** (**ETL**) operations to provide the necessary data for ML training purposes. In this step, we can split and version data for model training in the required format (for example, the training or test set). As a result of this step, any experiment (that is, model training) can be audited and is back-traceable.

For a better understanding of the data ingestion step, here is the previously described use case implementation:

Use case implementation

As you have access to the pet park's data lake, you can now procure data to get started. Using data pipelines (part of the data ingestion step), you do the following:

1. Extract, transform, and load 100,000 images of cats and dogs.

2. Split and version this data into a train and test split (with an 80% and 20% split).

Versioning this data will enable end-to-end traceability for trained models.

Congrats – now you are ready to start training and testing the ML model using this data.

- **Model training**: After procuring the required data for ML model training in the previous step, this step will enable model training; it has modular scripts or code that perform all the traditional steps in ML, such as data preprocessing, feature engineering, and feature scaling before training or retraining any model. Following this, the ML model is trained while performing hyperparameter tuning to fit the model to the dataset (training set). This step can be done manually, but efficient and automatic solutions such as **Grid Search** or **Random Search** exist. As a result, all important steps of ML model training are executed with a ML model as the output of this step.

Use case implementation

In this step, we implement all the important steps to train the image classification model. The goal is to train a ML model to classify cats and dogs. For this case, we train a **convolutional neural network** (**CNN** – https:// towardsdatascience.com/wtf-is-image-classification-8e78a8235acb) for the image classification service. The following steps are implemented: data preprocessing, feature engineering, and feature scaling before training, followed by training the model with hyperparameter tuning. As a result, we have a CNN model to classify cats and dogs with 97% accuracy.

- **Model testing**: In this step, we evaluate the trained model performance on a separated set of data points named test data (which was split and versioned in the data ingestion step). The inference of the trained model is evaluated according to selected metrics as per the use case. The output of this step is a report on the trained model's performance.

Use case implementation

We test the trained model on test data (we split data earlier in the *Data ingestion* step) to evaluate the trained model's performance. In this case, we look for precision and the recall score to validate the model's performance in classifying cats and dogs to assess false positives and true positives to get a realistic understanding of the model's performance. If and when we are satisfied with the results, we can proceed to the next step, or else reiterate the previous steps to get a decent performing model for the pet park image classification service.

- **Model packaging**: After the trained model has been tested in the previous step, the model can be serialized into a file or containerized (using Docker) to be exported to the production environment.

Use case implementation

The model we trained and tested in the previous steps is serialized to an ONNX file and is ready to be deployed in the production environment.

- **Model registering**: In this step, the model that was serialized or containerized in the previous step is registered and stored in the model registry. A registered model is a logical collection or package of one or more files that assemble, represent, and execute your ML model. For example, multiple files can be registered as one model. For instance, a classification model can be comprised of a vectorizer, model weights, and serialized model files. All these files can be registered as one single model. After registering, the model (all files or a single file) can be downloaded and deployed as needed.

Use case implementation

The serialized model in the previous step is registered on the model registry and is available for quick deployment into the pet park production environment.

By implementing the preceding steps, we successfully execute the ML pipeline designed for our use case. As a result, we have trained models on the model registry ready to be deployed in the production setup. Next, we will look into the workings of the deployment pipeline.

Deploy

The deploy module enables operationalizing the ML models we developed in the previous module (build). In this module, we test our model performance and behavior in a production or production-like (test) environment to ensure the robustness and scalability of the ML model for production use. *Figure 1.12* depicts the deploy pipeline, which has two components – production testing and production release – and the deployment pipeline is enabled by streamlined CI/CD pipelines connecting the development to production environments:

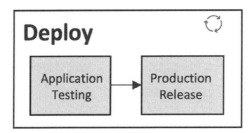

Figure 1.12 – MLOps – deploy pipeline

It works from left to right. Let's look at the functionality of each step in detail:

- **Application testing**: Before deploying an ML model to production, it is vital to test its robustness and performance via testing. Hence we have the "application testing" phase where we rigorously test all the trained models for robustness and performance in a production-like environment called a test environment. In the application testing phase, we deploy the models in the test environment (pre-production), which replicates the production environment.

  The ML model for testing is deployed as an API or streaming service in the test environment to deployment targets such as Kubernetes clusters, container instances, or scalable virtual machines or edge devices as per the need and use case. After the model is deployed for testing, we perform predictions using test data (which is not used for training the model; test data is sample data from a production environment) for the deployed model, during which model inference in batch or periodically is done to test the model deployed in the test environment for robustness and performance.

  The performance results are automatically or manually reviewed by a quality assurance expert. When the ML model's performance meets the standards, then it is approved to be deployed in the production environment where the model will be used to infer in batches or real time to make business decisions.

Use case implementation

We deploy the model as an API service on an on-premises computer in the pet park, which is set up for testing purposes. This computer is connected to a CCTV camera in the park to fetch real-time inference data to predict cats or dogs in the video frames. The model deployment is enabled by the CI/CD pipeline. In this step, we test the robustness of the model in a production-like environment, that is, whether the model is performing inference consistently, and an accuracy, fairness, and error analysis. At the end of this step, a quality assurance expert certifies the model if it meets the standards.

- **Production release**: Previously tested and approved models are deployed in the production environment for model inference to generate business or operational value. This production release is deployed to the production environment enabled by CI/CD pipelines.

Use case implementation

We deploy a previously tested and approved model (by a quality assurance expert) as an API service on a computer connected to CCTV in the pet park (production setup). This deployed model performs ML inference on the incoming video data from the CCTV camera in the pet park to classify cats or dogs in real time.

Monitor

The monitor module works in sync with the deploy module. Using explainable monitoring (discussed later in detail, in *Chapter 11, Key Principles for Monitoring Your ML System*), we can monitor, analyze, and govern the deployed ML application (ML model and application). Firstly, we can monitor the performance of the ML model (using pre-defined metrics) and the deployed application (using telemetry data). Secondly, model performance can be analyzed using a pre-defined explainability framework, and lastly, the ML application can be governed using alerts and actions based on the model's quality assurance and control. This ensures a robust monitoring mechanism for the production system:

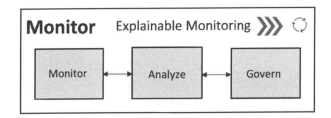

Figure 1.13 – MLOps – monitor pipeline

Let's see each of the abilities of the monitor module in detail:

- **Monitor**: The monitoring module captures critical information to monitor data integrity, model drift, and application performance. Application performance can be monitored using telemetry data. It depicts the device performance of a production system over a period of time. With telemetry data such as accelerometer, gyroscope, humidity, magnetometer, pressure, and temperature we can keep a check on the production system's performance, health, and longevity.

Use case implementation

In real time, we will monitor three things – data integrity, model drift, and application performance – for the deployed API service on the park's computer. Metrics such as accuracy, F1 score, precision, and recall are tracked to data integrity and model drift. We monitor application performance by tracking the telemetry data of the production system (the on-premises computer in the park) running the deployed ML model to ensure the proper functioning of the production system. Telemetry data is monitored to foresee any anomalies or potential failures and fix them in advance. Telemetry data is logged and can be used to assess production system performance over time to check its health and longevity.

- **Analyze**: It is critical to analyze the model performance of ML models deployed in production systems to ensure optimal performance and governance in correlation to business decisions or impact. We use model explainability techniques to measure the model performance in real time. Using this, we evaluate important aspects such as model fairness, trust, bias, transparency, and error analysis with the intention of improving the model in correlation to business.

Over time, the statistical properties of the target variable we are trying to predict can change in unforeseen ways. This change is called "model drift," for example, in a case where we have deployed a recommender system model to suggest suitable items for users. User behavior may change due to unforeseeable trends that could not be observed in historical data that was used for training the model. It is essential to consider such unforeseen factors to ensure deployed models provide the best and most relevant business value. When model drift is observed, then any of these actions should be performed:

a) The product owner or the quality assurance expert needs to be alerted.

b) The model needs to be switched or updated.

c) Re-training the pipeline should be triggered to re-train and update the model as per the latest data or needs.

Use case implementation

We monitor the deployed model's performance in the production system (a computer connected to the CCTV in the pet park). We will analyze the accuracy, precision, and recall scores for the model periodically (once a day) to ensure the model's performance does not deteriorate below the threshold. When the model performance deteriorates below the threshold, we initiate system governing mechanisms (for example, a trigger to retrain the model).

- **Govern**: Monitoring and analyzing is done to govern the deployed application to drive optimal performance for the business (or the purpose of the ML system). After monitoring and analyzing the production data, we can generate certain alerts and actions to govern the system. For example, the product owner or the quality assurance expert gets alerted when model performance deteriorates (for example, low accuracy, high bias, and so on) below a pre-defined threshold. The product owner initiates a trigger to retrain and deploy an alternative model. Lastly, an important aspect of governance is "compliance" with the local and global laws and rules. For compliance, model explainability and transparency are vital. For this, model auditing and reporting are done to provide end-to-end traceability and explainability for production models.

Use case implementation

We monitor and analyze the deployed model's performance in the production system (a computer connected to the CCTV in the pet park). Based on the analysis of accuracy, precision, and recall scores for the deployed model, periodically (once a day), alerts are generated when the model's performance deteriorates below the pre-defined threshold. The product owner of the park generates actions, and these actions are based on the alerts. For example, an alert is generated notifying the product owner that the production model is 30% biased to detect dogs more than cats. The product owner then triggers the model re-training pipeline to update the model using the latest data to reduce the bias, resulting in a fair and robust model in production. This way, the ML system at the pet park in Barcelona is well-governed to serve the business needs.

This brings us to the end of the MLOps pipeline. All models trained, deployed, and monitored using the MLOps method are end-to-end traceable and their lineage is logged in order to trace the origins of the model, which includes the source code the model used to train, the data used to train and test the model, and parameters used to converge the model. Full lineage is useful to audit operations or to replicate the model, or when a blocker is hit, the logged ML model lineage is useful to backtrack the origins of the model or to observe and debug the cause of the blocker. As ML models generate data in production during inference, this data can be tied to the model training and deployment lineage to ensure the end-to-end lineage, and this is important for certain compliance requirements. Next, we will look into key drivers enabling the MLOps pipeline.

Drivers

These are the key drivers for the MLOps pipeline: data, code, artifacts, middleware, and infrastructure. Let's look into each of the drivers to get an overview of how they enable the MLOps pipeline:

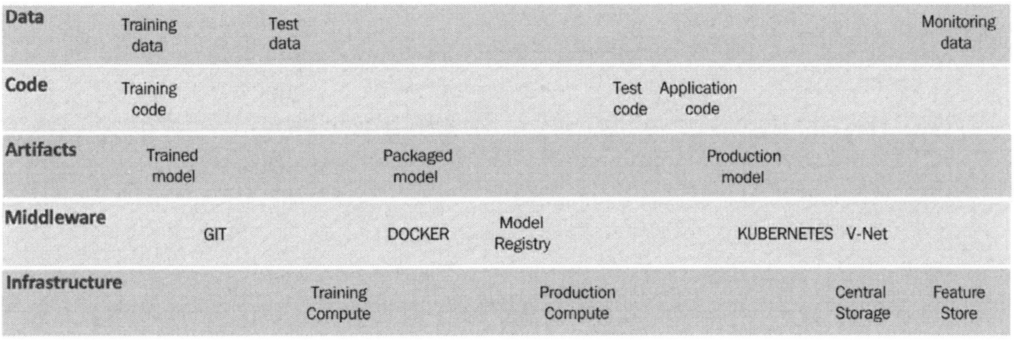

Data	Training data	Test data					Monitoring data
Code	Training code			Test code	Application code		
Artifacts	Trained model		Packaged model		Production model		
Middleware	GIT		DOCKER	Model Registry		KUBERNETES V-Net	
Infrastructure		Training Compute		Production Compute		Central Storage	Feature Store

Figure 1.14 – MLOps drivers

Each of the key drivers for the MLOps pipeline are defined as follows:

- **Data**: Data can be in multiple forms, such as text, audio, video, and images. In traditional software applications, data quite often tends to be structured, whereas, for ML applications, it can be structured or unstructured. To manage data in ML applications, data is handled in these steps: data acquisition, data annotation, data cataloging, data preparation, data quality checking, data sampling, and data augmentation. Each step involves its own life cycle. This makes a whole new set of processes and tools necessary for ML applications. For efficient functioning of the ML pipeline, data is segmented and versioned into training data, testing data, and monitoring data (collected in production, for example, model inputs, outputs, and telemetry data). These data operations are part of the MLOps pipeline.

- **Code**: There are three essential modules of code that drive the MLOps pipeline: training code, testing code, and application code. These scripts or code are executed using the CI/CD and data pipelines to ensure the robust working of the MLOps pipeline. The source code management system (for example, using Git or Mercurial) will enable orchestration and play a vital role in managing and integrating seamlessly with CI, CD, and data pipelines. All of the code is staged and versioned in the source code management setup (for example, Git).

- **Artifacts**: The MLOps pipeline generates artifacts such as data, serialized models, code snippets, system logs, ML model training, and testing metrics information. All these artifacts are useful for the successful working of the MLOps pipeline, ensuring its traceability and sustainability. These artifacts are managed using middleware services such as the model registry, workspaces, logging services, source code management services, databases, and so on.

- **Middleware**: Middleware is computer software that offers services to software applications that are more than those available from the operating systems. Middleware services ensure multiple applications to automate and orchestrate processes for the MLOps pipeline. We can use a diverse set of middleware software and services depending on the use cases, for example, Git for source code management, VNets to enable the required network configurations, Docker for containerizing our models, and Kubernetes for container orchestration to automate application deployment, scaling, and management.

- **Infrastructure**: To ensure the successful working of the MLOps pipeline, we need essential compute and storage resources to train Test and deploy the ML models. Compute resources enable us to train, deploy and monitor our ML models. Two types of storages resources can facilitate ML operations, central storage and feature stores. A central storage stores the logs, artifacts, training, testing and monitoring data. A feature store is optional and complementary to central storage. It extracts, transforms and stores needed features for ML model training and inference using a feature pipeline. When it comes to the infrastructure, there are various options such as on-premises resources or **infrastructure as a service (IaaS)**, which is cloud services. These days, there are many cloud players providing IaaS, such as Amazon, Microsoft, Google, Alibaba, and so on. Having the right infrastructure for your use case will enable robust, efficient, and frugal operations for your team and company.

A fully automated workflow is achievable with smart optimization and synergy of all these drivers with the MLOps pipeline. Some direct advantages of implementing an automated MLOps workflow is a spike in IT teams' efficiency (by reducing the time spent by data scientists and developers on mundane and repeatable tasks) and the optimization of resources, resulting in cost reductions, and both of these are great for any business.

Summary

In this chapter, we have learned about the evolution of software development and infrastructure to facilitate ML. We delved into the concepts of MLOps, followed by getting acquainted with a generic MLOps workflow that can be implemented in a wide range of ML solutions across multiple industries.

In the next chapter, you will learn how to characterize any ML problem into an MLOps-driven solution and start developing it using an MLOps workflow.

2
Characterizing Your Machine Learning Problem

In this chapter, you will get a fundamental understanding of the various types of **Machine Learning (ML)** solutions that can be built for production, and will learn to categorize the relevant operations in line with the business and technological needs of your organization. You will learn how to curate an implementation roadmap for operationalizing ML solutions, followed by procuring the necessary tools and infrastructure for any given problem. By the end of this chapter, you will have a solid understanding of how to architect robust and scalable ML solutions and procure the required data and tools for implementing these solutions.

ML Operations (MLOps) aims to bridge academia and industry using state-of-the-art engineering principles, and we will explore different elements from both industry and academia to get a holistic understanding and awareness of the possibilities. Before beginning to craft your MLOps solution, it is important to understand the various possibilities, setups, problems, solutions, and methodologies on offer for solving business-oriented problems. To achieve this understanding, we're going to cover the following main topics in this chapter:

- The ML solution development process
- Types of ML models

- Characterizing your MLOps
- An implementation roadmap for your solution
- Procuring the necessary data, tools, and infrastructure
- Introduction to a real-life business problem

Without further ado, let's jump in and explore the possibilities ML can enable by taking an in-depth look into the ML solution development process and examining different types of ML models to solve business problems.

The ML solution development process

ML offers many possibilities to augment and automate business. To get the best from ML, teams and people engaged in ML-driven business transformation need to understand both ML and the business itself. Efficient business transformation begins with having a rough understanding of the business, including aspects such as value-chain analysis, use-case identification, data mapping, and business simulations to validate the business transformation. *Figure 2.1* presents a process to develop ML solutions to augment or automate business operations:

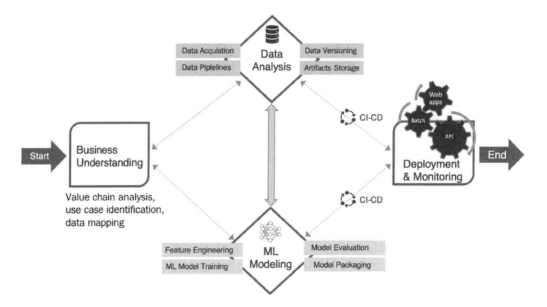

Figure 2.1 – ML solution development process

Business understanding is the genesis of developing an ML solution. After having a decent business understanding, we proceed to data analysis, where the right data is acquired, versioned, and stored. Data is consumed for ML modeling using data pipelines where feature engineering is done to get the right features to train the model. We evaluate the trained models and package them for deployment. Deployment and monitoring are done using a pipeline taking advantage of **Continuous Integration/Continuous Deployment (CI/CD)** features that enable real-time and continuous deployment to serve trained ML models to the users. This process ensures robust and scalable ML solutions.

Types of ML models

As there is a selection of ML and deep learning models that address the same business problem, it is essential to understand the landscape of ML models in order to make an efficient algorithm selection. There are around 15 types of ML techniques, these being categorized into 4 categories, namely **learning models**, **hybrid models**, **statistical models**, and **Human-In-The-Loop (HITL)** models, as shown in the following matrix (where each grid square reflects one of these categories) in *Figure 2.2*. It is worth noting that there are other possible ways of categorizing ML models and none of them are fully complete, and as such, these categorizations will serve appropriately for some scenarios and not for others. Here is our recommended categorization with which to look at ML models:

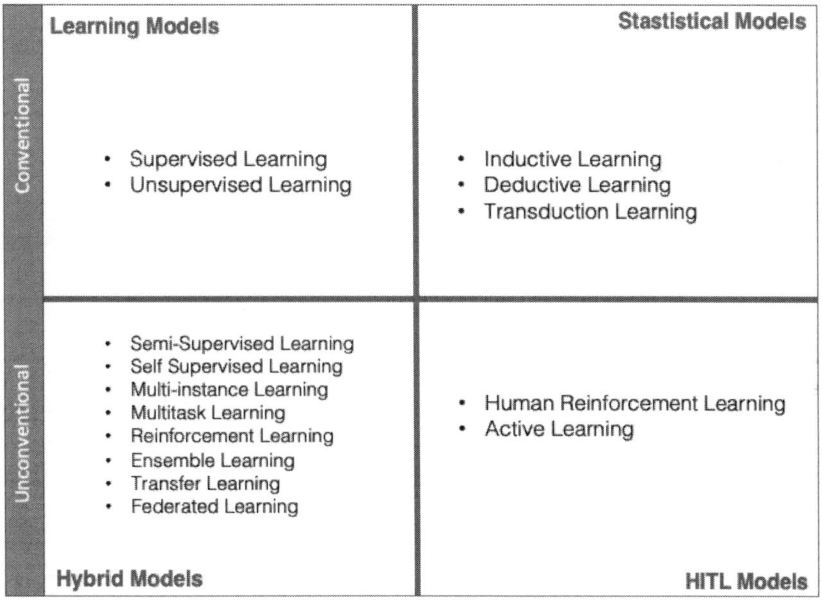

	Learning Models	Stastistical Models
Conventional	• Supervised Learning • Unsupervised Learning	• Inductive Learning • Deductive Learning • Transduction Learning
Unconventional	• Semi-Supervised Learning • Self Supervised Learning • Multi-instance Learning • Multitask Learning • Reinforcement Learning • Ensemble Learning • Transfer Learning • Federated Learning	• Human Reinforcement Learning • Active Learning
	Hybrid Models	**HITL Models**

Figure 2.2 – Types of ML models

Learning models

First, we'll take a look at two types of standard learning models, **supervised learning** and **unsupervised learning**:

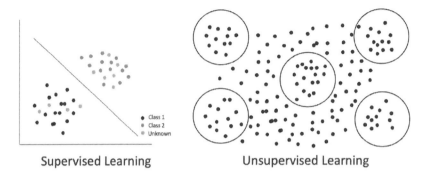

Figure 2.3 – Supervised versus unsupervised learning

Supervised learning

Supervised learning models or algorithms are trained based on labeled data. In the training data, the result of the input is marked or known. Hence a model is trained to predict the outcome when given an input based on the labeled data it learns from, and you tell the system which output corresponds with a given input in the system.

Supervised learning models are very effective on narrow AI cases and well-defined tasks but can only be harnessed where there is sufficient and comprehensive labeled data. We can see in *Figure 2.3*, in the case of supervised learning, that the model has learned to predict and classify an input.

Consider the example of an image classification model used to classify images of cats and dogs. A supervised learning model is trained on labeled data consisting of thousands of correctly labeled images of cats and dogs. The trained model then learns to classify a given input image as containing a dog or a cat.

Unsupervised learning

Unsupervised learning has nothing to do with a machine running around and doing things without human supervision. Unsupervised learning models or algorithms learn from unlabeled data. Unsupervised learning can be used to mine insights and identify patterns from unlabeled data. Unsupervised algorithms are widely used for clustering or anomaly detection without relying on any labels. These algorithms can be pattern-finding algorithms; when data is fed to such an algorithm, it will identify patterns and turn those into a recipe for taking a new data input without a label and applying the correct label to it.

Unsupervised learning is used mainly for analytics, though you could also use it for automation and ML. It is recommended not to use these algorithms in production due to their dynamic nature that changes outputs on every training cycle. However, they can be useful to automate certain processes such as segmenting incoming data or identifying anomalies in real time.

Let's discuss an example of clustering news articles into relevant groups. Let's assume you have thousands of news articles without any labels and you would like to identify the types or categories of articles. To perform unsupervised learning on these articles, we can input a bunch of articles into the algorithm and converge it to put similar things together (that is, clustering) in four groups. Then, we look at the clusters and discover that similar articles have been grouped together in categories such as politics, sports, science, and health. This is a way of mining patterns in the data.

Hybrid models

There have been rapid developments in ML by combining conventional methods to develop hybrid models to solve diverse business and research problems. Let's look into some hybrid models and how they work. *Figure 2.4* shows various hybrid models:

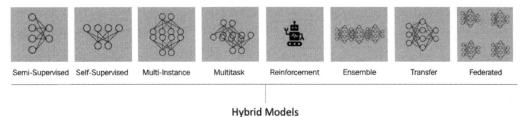

| Semi-Supervised | Self-Supervised | Multi-Instance | Multitask | Reinforcement | Ensemble | Transfer | Federated |

Hybrid Models

Figure 2.4 – Types of hybrid models

Semi-supervised learning

Semi-supervised learning is a hybrid of supervised learning, used in cases where only a few samples are labeled and a large number of samples are not labeled. Semi-supervised learning enables efficient use of the data available (though not all of it is labeled), including the unlabeled data. For example, a text document classifier is a typical example of a semi-supervised learning program. It will be very difficult to locate a large number of labeled text documents in this case, so semi-supervised learning is ideal. This is due to the fact that making someone read through entire text documents just to assign a basic classification is inefficient. As a result, semi-supervised learning enables the algorithm to learn from a limited number of labeled text documents while classifying the large number of unlabeled text documents present in the training data.

Self-supervised learning

Self-supervised learning problems are unsupervised learning problems where data is not labeled; these problems are translated into supervised learning problems in order to apply algorithms for supervised learning to solve them sustainably. Usually, self-supervised algorithms are used to solve an alternate task in which they supervise themselves to solve the problem or generate an output. One example of self-supervised learning is **Generative Adversarial Networks (GANs)**; these are commonly used to generate synthetic data by training on labeled and/or unlabeled data. With proper training, GAN models can generate a relevant output in a self-supervised manner. For example, a GAN could generate a human face based on a text description input, such as *gender: male, age: 30, color: brown*, and so on.

Multi-instance learning

Multi-instance learning is a supervised learning problem in which data is not labeled by individual data samples, but cumulatively in categories or classes. Compared to typical supervised learning, where labeling is done for each data sample, such as news articles labeled in categories such as politics, science, and sports, with multi-instance learning, labeling is done categorically. In such scenarios, individual samples are collectively labeled in multiple classes, and by using supervised learning algorithms, we can make predictions.

Multitask learning

Multitask learning is an incarnation of supervised learning that involves training a model on one dataset and using that model to solve multiple tasks or problems. For example, for natural language processing, we use word embeddings or **Bidirectional Encoder Representations from Transformers (BERT)** embeddings models, which are trained on one large corpus of data. (BERT is a pre-trained model, trained on a large text corpus. The model has a deep understanding of how a given human language works.) And these models can be used to solve many supervised learning tasks such as text classification, keyword extraction, sentiment analysis, and more.

Reinforcement learning

Reinforcement learning is a type of learning in which an agent, such as a robot system, learns to operate in a defined environment to perform sequential decision-making tasks or achieve a pre-defined goal. Simultaneously, the agent learns based on continuously evaluated feedback and rewards from the environment. Both feedback and rewards are used to shape the learning of the agent, as shown in *Figure 2.5*. An example is Google's AlphaGo, which recently outperformed the world's leading Go player. After 40 days of self-training using feedback and rewards, AlphaGo was able to beat the world's best human Go player:

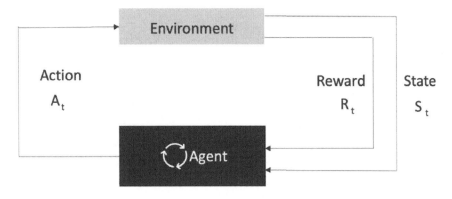

Figure 2.5 – Reinforcement learning

Ensemble learning

Ensemble learning is a hybrid model that involves two or more models trained on the same data. Predictions are made using each model individually and a collective prediction is made as a result of combining all outputs and averaging them to determine the final outcome or prediction. An example of this is the random forest algorithm, which is an ensemble learning method for classification or regression tasks. It operates by composing several decision trees while training, and creates a prediction as output by averaging the predictions of all the decision trees.

Transfer learning

We humans have an innate ability to transfer knowledge to and from one another. This same principle is translated to ML, where a model is trained to perform a task and it is transferred to another model as a starting point for training or fine-tuning for performing another task. This type of learning is popular in deep learning, where pre-trained models are used to solve computer vision or natural language processing problems by fine-tuning or training using a pre-trained model. Learning from pre-trained models gives a huge jumpstart as models don't need to be trained from scratch, saving large amounts of training data. For example, we can train a sentiment classifier model using training data containing only a few labeled data samples. This is possible with transfer learning using a pre-trained BERT model (which is trained on a large corpus of labeled data). This enables the transfer of learning from one model to another.

Federated learning

Federated learning is a way of performing ML in a collaborative fashion (synergy between cloud and edge). The training process is distributed across multiple devices, storing only a local sample of the data. Data is neither exchanged nor transferred between devices or the cloud to maintain data privacy and security. Instead of sharing data, locally trained models are shared to learn from each other to train global models. Let's discuss an example of federated learning in hospitals (as shown in *Figure 2.6*) where patient data is confidential and cannot be shared with third parties. In this case, ML training is done locally in the hospitals (at the edge) and global models are trained centrally (on the cloud) without sharing the data. Models trained locally are fine-tuned to produce global models. Instead of ingesting data in the central ML pipeline, locally trained models are ingested. Global models learn by tuning their parameters from local models to converge on optimal performance, concatenating the learning of local models:

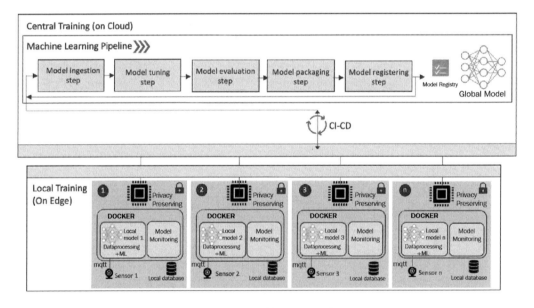

Figure 2.6 – Federated learning architecture

Statistical models

In some cases, statistical models are efficient at making decisions. It is vital to know where statistical models can be used to get the best value or decisions. There are three types of statistical models: inductive learning, deductive learning, and transductive learning. *Figure 2.7* shows the relationship between these types of statistical models:

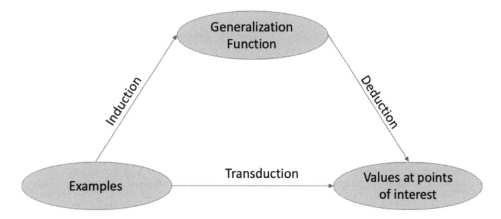

Figure 2.7 – Relationship between the three types of statistical models

Inductive learning is a statistical method that generalizes from specific examples in the training data, using this evidence to determine the most likely outcome. It involves a process of learning by example, where a system tries to generalize a general function or rule from a set of observed instances. For example, when we fit an ML model, it is a process of induction. The ML model is a generalization of the specific examples in the training dataset. For instance, using linear regression when fitting the model to the training data generalizes specific examples in the training data by the function $Y = a + bX$. Such generalizations are made in inductive learning.

Deductive learning refers to using general rules to determine specific outcomes. The outcomes of deductive learning are deterministic and specific, whereas for inductive reasoning, the conclusions are probabilistic or generalized. In a way, deduction is the reverse of induction. If induction goes from the specific to the general, deduction goes from the general to the specific.

Transductive learning is a method for reasoning about outcomes based on specific training data samples (in the training dataset). This method is different from inductive learning, where predictions are generalized over the training data. In transductive learning, specific or similar data samples from the training data are compared to reason about or predict an outcome. For example, in the case of the k-nearest neighbors algorithm, it uses specific data samples on which to base its outcome rather than generalizing the outcome or modeling with the training data.

HITL models

There are two types of **HITL** models: **human-centered reinforcement learning** models and **active learning** models. In these models, human-machine collaboration enables the algorithm to mimic human-like behaviors and outcomes. A key driver for these ML solutions is the *human in the loop (hence HITL)*. Humans validate, label, and retrain the models to maintain the accuracy of the model:

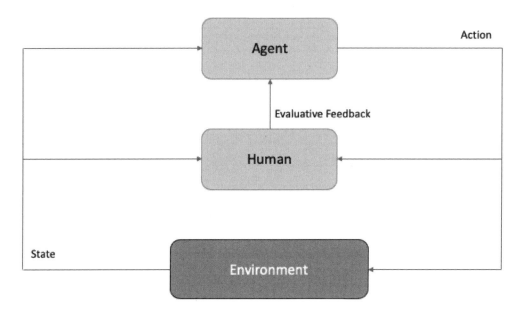

Figure 2.8 – Workflow of human-centered reinforcement learning

Human-centered reinforcement learning is a hybrid of reinforcement learning, as it involves humans in the loop to monitor the agent's learning and provide evaluative feedback to shape the learning of the agent. Human-centered reinforcement learning is also known as *interactive reinforcement learning*. Each time the agent takes action, the observing human expert can provide evaluative feedback that describes the quality of the selected action taken by the agent based on the human expert's knowledge, as shown in *Figure 2.8.*

Based on the feedback received from the task environment and human expert, the agent augments its behavior and actions. Human reinforcement learning is highly efficient in environments where the agent has to learn or mimic human behavior. To learn more, read the paper *Human-Centered Reinforcement Learning: A Survey* (`https://ieeexplore.ieee.org/abstract/document/8708686`).

Active learning is a method where the trained model can query a HITL (the human user) during the inference process to resolve incertitude during the learning process. For example, this could be a question-answering chatbot asking the human user for validation by asking yes or no questions.

These are the types of ML solutions possible to build for production to solve problems in the real world. Now that you are aware of the possibilities for crafting ML solutions, as the next step, it is critical to categorize your MLOps in line with your business and technological needs. It's important for you to be able to identify the right requirements, tools, methodology, and infrastructure needed to support your business and MLOps, hence we will look into structuring MLOps in the next section.

Structuring your MLOps

The primary goal of MLOps is to make an organization or set of individuals collaborate efficiently to build data and ML-driven assets to solve their business problems. As a result, overall performance and transparency are increased. Working in silos or developing functionalities repeatedly can be extremely costly and time-consuming.

In this section, we will explore how MLOps can be structured within organizations. Getting the MLOps process right is of prime importance. By selecting the right process and tools for your MLOps, you and your team are all set to implement a robust, scalable, frugal, and sustainable MLOps process. For example, I recently helped one of my clients in the healthcare industry to build and optimize their MLOps, which resulted in 76% cost optimization (for storage and compute resources) compared to their previous traditional operations.

The client's team of data scientists witnessed having 30% of their time freed up from mundane and repetitive daily tasks (for example, data wrangling, ML pipeline, and hyperparameter tuning) – such can be the impact of having an efficient MLOps process. By implementing efficient MLOps, your team can be assured of efficiency, high performance, and great collaboration that is repeatable and traceable within your organization.

MLOps can be categorized into **small data ops**, **big data ops**, **large-scale MLOps**, and **hybrid MLOps** (this categorization is based on the author's experience and is a recommended way to approach MLOps for teams and organizations):

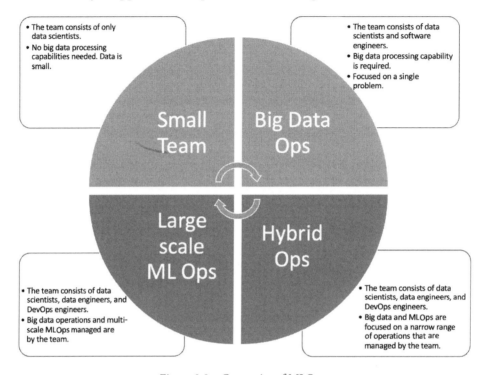

* The team consists of only data scientists.
* No big data processing capabilities needed. Data is small.

* The team consists of data scientists and software engineers.
* Big data processing capability is required.
* Focused on a single problem.

* The team consists of data scientists, data engineers, and DevOps engineers.
* Big data operations and multi-scale MLOps managed are by the team.

* The team consists of data scientists, data engineers, and DevOps engineers.
* Big data and MLOps are focused on a narrow range of operations that are managed by the team.

Figure 2.9 – Categories of MLOps

As shown in *Figure 2.9*, MLOps within organizations can be broadly categorized into four different categories depending on team size, and the ML applications, business models, data scale, tools, and infrastructure used to execute operations. In terms of data, many scenarios do not need big data (anything above 1 TB) operations, as simple operations can be effective for small- or medium-scale data. The differences between data scales are as follows:

* **Big data**: A quantity of data that cannot fit in the memory of a single typical computer; for instance, > 1 TB

* **Medium-scale data**: A quantity of data that can fit in the memory of a single server; for instance, from 10 GB to 1 TB

* **Small-scale data**: A quantity of data that easily fits in the memory of a laptop or a PC; for instance, < 10 GB

With these factors in mind, let's look into the MLOps categories to identify the suitable process and scale for implementing MLOps for your business problems or organization.

Small data ops

A small start-up with a team of data scientists seeking to build ML models for narrow and well-defined problems can be agile and highly collaborative. Usually, in such cases, ML models are trained locally on the respective data scientists' computers and then forgotten about, or scaled out and deployed on the cloud for inference. In these scenarios, there can be some general pitfalls, such as the team lacking a streamlined CI/CD approach for deploying models. However, they might manage to have central or distributed data sources that are managed carefully by the team, and the training code can be versioned and maintained in a central repository. When operations start to scale, such teams are prone to the following:

- Running into situations where much of the work is repeated by multiple people including tasks such as crafting data, ML pipelines doing the same job, or training similar types of ML models.

- Working in silos and having minimal understanding of the parallel work of their teammates. This leads to less transparency.

- Incurring huge costs, or higher costs than expected, due to the mundane and repeated work.

- Code and data starting to grow independently.

- Artifacts not being audited and hence are non-repeatable.

Any of these can be costly and unsustainable for the team. If you are working in a team or have a setup like the following, you can categorize your operations as small data ops:

- The team consists of only data scientists.

- You only work with Python environments and manage everything in the Python framework. Choosing Python can be a result of having many ML libraries and tools ready to plug and play for quick prototyping and building solutions. The number of ML libraries for a language such as Java, for example, is quite a lot smaller compared to those available for Python.

- Little to no big data processing is required as the data scientists use small data (<10 GB).

- Quick ML model development starts with a local computer, then scales out to the cloud for massive computation resources.

- High support requirements for open source technologies such as PyTorch, TensorFlow, and scikit-learn for any type of ML, from classical learning to deep, supervised, and unsupervised learning.

Big data ops

This can be a team of experienced data scientists and engineers working in a start-up or an SME where they have the requirement for large-scale big data processing to perform ML training or inference. They use big data tools such as **Kafka**, **Spark**, or **Hadoop** to build and orchestrate their data pipelines. High-powered processors such as GPUs or TPUs are used in such scenarios to speed up data processing and ML training. The development of ML models is led by data scientists and deploying the models is orchestrated by data/software engineers. A strong focus is given to developing models and less importance is placed on monitoring the models. As they continue with their operations, this type of team is prone to the following:

- A lack of traceability for model training and monitoring
- A lack of reproducible artifacts
- Incurring huge costs, or more than expected, due to mundane and repeated work
- Code and data starting to grow independently

Any of these can be costly and unsustainable for a team.

If you are working in a team or have a setup as described in the following points, you can categorize your operations as big data ops:

- The team consists of data scientists/engineers.
- There are high requirements for big data processing capacity.
- Databricks is a key framework to share and collaborate inside teams and between organizations.
- ML model development happens in the cloud by utilizing one of many ML workflow management tools such as **Spark MLlib**.
- There are low support requirements for open source technologies such as PyTorch and TensorFlow for deep learning.

Hybrid MLOps

Hybrid teams operate with experienced data scientists, data engineers, and DevOps engineers, and these teams make use of ML capabilities to support their business operations. They are further ahead in implementing MLOps compared to other teams. They work with big data and open source software tools such as PyTorch, TensorFlow, and scikit-learn, and hence have a requirement for efficient collaboration. They often work on well-defined problems by implementing robust and scalable software engineering practices. However, this team is still prone to challenges such as the following:

- Incurring huge costs, or more than expected, due to mundane and repeated work to be done by data scientists, such as repeating data cleaning or feature engineering.

- Inefficient model monitoring and retraining mechanisms.

Any of these can be costly and unsustainable for the team.

If you are working in a team or have a setup as described in the following points, you can categorize your operations as Hybrid Ops:

- The team consists of data scientists, data engineers, and DevOps engineers.

- High requirement for efficient and effective collaboration.

- High requirement for big data processing capacity.

- High support requirements for open source technologies such as PyTorch, TensorFlow, and scikit-learn for any kind of ML, from classical to deep learning, and from supervised to unsupervised learning.

Large-scale MLOps

Large-scale operations are common in big companies with large or medium-sized engineering teams consisting of data scientists, data engineers, and DevOps engineers. They have data operations on the scale of big data, or with various types of data on various scales, veracity, and velocity. Usually, their teams have multiple legacy systems to manage to support their business operations. Such teams or organizations are prone to the following:

- Incurring huge costs, or more than expected, due to mundane and repeated work.

- Code and data starting to grow independently.

- Having bureaucratic and highly regulated processes and quality checks.

- Highly entangled systems and processes – when one thing breaks, everything breaks.

Any of these can be costly and unsustainable for the team.

If you are working in a team or have a setup as described in the following points, you can categorize your operations as large-scale ops:

- The team consists of data scientists, data engineers, and DevOps engineers.

- Large-scale inference and operations.

- Big data operations.

- ML model management on multiple resources.

- Big or multiple teams.

- Multiple use cases and models.

Once you have characterized your MLOps as per your business and technological needs, a solid implementation roadmap ensures smooth development and implementation of a robust and scalable MLOps solution for your organization. For example, a fintech start-up processing 0-1,000 transactions a day would need small-scale data ops compared to a larger financial institution that needs large-scale MLOps. Such categorization enables a team or organization to be more efficient and robust.

An implementation roadmap for your solution

Having a well-defined method and milestones ensures the successful delivery of the desired ML solution (using MLOps methods). In this section, we will discuss a generic implementation roadmap that can facilitate MLOps for any ML problem in detail. The goal of this roadmap is to solve the problem with the right solution:

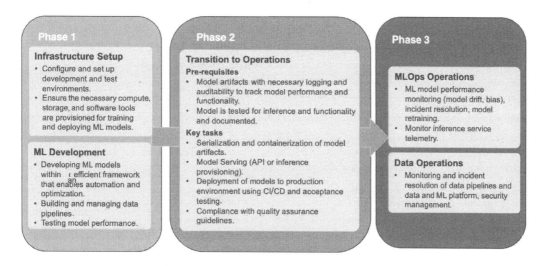

Phase 1

Infrastructure Setup
- Configure and set up development and test environments.
- Ensure the necessary compute, storage, and software tools are provisioned for training and deploying ML models.

ML Development
- Developing ML models within an efficient framework that enables automation and optimization.
- Building and managing data pipelines.
- Testing model performance.

Phase 2

Transition to Operations
Pre-requisites
- Model artifacts with necessary logging and auditability to track model performance and functionality.
- Model is tested for inference and functionality and documented.

Key tasks
- Serialization and containerization of model artifacts.
- Model Serving (API or inference provisioning).
- Deployment of models to production environment using CI/CD and acceptance testing.
- Compliance with quality assurance guidelines.

Phase 3

MLOps Operations
- ML model performance monitoring (model drift, bias), incident resolution, model retraining.
- Monitor inference service telemetry.

Data Operations
- Monitoring and incident resolution of data pipelines and data and ML platform, security management.

Figure 2.10 – Implementation roadmap for an MLOps-based solution

Using the preceding roadmap, we can transition from ML development to MLOps with clear milestones, as shown in these three phases for MLOps implementation. Now, let's look into these three phases of the roadmap in more detail. It's worth noting that after the following section on theory, we will get into the practical implementation of the roadmap and work on a real-world business use case.

Phase 1 – ML development

This is the genesis of implementing the MLOps framework for your problem; before beginning to implement the requirements, the problem and solution must be clear and vivid. In this phase, we take into account the system requirements to design and implement a robust and scalable MLOps framework. We begin by selecting the right tools and infrastructure needed (storage, compute, and so on) to implement the MLOps.

When the infrastructure is set up, we should be provisioned with the necessary workspace and the development and test environments to execute ML experiments (training and testing). We train the ML models using the development environment and test the models for performance and functionality using test data in the development or test environments, depending on the workflow or requirement. When infrastructure is set up and the first ML model is trained, tested, serialized, and packaged, phase 1 of your MLOps framework is set up and validated for robustness. Serializing and containerizing is an important process to standardize and get the models ready for deployments.

Next, we move to implement phase 2.

Phase 2 – Transition to operations

Phase 2 is about transitioning to operations, and it involves serializing and containerizing the models trained in phase 1 and getting them ready for deployment. This enables standardized, efficient deployments. The models are served in the form of APIs or independent artifacts for batch inference. When a model is packaged and ready to be served, it is deployed in the production environment using streamlined CI/CD pipelines upon passing quality assurance checks. By the end of phase 2, you will have packaged models served and deployed in the production environment performing inference in real time.

Phase 3 – Operations

Phase 3 is the core operations phase for deployed models in phase 2. In this phase, we monitor the deployed model performance in terms of model drift, bias, or other metrics (we will delve into these terms and metrics in the coming chapters). Based on the model's performance, we can enable continual learning via periodic model retraining and enable alerts and actions. Simultaneously, we monitor logs in telemetry data for the production environment to detect any possible errors and resolve them on the go to ensure the uninterrupted working of the production system. We also manage data pipelines, the ML platform, and security on the go. With the successful implementation of this phase, we can monitor the deployed models and retrain them in a robust, scalable, and secure manner.

In most cases, all three phases need to be implemented for your ML solution, but in some cases just phases 1 and 2 are enough; for instance, when the ML models make batch inferences and need not do inference in real time. By achieving these milestones and implementing all three phases, we have set up a robust and scalable ML life cycle for our applications systematically and sustainably.

Procuring data, requirements, and tools

Implementing successful MLOps depends on certain factors such as procuring appropriate training data, and having high standards, and appropriate requirements, tools, and infrastructure.

In this section, we will delve into these factors that make robust and scalable MLOps.

Data

I used to believe that learning about data meant mastering tools such as Python, SQL, and regression. The tool is only as good as the person and their understanding of the context around it. The context and domain matter, from data cleaning to modeling to interpretation. The best tools in the world won't fix a bad problem definition (or lack of one). Knowing what problem to solve is a very context-driven and business-dependent decision. Once you are aware of the problem and context, it enables you to discern the right training data needed to solve the problem.

Training data is a vital part of ML systems. It plays a vital role in developing ML systems compared to traditional software systems. As we have seen in the previous chapter, both code and training data work in parallel to develop and maintain an ML system. It is not only about the algorithm but also about the data. There are two aspects to ensure you have the right data for algorithm training, which are to provide both the right quantity and quality of data:

- **Data quantity**: Data scientists echo a common argument about their models, arguing that model performance is not good because the quantity of data they were given was not sufficient to produce good model performance. If they had more data, the performance would have been better – are you familiar with such arguments? In most cases, more data might not really help, as quality also is an important factor. For instance, your models can learn more insights and characteristics from your data if you have more samples for each class. For example, if you analyze anomalous financial transactions with many samples in your data, you will discover more types of anomalous transactions. If there is only one anomalous case, then ML is not useful.

  The data requirements for ML projects should not solely focus on data quantity itself, but also on the quality, which means the focus should not be on the number of data samples but rather on the diversity of data samples. However, in some cases, there are constraints on the quantity of data available to tackle some problems. For example, let's suppose we work on models to predict the churn rate for an insurance company. In that case, we can be restricted to considering data from a limited period or using a limited number of samples due to the availability of data for a certain time period; for example, 5 years (whereas the insurance company might have operated for the last 50 years). The goal is to acquire data of the maximum possible quantity and quality to train the best-performing ML models.

- **Data quality**: Data quality is an important factor for training ML models; it impacts model performance. The more comprehensive or higher the quality of the data, the better the ML model or application will work. Hence the process before the training is important: cleaning, augmenting, and scaling the data. There are some important dimensions of data quality to consider, such as consistency, correctness, and completeness.

Data consistency refers to the correspondence and coherence of the data samples throughout the dataset. Data correctness is the degree of accuracy and the degree to which you can rely on the data to truly reflect events. Data correctness is dependent on how the data was collected. The sparsity of data for each characteristic (for example, whether the data covers a comprehensive range of possible values to reflect an event) reflects data completeness.

With an appropriate quantity of good-quality data, you can be sure that your ML models and applications will perform above the required standards. Hence, having the right standards is vital for the application to perform and solve business problems in the most efficient ways.

Requirements

The product or business/tech problem owner plays a key role in facilitating the building of a robust ML system efficiently by identifying requirements and tailoring them with regard to the scope of data, collection of data, and required data formats. These requirements are vital inputs for developers of ML systems, such as data scientists or ML engineers, to start architecting the solution to address the problem by analyzing and correlating the given dataset based on the requirements. ML solution requirements should consist of comprehensive data requirements. Data requirement specifications consist of information about the quality and quantity of the data. The requirements can be more extensive; for example, they can contain estimations about anticipated or expected predictive performance expressed in terms of the performance metrics determined during requirements analysis and elicitation.

Meticulous specifications can be made, such as the specification of expected or anticipated performance on the training data, as these can be rapidly validated after the model training process. Whereas, based on the training performance, inference or runtime (including in production and operations) performance can be assessed during operations. The requirements made by the product owner or business owner should consider important factors such as ethical and explainability factors. Discrimination or bias (such as who or what is predicted or classified) is critical for the application and which properties should be preserved as part of data privacy (for example, some properties should not be used for predictions or classification, such as race, age, or gender). Explainability requirements must explicitly be taken into account to explain situations and decisions of the ML solution or system to the users of the system. Lastly, the requirements must stipulate regulations and restrictions concerning the use of the data and validation of decisions made by the ML system. The following table shows some requirements to consider to ensure that you build a robust and scalable ML solution:

Elicitiation	Analysis	Specifications	Verification and Validation
• Elicit additional data sources. • Important stakeholders: Data scientists and legal experts. • Protected characteristics.	• Discuss performance measures. • Discuss conditions for data preparation, definitions of outliers, and derived data.	• Quantitative targets. • Data requirements. • Explainability. • Freedom from discrimination. • Legal and regulatory constraints.	• Analyse operational data. • Look for bias in data. • Retrain ML models. • Detect data anomalies.

Figure 2.11 – Requirements mapping for ML solutions

The table in *Figure 2.11* illustrates the flow of the requirements characterization process, from elicitation to analysis to specifications to verification and validation of the system. This process ensures best-fit resources are procured to build and deploy an efficient ML system to solve your problem. When the requirements are well defined, selecting the right tools and infrastructure that support the established process and ensure the standards are met is crucial.

Tools and infrastructure

The MLOps landscape has been developing rapidly over the last two years; many tools and frameworks have evolved as part of the infrastructural offering. You can visit `https://landscape.lfai.foundation/` to see how many mainstream options have been developed to orchestrate ML, deep learning, reinforcement learning, development environments, data pipelines, model management, explainable AI, security, and distributed computing.

There is a surge in services provided by popular cloud service providers such as Microsoft, AWS, and Google, which are complemented by data processing tools such as Airflow, Databricks, and Data Lake. These are crafted to enable ML and deep learning, for which there are great frameworks available such as scikit-learn, Spark MLlib, PyTorch, TensorFlow, MXNet, and CNTK, among others. Tools and frameworks are many, but procuring the right tools is a matter of choice and the context of your ML solution and operations setup. Having the right tools will ensure high efficiency and automation for your MLOps workflow. The options are many, the sky's the limit, but we have to start from somewhere to reach the sky. For this reason, we will look to give you some hands-on experience from here onward. It is always better to learn from real-life problems, and we will do so by using the real-life business problem described in the next section.

Discussing a real-life business problem

We will be implementing the following business problem to get hands-on experience. I recommend you read this section multiple times to get a good understanding of the business problem; it makes it easier to implement it.

> **Important note**
>
> Problem context:
>
> You work as a data scientist in a small team with three other data scientists for a cargo shipping company based in the port of Turku in Finland. 90% of the goods imported into Finland come via cargo ships at the ports across the country. For cargo shipping, weather conditions and logistics can be challenging at times at the ports. Rainy conditions can distort operations and logistics at the ports, which can affect the supply chain operations. Forecasting rainy conditions in advance gives the possibility to optimize resources such as human resources, logistics, and transport resources for efficient supply chain operations at ports. Business-wise, forecasting rainy conditions in advance enables ports to reduce operational costs by up to ~20% by enabling efficient planning and scheduling of human resources, logistics, and transport resources for supply chain operations.
>
> Task:
>
> You as a data scientist are tasked with developing an ML-driven solution to forecast weather conditions 4 hours in advance at the port of Turku in Finland. That will enable the port to optimize its resources, thereby enabling cost-savings of up to 20%. To get started, you are provided with a historic weather dataset covering a timeline of 10 years from the port of Turku (the dataset can be accessed in the next chapter). Your task is to build a continuous-learning-driven ML solution to optimize operations at the port of Turku.

To solve this problem, we will use Microsoft Azure, one of the most widely used cloud services, and MLflow, an open source ML development tool, to get hands-on with using resources. This way, we will get experience working on the cloud and with open source software. Before starting the hands-on implementation in the next chapter, please make sure to do the following:

1. Create a free Azure subscription from `https://azure.microsoft.com/` (takes 5 minutes).

2. Create an Azure Machine Learning service application with the name `MLOps_WS`. This can be done from your Azure portal by clicking **Create a resource**. Then type `Machine Learning` into the search field and select the **Machine Learning** option. Then, follow the detailed instructions in the next chapter (*Chapter 3, Code Meets Data*) to create the Azure Machine Learning service resource with the name `MLOps_WS`.

Now, with this, you are all set to get hands-on with implementing an MLOps framework for the preceding business problem.

Summary

In this chapter, we have learned about the ML solution development process, how to identify a suitable ML solution to a problem, and how to categorize operations to implement suitable MLOps. We got a glimpse into a generic implementation roadmap and saw some tips for procuring essentials such as tools, data, and infrastructure to implement your ML application. Lastly, we went through the business problem to be solved in the next chapter by implementing an MLOps workflow (discussed in *Chapter 1, Fundamentals of MLOps Workflow*) in which we'll get some hands-on experience in MLOps.

In the next chapter, we will go from theory to practical implementation. The chapter gets hands-on when we start with setting up MLOps tools on Azure and start coding to clean the data to address the business problem and get plenty of hands-on experience.

3
Code Meets Data

In this chapter, we'll get started with hands-on **MLOps** implementation as we learn by solving a business problem using the MLOps workflow discussed in the previous chapter. We'll also discuss effective methods of source code management for **machine learning** (**ML**), explore data quality characteristics, and analyze and shape data for an ML solution.

We begin this chapter by categorizing the business problem to curate a best-fit MLOps solution for it. Following this, we'll set up the required resources and tools to implement the solution. 10 guiding principles for source code management for ML are discussed to apply clean code practices. We will discuss what constitutes good-quality data for ML and much more, followed by processing a dataset related to the business problem and ingesting and versioning it to the ML workspace. Most of the chapter is hands-on and designed to equip you with a good understanding of and experience with MLOps. For this, we're going to cover the following main topics in this chapter:

- Business problem analysis and categorizing the problem
- Setting up resources and tools
- 10 principles of source code management for machine learning
- Good data for machine learning
- Data preprocessing
- Data registration and versioning
- Toward an ML pipeline

Without further ado, let's jump into demystifying the business problem and implementing the solution using an MLOps approach.

Business problem analysis and categorizing the problem

In the previous chapter, we looked into the following business problem statement. In this section, we will demystify the problem statement by categorizing it using the principles to curate an implementation roadmap. We will glance at the dataset given to us to address the business problem and decide what type of ML model will address the business problem efficiently. Lastly, we'll categorize the MLOps approach for implementing robust and scalable ML operations and decide on tools for implementation.

> **Here is the problem statement:**
>
> You work as a data scientist with a small team of data scientists for a cargo shipping company based in Finland. 90% of goods are imported into Finland via cargo shipping. You are tasked with saving 20% of the costs for cargo operations at the port of Turku, Finland. This can be achieved by developing an ML solution that predicts weather conditions at the port 4 hours in advance. You need to monitor for possible rainy conditions, which can distort operations at the port with human resources and transportation, which in turn affects supply chain operations at the port. Your ML solution will help port authorities to predict possible rain 4 hours in advance; this will save 20% of costs and enable smooth supply chain operations at the port.

The first step in solving a problem is to simplify and categorize it using an appropriate approach. In the previous chapter, we discussed how to categorize a business problem to solve it using ML. Let's apply those principles to chart a clear roadmap to implementing it.

First, we'll see what type of model we will train to yield the maximum business value. Secondly, we will identify the right approach for our MLOps implementation.

In order to decide on the type of model to train, we can start by having a glance at the dataset available on GitHub: `https://github.com/PacktPublishing/EngineeringMLOps`.

Here is a snapshot of `weather_dataset_raw.csv`, in *Figure 3.1*. The file size is 10.7 MB, the number of rows is 96,453, and the file is in CSV format:

S_No		Timestamp	Location	Temperature_C	Apparent_ Temperature_C	Humidity	Wind_speed_kmph	Wind_bearing _degrees	Visibility_km	Pressure _millibars	Weather _conditions
0	0	2006-04-01 00:00:00+02:00	Port of Turku, Finland	9.472222	7.388889	0.89	14.1197	251	15.8263	1015.13	rain
1	1	2006-04-01 01:00:00+02:00	Port of Turku, Finland	9.355556	7.227778	0.86	14.2646	259	15.8263	1015.63	rain
2	2	2006-04-01 02:00:00+02:00	Port of Turku, Finland	9.377778	9.377778	0.89	3.9284	204	14.9569	1015.94	rain
3	3	2006-04-01 03:00:00+02:00	Port of Turku, Finland	8.288889	5.944444	0.83	14.1036	269	15.8263	1016.41	NaN
4	4	2006-04-01 04:00:00+02:00	Port of Turku, Finland	8.755556	6.977778	0.83	11.0446	259	15.8263	1016.51	rain

Figure 3.1 – Dataset snapshot

By assessing the data, we can categorize the business problem as follows:

- **Model type**: In order to save 20% of the operational costs at the port of Turku, a supervised learning model is required to predict by classifying whether it will rain or not rain. Data is labeled, and the `Weather condition` column depicts whether an event has recorded rain, snow, or clear conditions. This can be framed or relabeled as `rain` or `no rain` and used to perform binary classification. Hence, it is straightforward to solve the business problem with a supervised learning approach.

- **MLOps approach**: By observing the problem statement and data, here are the facts:

  (a) Data: The training data is 10.7 MB. The data size is reasonably small (it cannot be considered big data).

  (b) Operations: We need to train, test, deploy, and monitor an ML model to forecast the weather at the port of Turku every hour (4 hours in advance) when new data is recorded.

  (c) Team size: A small/medium team of data scientists, no DevOps engineers.

Based on the preceding facts, we can categorize the operations into **small team ops**; there is no need for big data processing and the team is small and agile. Now we will look at some suitable tools to implement the operations needed to solve the business problem at hand.

For us to get a holistic understanding of MLOps implementation, we will implement the business problems using two different tools simultaneously:

- **Azure Machine Learning** (Microsoft Azure)
- **MLflow** (an open source cloud and platform-agnostic tool)

We use these two tools to see how things work from a pure cloud-based approach and from an open source / cloud-agnostic approach. All the code and CI/CD operations will be managed and orchestrated using Azure DevOps, as shown in *Figure 3.2*:

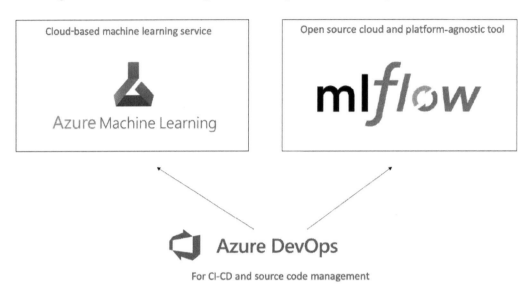

Figure 3.2 – MLOps tools for the solution

Now, we will set up the tools and resources needed to implement the solution for the business problem. As we will use Python as the primary programming language, it is a pre-requisite to have **Python 3** installed within your Mac, Linux, or Windows OS.

Setting up the resources and tools

If you have these tools already installed and set up on your PC, feel free to skip this section; otherwise, follow the detailed instructions to get them up and running.

Installing MLflow

We get started by installing MLflow, which is an open source platform for managing the ML life cycle, including experimentation, reproducibility, deployment, and a central model registry.

To install MLflow, go to your terminal and execute the following command:

```
pip3 install mlflow
```

After successful installation, test the installation by executing the following command to start the `mlflow` tracking UI:

```
mlflow ui
```

Upon running the `mlflow` tracking UI, you will be running a server listening at port `5000` on your machine, and it outputs a message like the following:

```
[2021-03-11 14:34:23 +0200]  [43819]  [INFO]  Starting gunicorn
20.0.4
[2021-03-11 14:34:23 +0200]  [43819]  [INFO]  Listening at:
http://127.0.0.1:5000 (43819)
[2021-03-11 14:34:23 +0200]  [43819]  [INFO]  Using worker: sync
[2021-03-11 14:34:23 +0200]  [43821]  [INFO]  Booting worker with
pid: 43821
```

You can access and view the `mlflow` UI at `http://localhost:5000`. When you have successfully installed `mlflow` and run the tracking UI, you are ready to install the next tool.

Azure Machine Learning

Azure Machine Learning provides a cloud-based ML platform for training, deploying, and managing ML models. This service is available on Microsoft Azure, so the pre-requisite is to have a free subscription to Microsoft Azure. Please create a free account with around $170 of credit, which is sufficient to implement the solution, here: `https://azure.microsoft.com/`.

When you have access/a subscription to Azure, move on to the next section to get Azure Machine Learning up and running.

Creating a resource group

A **resource group** is a collection of related resources for an Azure solution. It is a container that ties up all the resources related to a service or solution. Creating a resource group enables easy access and management of a solution. Let's get started by creating your own resource group:

1. Open the Azure portal.

2. Access the portal menu (go to the portal's home page if you are not there by default) and hover over the resource group icon in the navigation section. A **Create** button will appear; click on it to create a new resource group:

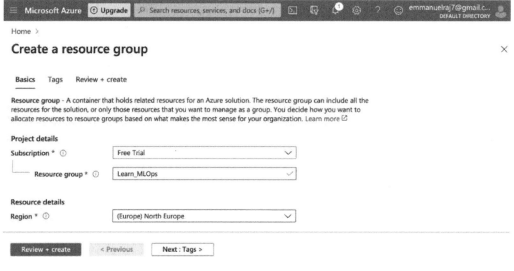

Figure 3.3 – Creating a resource group

3. Create a resource group with the name of your choice (Learn_MLOps is recommended), as shown in *Figure 3.3*.

4. Select a region close to you to get the optimal performance and pricing. For example, in *Figure 3.3* a resource group with the name Learn MLOps and region **(Europe) North Europe** is ready to be created. After you click the **Review + Create** button and Azure validates the request, the final **Create** button will appear. The final **Create** button should be pressed to create the new resource group.

When the resource group is reviewed and created, you can set up and manage all the services related to the ML solution in this resource group. The newly created resource group will be listed in the resource group list.

Creating an Azure Machine Learning workspace

An ML workspace is a central hub for tracking and managing your ML training, deploying, and monitoring experiments. To create an Azure Machine Learning workspace, go to the Azure portal menu, click on **Create a resource**, then search for `Machine Learning` and select it. You will see the following screen:

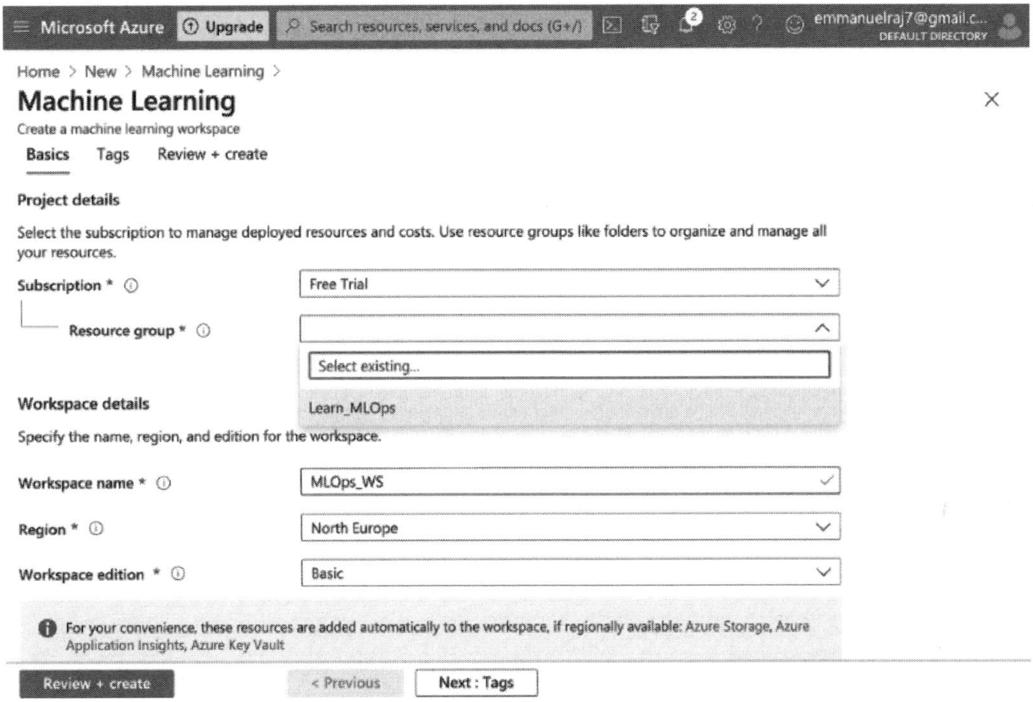

Figure 3.4 – Creating an Azure Machine Learning workspace

Name the workspace with the name of your choice (for example, we've named it **MLOps_WS** in *Figure 3.4*). Select the resource group you created earlier to tie this ML service to it (**Learn_MLOps** is selected in *Figure 3.4*). Finally, hit the **Review + create** button and you will be taken to a new screen with the final **Create** button. Press the final **Create** button to create your Azure Machine Learning workspace.

After creating the Azure Machine Learning workspace (`Learn_MLOps`), the Azure platform will deploy all the resources this service needs. The resources deployed with the Azure Machine Learning instance (`Learn_MLOps`), such as Blob Storage, Key Vault, and Application Insights, are provisioned and tied to the workspace. These resources will be consumed or used via the workspace and the SDK.

You can find detailed instructions on creating an Azure Machine Learning instance here: `https://docs.microsoft.com/en-us/azure/machine-learning/how-to-manage-workspace`.

Installing Azure Machine Learning SDK

Go to the terminal or command line in your PC and install the Azure Machine Learning SDK, which will be extensively used in the code to orchestrate the experiment. To install it, run the following command:

```
pip3 install --upgrade azureml-sdk
```

You can find detailed instructions here: `https://docs.microsoft.com/en-us/python/api/overview/azure/ml/install?view=azure-ml-py`.

Azure DevOps

All the source code and CI/CD-related operations will be managed and orchestrated using Azure DevOps. The code we manage in the repository in Azure DevOps will be used to train, deploy, and monitor ML models enabled by CI/CD pipelines. Let's start by creating an Azure DevOps subscription:

1. Create a free account at `dev.azure.com`. A free account can be created using a pre-existing Microsoft or GitHub account.

2. Create a project named `Learn_MLOps` (make it public or private depending on your preference).

3. Go to the **repos** section. In the **Import a repository** section, press the **Import** button.

4. Import a repository from a public GitHub project from this repository: `https://github.com/PacktPublishing/EngineeringMLOps` (as shown in *Figure 3.5*):

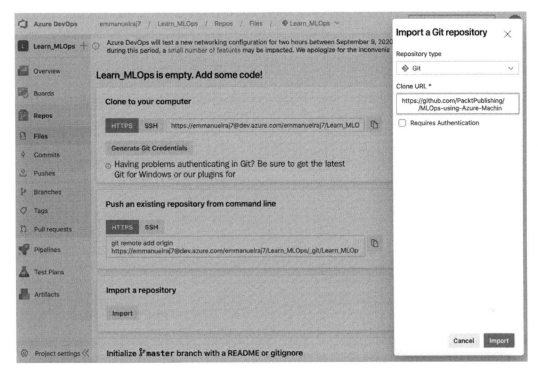

Figure 3.5 – Import the GitHub repository into the Azure DevOps project

After importing the GitHub repository, files from the imported repository will be displayed.

JupyterHub

Lastly, we'll need an interactive data analysis and visualization tool to process data using our code. For this, we use **JupyterHub**. This is a common data science tool used widely by data scientists to process data, visualize data, and train ML models. To install it, follow two simple steps:

1. Install JupyterHub via the command line on your PC:

```
python3 -m pip install jupyterhub
```

You may find detailed instructions here: `https://jupyterhub.readthedocs.io/en/stable/quickstart.html`.

2. Install Anaconda.

Anaconda is needed as it installs dependencies, setup environments, and services to support the JupyterHub. Download Anaconda and install it as per the detailed instructions here: `https://docs.anaconda.com/anaconda/install/`.

Now that we are set up for the hands-on implementation, let's look at what it takes to manage good code and data.

10 principles of source code management for ML

Here are 10 principles that can be applied to your code to ensure the quality, robustness, and scalability of your code:

- **Modularity:** It is better to have modular code than to have one big chunk. Modularity encourages reusability and facilitates upgrading by replacing the required components. To avoid needless complexity and repetition, follow this golden rule:

    Two or more ML components should be paired only when one of them uses the other. If none of them uses each other, then pairing should be avoided.

    An ML component that is not tightly paired with its environment can be more easily modified or replaced than a tightly paired component.

- **Single task dedicated functions:** Functions are important building blocks of pipelines and the system, and they are small sections of code that are used to perform particular tasks. The purpose of functions is to avoid repetition of commands and enable reusable code. They can easily become a complex set of commands to facilitate tasks. For readable and reusable code, it is more efficient to have a single function dedicated to a single task instead of multiple tasks. It is better to have multiple functions than one long and complex function.

- **Structuring:** Functions, classes, and statements should be structured in a readable, modular, and concise form. Nobody wants to see an error like `Error 300`. Structuring blocks of code and trying to limit the maximum levels of indentation for functions and classes can enhance the readability of the code.

- **Clean code:** If you have to explain the code, it's not that good. Clean code is self-explanatory. It focuses on high readability, optimal modularity, reusability, non-repeatability, and optimal performance. Clean code reduces the cost of maintaining and upgrading your ML pipelines. It enables a team to perform efficiently and can be extended to other developers.

  To understand this in depth, read *Clean Code: A Handbook of Agile Software Craftsmanship* by **Robert C Martin**.

- **Testing:** It is vital to ensure the robustness of a system, and testing plays an important role in this. In general, testing extends to unit testing and acceptance testing. Unit testing is a method by which components of source code are tested for robustness with coerced data and usage methods to determine whether the component is fit for the production system. Acceptance tests are done to test the overall system to ensure the system realizes user requirements; end-to-end business flows are verified in real-time scenarios. Testing is vital to ensure the efficient working of code: "if it isn't tested, it is broken."

To learn more about the implementation of unit testing, read this documentation: https://docs.python.org/3/library/unittest.html.

- **Version control (code, data and models):** Git is used for version control of code in ML systems. The purpose of version control is to ensure that all the team members working on the system have access to up-to-date code and that code is not lost when there is a hardware failure. One rule of working with Git should be to not break the master (branch). This means when you have working code in the repository and you add new features or make improvements, you do this in a feature branch, which is merged to the master branch when the code is working and reviewed. Branches should be given a short descriptive name, such as feature/label-encoder. Branch naming and approval guidelines should be properly communicated and agreed upon with the team to avoid any complexity and unnecessary conflicts. Code review is done with pull requests to the repository of the code. Usually, it is best to review code in small sets, less than 400 lines. In practice, it often means one module or a submodule at a time.

  Versioning of data is essential for ML systems as it helps us to keep track of which data was used for a particular version of code to generate a model. Versioning data can enable reproducing models and compliance with business needs and law. We can always backtrack and see the reason for certain actions taken by the ML system. Similarly, versioning of models (artifacts) is important for tracking which version of a model has generated certain results or actions for the ML system. We can also track or log parameters used for training a certain version of the model. This way, we can enable end-to-end traceability for model artifacts, data, and code. Version control for code, data, and models can enhance an ML system with great transparency and efficiency for the people developing and maintaining it.

- **Logging:** In production, a logger is useful as it is possible to monitor and identify important information. The `print` statements are good for testing and debugging but not ideal for production. The logger contains information, especially system information, warnings, and errors, that are quite useful in the monitoring of production systems.

- **Error handling:** Error handling is vital for handling edge cases, especially ones that are hard to anticipate. It is recommended to catch and handle exceptions even if you think you don't need to, as prevention is better than cure. Logging combined with exception handling can be an effective way of dealing with edge cases.

- **Readability:** Code readability enables information transfer, code efficiency, and code maintainability. It can be achieved by following principles such as following industry-standard coding practices such as PEP-8 (https://www.python. org/dev/peps/pep-0008/) or the JavaScript standard style (depending on the language you are using). Readability is also increased by using docstrings. A docstring is a text that is written at the beginning of, for example, a function, describing what it does and possibly what it takes as input. In some cases, it is enough to have a one-liner explanation, such as this:

```python
def swap(a,b):
    """Swaps the variables a and b. Returns the swapped
    variables"""
    return b, a
```

A longer docstring is needed for a more complex function. Explaining the arguments and returns is a good idea:

```python
def function_with_types_in_docstring(param1, param2):
    """Example function with types documented in the
    docstring.

    `PEP 484`_ type annotations are supported. If attribute,
    parameter, and
    return types are annotated according to `PEP 484`_, they
    do not need to be
    included in the docstring:
    Args:
        param1 (int): The first parameter.
        param2 (str): The second parameter.

    Returns:
        bool: The return value. True for success, False
    otherwise.
    """
```

Commenting and documenting: Commenting and documentation are vital for maintaining sustainable code. It is not always possible to explain the code clearly. Comments can be useful in such cases to prevent confusion and explain the code. Comments can convey information such as copyright info, intent, clarification of code, possible warnings, and elaboration of code. Elaborate documentation of the system and modules can enable a team to perform efficiently, and the code and assets can be extended to other developers. For documentation, open source tools are available for documenting APIs such as Swagger (`https://swagger.io`) and Read the Docs (`https://readthedocs.org`). Using the right tools for documentation can enable efficiency and standardize knowledge for developers.

What is good data for ML?

Good ML models are a result of training on good-quality data. Before proceeding to ML training, a pre-requisite is to have good-quality data. Therefore, we need to process the data to increase its quality. So, determining the quality of data is essential. Five characteristics will enable us to discern the quality of data, as follows:

- **Accuracy**: Accuracy is a crucial characteristic of data quality, as having inaccurate data can lead to poor ML model performance and consequences in real life. To check the accuracy of the data, confirm whether the information represents a real-life situation or not.

- **Completeness**: In most cases, incomplete information is unusable and can lead to incorrect outcomes if an ML model is trained on it. It is vital to check the comprehensiveness of the data.

- **Reliability**: Contradictions or duplications in data can lead to the unreliability of the data. Reliability is a vital characteristic; trusting the data is essential, primarily when it is used to make real-life decisions using ML. To some degree, we can assess the reliability of data by examining bias and distribution. In case of any extremities, the data might not be reliable for ML training or might carry bias.

- **Relevance**: The relevance of data plays an essential role in contextualizing and determining if irrelevant information is being gathered. Having relevant data can enable appropriate decisions in real-life contexts using ML.

- **Timeliness**: Obsolete or out-of-date information costs businesses time and money; having up-to-date information is vital in some cases and can improve the quality of data. Decisions enabled by ML using untimely data can be costly and can lead to wrong decisions.

When these five characteristics are maximized, it ensures the highest data quality. With these principles in mind, let's delve into the implementation, where code meets data.

Firstly, let's assess the data and process it to get it ready for ML training. To get started, clone the repository you imported to your Azure DevOps project (from GitHub):

```
git clone https://xxxxxxxxx@dev.azure.com/xxxxx/Learn_MLOps/_
git/Learn_MLOps
```

Next, open your terminal and access the folder of the cloned repository and spin up the JupyterLab server for data processing. To do so, type the following command in the terminal:

```
jupyter lab
```

This will automatically open a window in your browser at `http://localhost:8888` where you can code and execute the code on the JupyterLab interface. In the `Code_meets_data_c3` folder, there is a Python script (`dataprocessing.py`) and a `.ipynb` notebook (`dataprocessing.ipynb`); feel free to run any of these files or create a new notebook and follow the upcoming steps.

We will perform computing for tasks as described in *Figure 3.6*. Data processing will be done locally on your PC, followed by ML training, deploying, and monitoring on compute targets in the cloud. This is to acquire experience of implementing models in various setups. In the rest of this chapter, we will do data processing (locally) to get the data to the best quality in order to do ML training (in the cloud, which is described in the next chapter).

S.no	Task	Compute (location)
1	Data processing	Local
2	ML training	Cloud
3	Deploying ML models	Cloud
4	Monitor ML models	Cloud

Figure 3.6 – Computation locations for data and ML tasks

To process raw data and get it ready for ML, you will do the compute and data processing on your local PC. We start by installing and importing the required packages and importing the raw dataset (as shown in the dataprocessing.ipynb and .py scripts). Python instructions in the notebooks must be executed in the existing notebook:

```
%matplotlib inline
import pandas as pd
import numpy as np
from matplotlib import pyplot as plt
from matplotlib.pyplot import figure
import seaborn as sns
from azureml.core import Workspace, Dataset
#import dataset
df = pd.read_csv('Dataset/weather_dataset_raw.csv')
```

With this, you have imported the dataset into a pandas DataFrame, df, for further processing.

Data preprocessing

Raw data cannot be directly passed to the ML model for training purposes. We have to refine or preprocess the data before training the ML model. To further analyze the imported data, we will perform a series of steps to preprocess the data into a suitable shape for the ML training. We start by assessing the quality of the data to check for accuracy, completeness, reliability, relevance, and timeliness. After this, we calibrate the required data and encode text into numerical data, which is ideal for ML training. Lastly, we will analyze the correlations and time series, and filter out irrelevant data for training ML models.

Data quality assessment

To assess the quality of the data, we look for accuracy, completeness, reliability, relevance, and timeliness. Firstly, let's check if the data is complete and reliable by assessing the formats, cumulative statistics, and anomalies such as missing data. We use pandas functions as follows:

```
df.describe()
```

By using the `describe` function, we can observe descriptive statistics in the output as follows:

	S_No	Temperature_C	Apparent_Temperature_C	Humidity	Wind_speed_kmph	Wind_bearing_degrees	Visibility_km	Pressure_millibars
count	96453.000000	96453.000000	96453.000000	96453.000000	96453.000000	96453.000000	96453.000000	96453.000000
mean	48226.000000	11.932678	10.855029	0.734899	10.810640	187.509232	10.347325	1003.235956
std	27843.727094	9.551546	10.696847	0.195473	6.913571	107.383428	4.192123	116.969906
min	0.000000	-21.822222	-27.716667	0.000000	0.000000	0.000000	0.000000	0.000000
25%	24113.000000	4.688889	2.311111	0.600000	5.828200	116.000000	8.339800	1011.900000
50%	48226.000000	12.000000	12.000000	0.780000	9.965900	180.000000	10.046400	1016.450000
75%	72339.000000	18.838889	18.838889	0.890000	14.135800	290.000000	14.812000	1021.090000
max	96452.000000	39.905556	39.344444	1.000000	63.852600	359.000000	16.100000	1046.380000

Figure 3.7 – Descriptive statistics of the DataFrame

Some observations can be made to conclude the data is coherent, and relevant as it depicts real-life statistics such as a mean temperature of ~11 C and a wind speed of ~10 kmph. Minimum temperatures in Finland tend to reach around ~-21 C, and there is an average visibility of 10 km. Facts like these depict the relevance and data origin conditions. Now, let's observe the column formats:

```
df.dtypes
```

Here are the formats of each column:

- `S_No`   int64
- `Timestamp`   object
- `Location`   object
- `Temperature_C`   float64
- `Apparent_Temperature_C`   float64
- `Humidity`   float64
- `Wind_speed_kmph`   float64
- `Wind_bearing_degrees`   int64
- `Visibility_km`   float64
- `Pressure_millibars`   float64
- `Weather_conditions`   object
- `dtype:`   object

Most of the columns are numerical (`float` and `int`), as expected. The `Timestamp` column is in `object` format, which needs to be changed to `DateTime` format:

```
df['Timestamp'] = pd.to_datetime(df['Timestamp'])
```

Using pandas' `to_datetime` function, we convert `Timestamp` to `DateTime` format. Next, let's see if there are any null values. We use pandas' `isnull` function to check this:

```
df.isnull().values.any()
```

Upon checking for any null values, if null values are discovered, as a next step the calibration of missing data is essential.

Calibrating missing data

It is not ideal to have missing values in the data as it is a sign of poor data quality. Missing data or values can be replaced using various techniques without compromising the correctness and reliability of data. After inspecting the data we have been working on, some missing values are observed. We use the `Forward fill` method to handle missing data:

```
df['Weather_conditions'].fillna(method='ffill', inplace=True,
axis=0)
```

NaN or null values have only been observed in the `Weather_conditions` column. We replace the NaN values by using the `fillna()` method from pandas and the forward fill (`ffill`) method. As weather is progressive, it is likely to replicate the previous event in the data. Hence, we use the forward fill method, which replicates the last observed non-null value until another non-null value is encountered.

Label encoding

As the machines do not understand human language or text, all the text has to be converted into numbers. Before that, let's process the text. We have a `Weather_conditons` column in text with values or labels such as `rain`, `snow`, and `clear`. These values are found using pandas' `value_counts()` function, as follows:

```
df['Weather_conditions'].value_counts()
```

`Weather_conditions` can be simplified by categorizing the column label into two labels, `rain` or `no_rain`. Forecasting in these two categories will enable us to solve the business problem for the cargo company:

```
df['Weather_conditions'].replace({"snow": "no_rain",  "clear":
"no_rain"}, inplace=True)
```

This will replace both `snow` and `clear` values with `no_rain` as both conditions imply no rain conditions at the port. Now that labels are processed, we can convert the `Weather_conditions` column into a machine-readable form or numbers using **label encoding**. Label encoding is a method of converting categorical values into a machine-readable form or numbers by assigning each category a unique value. As we have only two categories, `rain` and `no_rain`, label encoding can be efficient as it converts these values to 0 and 1. If there are more than two values, **one-hot encoding** is a good choice because assigning incremental numbers to categorical variables can give the variables higher priority or numerical bias during training. One-hot encoding prevents bias or higher preference for any variable, ensuring neutral privileges to each value of categorical variables. In our case, as we have only two categorical variables, we perform label encoding using scikit-learn as follows:

```
from sklearn.preprocessing import LabelEncoder
le = LabelEncoder()
y = df['Weather_conditions']
y = le.fit_transform(y)
```

Here, we import the `LabelEncoder()` function, which will encode the `Weather_conditions` column into 0s and 1s using the `fit_transform()` method. We can do this by replacing the previous textual column with a label encoded or machine-readable form to column `Weather_condition` as follows:

```
y = pd.DataFrame(data=y, columns=["Weather_condition"])
df = pd.concat([df,y], axis=1)
df.drop(['Weather_conditions'], axis=1, inplace=True)
```

Here, we concatenate our new label-encoded or machine-readable `Weather_condition` column to the DataFrame and drop the previous non-machine readable or textual `Weather_conditions` column. Data is now in machine-readable form and ready for further processing. You can check the transformed data by executing `df.head()` in the notebook (optional).

New feature – Future_weather_condition

As we are tasked with forecasting weather conditions 4 hours in the future, we create a new feature named `Future_weather_condition` by shifting `Current_weather_condition` by four rows, as each row is recorded with a time gap of an hour. `Future_weather_condition` is the label of future weather conditions 4 hours ahead. We will use this new feature as a dependent variable to forecast using ML:

```
df['Future_weather_condition'] = df.Current_weather_condition.
shift(4, axis = 0)
df.dropna(inplace=True)
```

We will use pandas' `dropna()` function on the DataFrame to discard or drop null values, because some rows will have null values due to shifting to a new column.

Data correlations and filtering

Now that the data is fully machine readable, we can observe the correlations using the **Pearson correlation coefficient** to observe how every single column is related to the other columns. Data and feature correlation is a vital step before feature selection for ML model training, especially when the features are continuous, like in our case. The Pearson correlation coefficient is a statistical linear correlation between each variable (X and y) that produces a value between $+1$ and -1. A value of $+1$ is a positive linear correlation, -1 is a negative linear correlation, and 0 is no linear correlation. It can be used to understand the relationship between continuous variables, though it is worth noting that Pearson correlation does not mean causation. We can observe Pearson correlation coefficients for our data using pandas as follows:

```
df.corr(method="pearson")
# Visualizing using heatmap
corrMatrix = df.corr()
sn.heatmap(corrMatrix, annot=True)
plt.show()
```

Here is the heatmap of the `Pearson` correlation results:

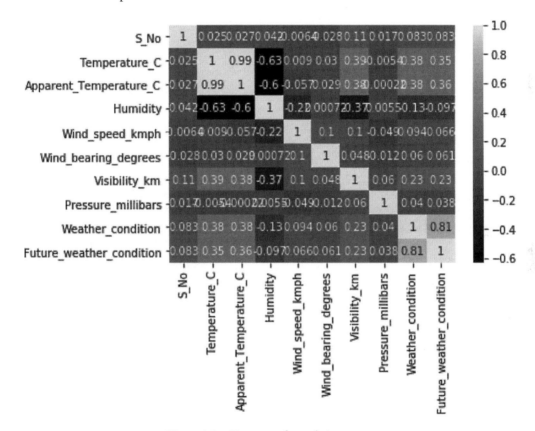

Figure 3.8 – Heatmap of correlation scores

From the heatmap in *Figure 3.8*, we can see that the `Temperature` and `Apparent_Temperature_C` coefficient is `0.99`. `S_No` (Serial number) is a continuous value, which is more or less like an incremental index for a DataFrame and can be discarded or filtered out as it does not provide great value. Hence both `Apparent_Temperature` and `S_No` are dropped or filtered. Now let's observe our dependent variable, `Future_weather_condition`, and its correlation with other independent variables:

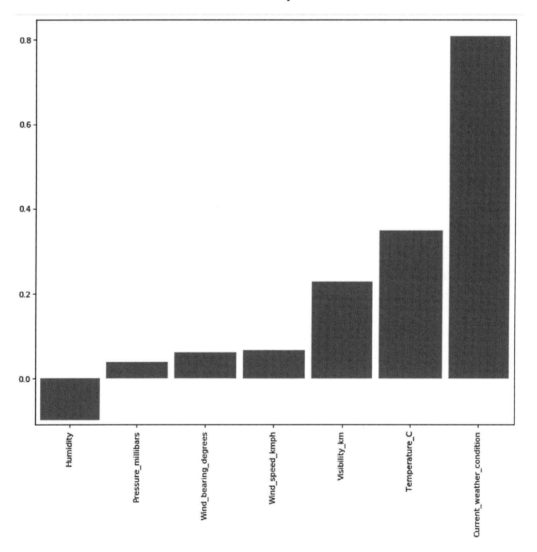

Figure 3.9 – Pearson correlation for Future_weather_condition

Anything between 0.5 and 1.0 has a positive correlation and anything between -0.5 and -1.0 has a negative correlation. Judging from the graph, there is a positive correlation with `Current_weather_condition`, and `Temperature_C` is also positively correlated with `Future_weather_c`.

Time series analysis

As the temperature is a continuous variable, it is worth observing its progression over time. We can visualize a time series plot using matplotlib as follows:

```
time = df['Timestamp]
temp = df['Temperature_C']
# plot graph
plt.plot(time, temp)
plt.show()
```

Here's the resulting plot:

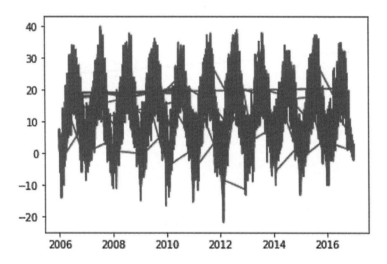

Figure 3.10 – Time series progression of Temperature in C

After assessing the time series progression of temperature in *Figure 3.10*, we can see that it depicts a stationary pattern since the mean, variance, and covariance are observed to be stationary over time. Stationary behaviors can be trends, cycles, random walks, or a combination of the three. It makes sense, as temperature changes over seasons and follows seasonal patterns. This brings us to the end of data analysis and processing; we are now ready to register the processed data in the workspace before proceeding to train the ML model.

Data registration and versioning

It is vital to register and version the data in the workspace before starting ML training as it enables us to backtrack our experiments or ML models to the source of data used for training the models. The purpose of versioning the data is to backtrack at any point, to replicate a model's training, or to explain the workings of the model as per the inference or testing data for explaining the ML model. For these reasons, we will register the processed data and version it to use it for our ML pipeline. We will register and version the processed data to the Azure Machine Learning workspace using the Azure Machine Learning SDK as follows:

```
subscription_id = '---insert your subscription ID here----'
resource_group = 'Learn_MLOps'
workspace_name = 'MLOps_WS'
workspace = Workspace(subscription_id, resource_group,
workspace_name)
```

Fetch your `subscription ID`, `resource_group` and `workspace_name` from the Azure Machine Learning portal, as shown in *Figure 3.11*:

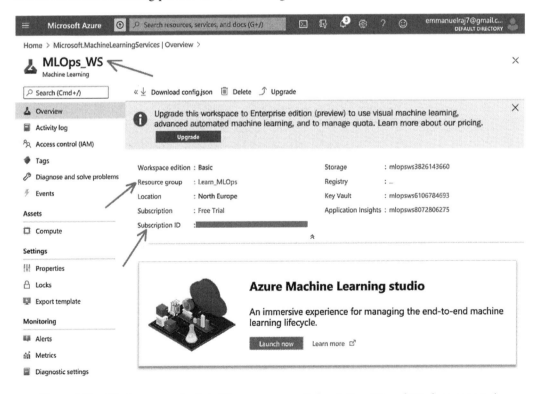

Figure 3.11 – Workspace credentials (Resource group, Subscription ID, and Workspace name)

By requesting the workspace credentials, a workspace object is obtained. When running the `Workspace()` function, your notebook will be connected to the Azure platform. You will be prompted to click on an authentication link and provide a random code and the Azure account details. After that, the script will confirm the authentication. Using the workspace object, we access the default data store and upload the required data files to the data store on Azure Blob Storage connected to the workspace:

```
# get the default datastore linked to upload prepared data
datastore = workspace.get_default_datastore()
#upload the local file from src_dir to target_path in datastore
datastore.upload(src_dir='Dataset', target_path='data')
dataset =  /
Dataset.Tablular.from_delimited_files(datastore.path('data/
weather_dataset_processed.csv'))
```

`Tabular.from_delimited_files()` may cause a failure in Linux or MacOS machines that do not have .NET Core 2.1 installed. For correct installation of this dependency, follow these instructions: `https://docs.microsoft.com/en-us/dotnet/core/install/linux`. After successfully executing the preceding commands, you will upload the data file to the data store and see the result shown in *Figure 3.12*. You can preview the dataset from the datastore as follows:

```
# preview the first 3 rows of the dataset from the datastore
dataset.take(3).to_pandas_dataframe()
```

When the data is uploaded to the data store, then we will register the dataset to the workspace and version it as follows:

```
weather_ds = dataset.register(workspace=workspace,
name=weather_ds_portofTurku, description='processed weather
data')
```

The register(...) function registers the dataset to the workspace, as shown in *Figure 3.12*. For detailed documentation, visit https://docs.microsoft.com/en-us/azure/machine-learning/how-to-create-register-datasets#register-datasets:

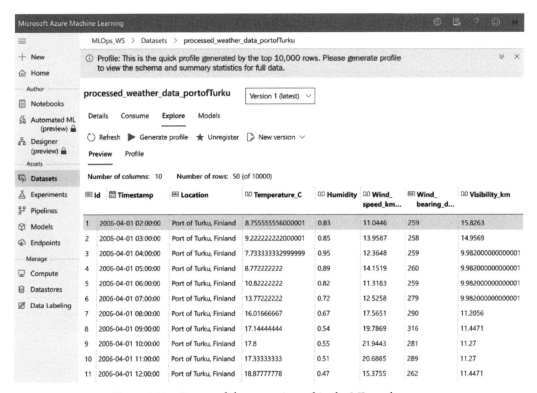

Figure 3.12 – Processed dataset registered in the ML workspace

Toward the ML Pipeline

So far, we have processed the data by working on irregularities such as missing data, selected features by observing correlations, created new features, and finally ingested and versioned the processed data to the Machine learning workspace. There are two ways to fuel the data ingestion for ML model training in the ML pipeline. One way is from the central storage (where all your raw data is stored) and the second way is using a feature store. As knowledge is power, Let's get to know the use of the feature store before we move to the ML pipeline.

Feature Store

A feature store compliments the central storage by storing important features and make them available for training or inference. A feature store is a store where you transform raw data into useful features that ML models can use directly to train and infer to make predictions. Raw Data typically comes from various data sources, which are structured, unstructured, streaming, batch, and real-time. It all needs to get pulled, transformed (using a feature pipeline), and stored somewhere, and that somewhere can be the feature store. The feature store then takes the data and makes it available for consumption. Data scientists tend to duplicate work (especially data processing). It can be avoided if we have a centralized feature store. Feature store allows data scientists to efficiently share and reuse features with other teams and thereby increase their productivity as they don't have to pre-process features from scratch.

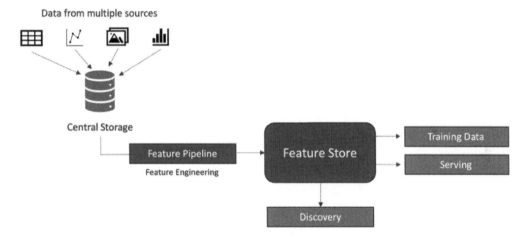

Figure 3.13: Feature store workflow

As we can see in *Figure 3.13*, a **Feature Store** is using a **Feature Pipeline** connected to a **Central Storage** (which stores data from multiple sources) to transform and store raw data into useful features for ML training. The features stored in the feature store can be retrieved for training, serving, or discovering insights or trends. Here are some benefits of using a feature Store:

- Efficient **Feature Engineering** for **Training Data**
- Avoid unnecessary data pre-processing before training
- Avoid repetitive feature engineering
- Features available for quick inferencing (testing)
- System support for serving of features

- Exploratory Data Analysis by feature Store

- Opportunity to reuse models features

- Quick Queries on features

- Reproducibility for training data sets

- Monitoring feature drift in production (we will learn about feature drift in *Chapter 12, Model Serving and Monitoring*)

- Features available for data drift monitoring

It is good to know the advantages of a feature store as it can be useful to fuel the ML pipeline (especially the data ingestion step), however not suitable for all cases. It depends on your use case. For our use case implementation, we will not use feature store but proceed to liaisoning data directly from central storage where we have preprocessed and registered the datasets we need for training and testing. With ingested and versioned data, you are set to proceed towards building your ML Pipeline. The ML pipeline will enable further feature engineering, feature scaling, curating training, and testing datasets that will be used to train ML models and tune hyperparameters for machine learning training. The ML pipeline and functionalities will be performed over cloud computing resources, unlike locally on your computer as we did in this chapter. It will be purely cloud-based.

Summary

In this chapter, we have learned how to identify a suitable ML solution to a business problem and categorize operations to implement suitable MLOps. We set up our tools, resources, and development environment. 10 principles of source code management were discussed, followed by data quality characteristics. Congrats! So far, you have implemented a critical building block of the MLOps workflow – data processing and registering processed data to the workspace. Lastly, we had a glimpse into the essentials of the ML pipeline.

In the next chapter, you will do the most exciting part of MLOps: building the ML pipeline. Let's press on!

4
Machine Learning Pipelines

In this chapter, we will explore and implement **machine learning** (**ML**) pipelines by going through hands-on examples using the MLOps approach. We will learn more by solving the business problem that we've been working on in *Chapter 3, Code Meets Data*. This theoretical and practical approach to learning will ensure that you will have comprehensive knowledge of architecting and implementing ML pipelines for your problems or your company's problems. A ML pipeline has modular scripts or code that perform all the traditional steps in ML, such as data preprocessing, feature engineering, and feature scaling before training or retraining any model.

We begin this chapter by ingesting the preprocessed data we worked on in the last chapter by performing feature engineering and scaling it to get it in shape for the ML training. We will discover the principles of ML pipelines and implement them on the business problem. Going ahead, we'll look into ML model training, hyperparameter tuning, and the testing of the trained models. Finally, we'll learn about packaging the models and their needed artifacts. We'll register the models for further evaluation and will deploy the ML models. We are going to cover the following main topics in this chapter:

- Going through the basics of ML pipelines

- Data ingestion and feature engineering

- ML training and hyperparameter optimization

- Model testing and defining metrics

- Model packaging

- Registering models and production artifacts

Going through the basics of ML pipelines

Before we jump into the implementation of the ML pipeline, let's get the basics right. We will reflect on ML pipelines and set up the needed resources for ML pipeline implementation and then we will get started with data ingestion. Let's demystify ML pipelines by reflecting on the ML pipeline we discussed in *Figure 14* of *Chapter 1, Fundamentals of MLOps Workflow*.

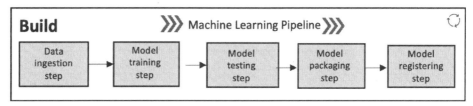

Figure 4.1 – Machine learning pipeline

As shown in *Figure 4.1*, a comprehensive ML pipeline consists of the following steps:

1. Data ingestion

2. Model training

3. Model testing

4. Model packaging

5. Model registering

We will implement all these steps of the pipeline using the Azure ML service (cloud-based) and MLflow (open source) simultaneously for the sake of a diverse perspective. Azure ML and MLflow are a power couple for MLOps: they exhibit the features shown in *Table 4.1*. They are also unique in their capabilities, as we can see from the following table.

Capability	MLflow Tracking and Deployment	Azure Machine Learning Python and SDK
Manage workspace		✓
Use data stores		✓
Log metrics	✓	✓

Capability	MLflow Tracking and Deployment	Azure Machine Learning Python and SDK
Upload artifacts	✓	✓
View metrics	✓	✓
Manage compute		✓
Deploy models	✓	✓
Monitor model performance		✓
Detect data drift		✓

Table 4.2 – MLflow versus Azure ML service

To implement the ML pipeline, we need a storage resource for our dataset and a computational resource for our ML models. As discussed before in *Chapter 2, Characterizing Your Machine Learning Problem*, we will perform the computation required to implement the ML pipeline and the business problem, as shown in *Figure 4.2*.

We process the data on our local computer or PC to get started and preprocess the data for our ML training. For ML training and pipeline implementation, we use compute resources provisioned on the cloud (Microsoft Azure). Even though ML training for the pipeline can be done on your local computer, we will use compute resources on the cloud to learn how to provision and use the needed compute resources for the ML pipeline.

S.no	Task	Compute (location)
1	Data Processing	local
2	Machine Learning training	Cloud
3	Deploying ML models	Cloud
4	Monitor ML models	Cloud

Figure 4.3 – Computation location for data and ML tasks

Without further ado, let's configure the needed compute resources for the ML pipeline using the following steps:

1. Go to your ML workspace.

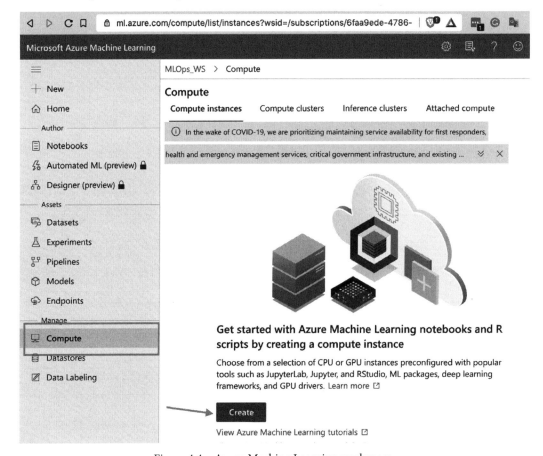

Figure 4.4 – Azure Machine Learning workspace

2. Go to the **Compute** option and click the **Create** button to explore compute options available on the cloud.

3. Select the suitable compute option for the ML model training to be optimal and efficient.

Select a suitable compute option based on your training needs and cost limitations and give it a name. For example, in *Figure 4.4*, a compute or virtual machine is selected for the experiment **Standard_D1_v2**: it is a CPU with 1 Core, 3.5 GB of RAM, and 50 GB of disk space. To select the suggested machine configuration or size, you must check **select from all options** in the **Virtual machine size** section. After selecting the desired virtual machine configuration or size, click the **Next** button to proceed and you will see the screen shown in *Figure 4.4*.

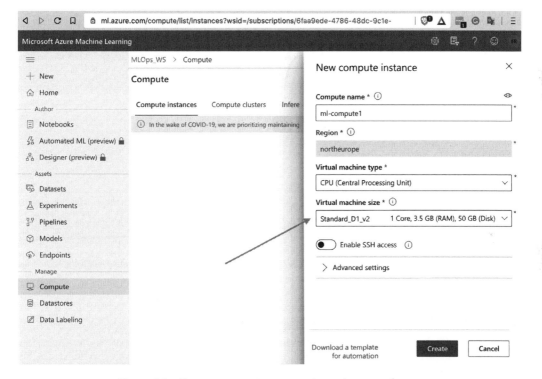

Figure 4.5 – Create a compute resource in an Azure workspace

Select a compute name that is unique within an Azure region (it is recommended to use something like `unique_code-ml-compute1`). The selected compute option in *Figure 4.4* is one of the cheapest compute options and this is sufficient for implementing the ML pipeline for the business problem. For faster implementation and training ML models, it is recommended to use the `STANDARD_DS11_V2` (2 cores, 14 GB RAM) virtual machine size. With this option, training a model will take around 12 minutes.

4. Provision the compute resource created previously. After naming and creating the needed compute resource, your compute resource is provisioned, ready, and running for ML training on the cloud, as shown in *Figure 4.5*.

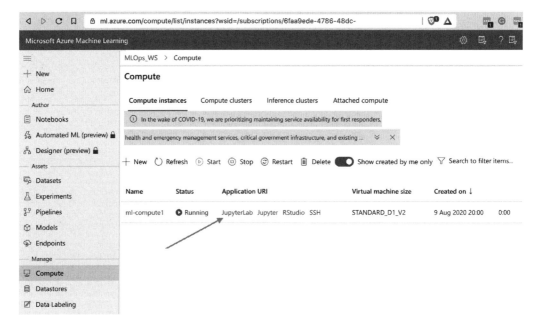

Figure 4.6 – Provisioned compute in an AzureML workspace

After it is provisioned, select the **JupyterLab** option. JupyterLab is an open source web-based user interface. It comes with features such as text editor, code editor, terminal, and custom components integrated in an extensible manner. We will use this as a programming interface connected to the provisioned compute to train the ML models.

Now we'll begin with the hands-on implementation of the ML pipeline. Follow these steps to implement the ML pipeline:

1. To start the implementation, clone the repository you have imported into the Azure DevOps project. To clone the repository, click on the **Clone** button in the upper-right corner from the **Repos** menu and then click on the **Generate Git Credentials** button. A hash password will be created.

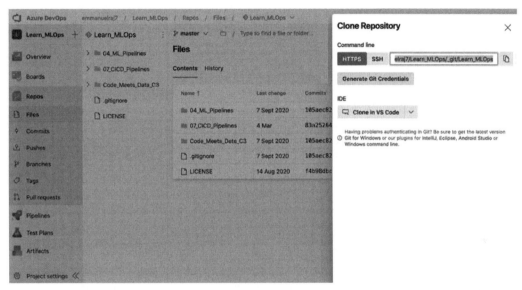

Figure 4.7 – Cloning an Azure DevOps Git repository (Generate Git Credentials)

2. Copy the HTTPS link from the **Command Line** section to get the Azure DevOps repository link, like this:

```
https://xxxxxxxxx@dev.azure.com/xxxxx/Learn_MLOps/_git/
Learn_MLOps
```

3. Copy the password generated from *step 1* and add it to the link from *step 2* by adding the password just after the first username separated by : before the @ character. Then it is possible to use the following `git clone` command without getting permission errors:

```
git clone https://user:password_hash@dev.azure.com/user/
repo_created
```

4. Once you are running JupyterLab, we will access the terminal to clone the repository to the azure compute. To access the terminal, you must select the **Terminal** option from the **Launcher** tab. Another way to access the terminal directly is by using the Terminal link from the Application URI column in the list of compute instances in the Azure ML workspace. Go to the **Terminal** option of JupyterLab and implement the following (as shown in *Figure 4.7*):

```
git clone https://xxxxxxxxx@dev.azure.com/xxxxx/Learn_
MLOps/_git/Learn_MLOps
```

Here is the output:

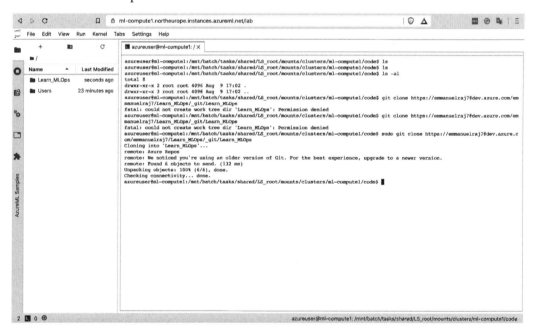

Figure 4.8 – Clone the Azure DevOps Git repository on Azure compute

5. Go to the `04_MLpipelines` folder and follow the implementation steps on `ML-pipeline.ipynb` from the cloned repository. All of the following steps are implemented in `ML-pipeline.ipynb`. It is recommended to follow the file instructions to have a better understanding of the implementation and execute the code yourself in a new file as per your setup.

   So far, we have provisioned the compute resource and cloned the GitHub repository in the compute.

6. Next, we start implementing the `ML-pipeline.ipynb` file by importing the needed libraries, such as `pandas`, `numpy`, `azureml`, `pickle`, `mlflow`, and others, as shown in the following code block:

```
import pandas as pd
import numpy as np
import warnings
from math import sqrt
warnings.filterwarnings('ignore')
from azureml.core.run import Run
from azureml.core.experiment import Experiment
from azureml.core.workspace import Workspace
from azureml.core.model import Model
from azureml.core.authentication import
ServicePrincipalAuthentication
from azureml.train.automl import AutoMLConfig
import pickle
from matplotlib import pyplot as plt
from matplotlib.pyplot import figure
import mlflow
```

7. Next, we use setup MLflow (for tracking experiments). Use the `get_mlflow_tracking_url()` function to get a tracking ID for where MLflow experiments and artifacts should be logged (in this case, we get the tracking ID for the provisioned training compute). Then use the `set_tracking_uri()` function to connect to a tracking URI (the uniform resource identifier of a specific resource) for the provisioned training compute. The tracking URI can be either for a remote server, a database connection string, or a local path to log data in a local directory. In our case, we point the tracking URI to the local path by default (on the provisioned training compute):

```
uri = workspace.get_mlflow_tracking_uri( )
mlflow.set_tracking_uri(uri)
```

The URI defaults to the `mlruns` folder where MLflow artifacts and logs will be saved for experiments.

By setting the tracking URI for your MLflow experiments, you have set the location for MLflow to save its artifacts and logs in the `mlruns` folder (on your provisioned compute). After executing these commands, check for the current path. You will find the `mlruns` folder.

Data ingestion and feature engineering

Data is essential to train ML models; without data, there is no ML. Data ingestion is a trigger step for the ML pipeline. It deals with the volume, velocity, veracity, and variety of data by extracting data from various data sources and ingesting the needed data for model training.

The ML pipeline is initiated by ingesting the right data for training the ML models. We will start by accessing the preprocessed data we registered in the previous chapter. Follow these steps to access and import the preprocessed data and get it ready for ML training:

1. Using the `Workspace()` function from the Azure ML SDK, access the data from the datastore in the ML workspace as follows:

```
from azureml.core import Workspace, Dataset
subscription_id = 'xxxxxx-xxxxxx-xxxxxx-xxxxxxx'
resource_group = 'Learn_MLOps'
workspace_name = 'MLOps_WS'
workspace = Workspace(subscription_id, resource_group,
workspace_name)
```

> **Note**
>
> Insert your own credentials, such as `subscription_id`, `resource_group`, and `workspace_name` and initiate a workspace object using these credentials.

When these instructions are successfully executed in the JupyterLab, you can run the remaining blocks of code in the next cells.

2. Import the preprocessed dataset that was prepared in the previous chapter. The preprocessed dataset is imported using the `.get_by_name()` function from the `Dataset` function from the Azureml SDK and the function is used to retrieve the needed dataset:

```
# Importing pre-processed dataset
dataset = Dataset.get_by_name (workspace,
 name='processed_weather_data_portofTurku')
print(dataset.name, dataset.version)
```

3. Upon successfully retrieving or mounting the dataset, you can confirm by printing `dataset.name` and `dataset.version`, which should print `processed_weather_data_portofTurku 1` or as per the name you have given the dataset previously.

4. After retrieving the preprocessed data, it is vital to split it into training and validation sets in order to train the ML model and test or evaluate it in the training phase and later stages. Hence, we split it into the training and validation sets, by splitting it in the 80% (training set) and 20% (test set) split-ratio as follows:

```
df_training = df.iloc[:77160]
df_test = df.drop(df_training.index)
df_training.to_csv('Data/training_data.csv',index=False)
df_test.to_csv('Data/test_data.csv',index=False)
```

5. After successfully splitting the data, these two datasets are stored and registered to the datastore (connected to the Azure ML workspace) as follows:

```
datastore = workspace.get_default_datastore()
datastore.upload(src_dir='Data', target_path='data')
training_dataset = /
Dataset.Tabular.from_delimited_files(datastore.
path('data/training_data.csv'))
```

```
validation_dataset = /
Dataset.Tabular.from_delimited_files(datastore.
path('data/validation_data.csv'))

training_ds = training_dataset.
register(workspace=workspace, name='training_dataset',
description='Dataset to use for ML training')
test_ds = validation_dataset.register(workspace=workspace,
                                      name='test_dataset',
description='Dataset for validation ML models')
```

By using the register() function, we are able to register the training and test datasets, which can be imported later from the datastore.

Next, we will import the training data and ingest it into the ML pipeline and use the test dataset later to test the model's performance on unseen data in production or for model analysis.

Data ingestion (training dataset)

To ingest training data into the ML pipeline, we start by importing it using the get_by_name() function and converting it to a pandas dataframe using the to_pandas_dataframe() function:

```
dataset = Dataset.get_by_name (workspace, name='training_
dataset')
print(dataset.name, dataset.version)
df = dataset.to_pandas_dataframe ( )
```

The training dataset is now retrieved and will be used to further train the ML models. The goal is to train classification models to predict whether it will rain or not. Hence, select the Temperature, Humidity, Wind_speed, Wind_bearing, Visibility, Pressure, and Current_weather_conditions features to train the binary classification models to predict weather conditions in the future (4 hours ahead).

Follow these steps to select features and scale them:

1. Before training the ML models, selecting the right features and scaling the data is vital. Therefore, we select features as follows. The values in the variable X represent the independent variables and the variable Y is the dependent variable (forecasted weather):

```
X = df[['Temperature_C', 'Humidity', 'Wind_speed_kmph',
 'Wind_bearing_degrees', 'Visibility_km', 'Pressure_
 millibars', 'Current_weather_condition']].values

y = df['Future_weather_condition'].values
```

2. Split the training data into the training and testing sets (for training validation after training) using the `train_test_split()` function from `sklearn`. Fixing the random seed (`random_state`) is needed to reproduce a training session by keeping the samples from the previous experiment with the same configuration. Hence, we will use `random_state=1`:

```
# Splitting the Training dataset into Train and Test set
for ML training
from sklearn.model_selection import train_test_split

X_train, X_val,  y_train, y_val = train_test_split(X, y,
 test_size=0.2, random_state=1)
```

With an 80% (training data) and 20% (test data) split, the training and test datasets are now ready for feature scaling and ML model training.

3. For the ML model training to be optimal and efficient, the data needs to be on the same scale. Therefore, we scale the data using `StandardScalar()` from `sklearn` to calibrate all the numeric values in the data on the same scale:

```
from sklearn.preprocessing import StandardScaler

sc = StandardScaler()

X_train = sc.fit_transform(X_train)

X_val = sc.transform(X_val)
```

With this step, the numeric values of the training data are scaled using `StandardScalar` and all the values are transformed in the range of `-1` to `1`, based on `X_train values`. Now we are ready to train ML models (the fun part)!

Machine learning training and hyperparameter optimization

We are all set to do the fun part, training ML models! This step enables model training; it has modular scripts or code that perform all the traditional steps in ML training, such as fitting and transforming data to train the model and hyperparameter tuning to converge the best model. The output of this step is a trained ML model.

To solve the business problem, we will train two well-known models using the **Support Vector Machine** classifier and the **Random Forest** classifier. These are chosen based on their popularity and consistency of results; you are free to choose models of your choice – there are no limitations in this step. First, we will train the Support Vector Machine classifier and then the Random Forest classifier.

Support Vector Machine

Support Vector Machine (SVM) is a popular supervised learning algorithm (used for classification and regression). The data points are classified using hyperplanes in an N-dimensional space. It is known for producing significant accuracy with less computation power. It is recommended to know SVM, in theory, to better understand the model training in practice. To learn more about SVM, head here: `https://www.kdnuggets.com/2017/02/yhat-support-vector-machine.html`.

Let's get started with training the SVM classifier:

1. We begin by initiating the training or experiment using the `Experiment()` function from the Azure SDK. The purpose of this function is to start a training run or experiment in order to monitor and log the model training performance in the Azure ML workspace:

    ```
    myexperiment = Experiment(workspace, "support-vector-
    machine")
    ```

2. Similarly, the MLflow experiment is also initiated to observe a different perspective:

    ```
    mlflow.set_experiment("mlflow-support-vector-machine")
    ```

    Now we have initiated an experiment in both the Azure ML workspace and MLflow. The following training step will be monitored and logged.

3. Next, we do hyperparameter tuning to find the best parameters to converge the best model. This can be done manually, but more efficient and automatic solutions such as Grid Search or Random Search exist. For training, the SVM classifier uses Grid Search as follows. We proceed by using the `SVC()` and `Grid SearchCV()` functions from `sklearn` and logging the run on Azure ML and MLflow:

```
from sklearn.svm import SVC
from sklearn import svm
from sklearn.model_selection import GridSearchCV
parameters = {'kernel':('linear', 'rbf'), 'C':[1, 10]}
svc = svm.SVC( )
# initialize a run in Azureml and mlflow experiments
run = myexperiment.start_logging()
mlflow.start_run()
run.log("dataset name", dataset.name)
run.log("dataset Version", dataset.version)
svc_grid = GridSearchCV(svc, parameters)
svc_grid.fit(X_train, y_train)
```

The goal of this run or experiment is to train the best SVM model with the best parameters. Grid Search is used to test the different parameter combinations and optimize the convergence of the algorithm to the best performance. Grid Search takes some time to execute (around 15 minutes on the `STANDARD_DS11_V2` (2 cores, 14 GB RAM) compute machine). The result or the output of the Grid Search suggests the best performing parameters to be `C=1` and the kernel as `rbf`. Using `run.log()`, we have logged the dataset used to train the model (the training set) and keep track of the experiment. This data is logged to the Azure ML workspace and the MLflow experiments.

4. Finally, using the best parameters, a new model is trained using `C=1` and `kernel='rbf '` as follows:

```
svc = SVC(C=svc_grid.get_params(deep=True)
['estimator__C'], kernel=svc_grid.get_params(deep=True)
['estimator__kernel'])

svc.fit(X_train, y_train)
# Logging training parameters to AzureML and MLFlow
experiments
```

```
run.log("C", svc_grid.get_params(deep=True)
['estimator__C'])
```

```
run.log("Kernel", svc_grid.get_params(deep=True)
['estimator__kernel'])
```

After training the SVC classifier, the following output
is shown:

```
SVC(C=1.0, cache_size=200, class_weight=None, coef0=0.0,
    decision_function_shape='ovr', degree=3, gamma='auto_
deprecated',
    kernel='rbf', max_iter=-1, probability=False, random_
state=None,
    shrinking=True, tol=0.001, verbose=False)
```

With this, we have trained the SVM model! We will now train the Random Forest classifier model.

Random Forest classifier

Random Forest is another popular supervised learning model (used for classification and regression). Random Forest is an ensemble learning method that operates with a multitude of decision trees. Before performing the model training, it is recommended to know the theoretical working of the Random Forest model. To know more about the Random Forest model, visit https://www.kdnuggets.com/2020/01/random-forest-powerful-ensemble-learning-algorithm.html.

1. To start training the Random Forest classifier, initialize the experiment in the Azure ML workspace and the MLflow experiment as follows:

    ```
    myexperiment = Experiment(workspace, "support-vector-
    machine")
    mlflow.set_experiment("mlflow-support-vector-machine")
    ```

2. After the experiment is successfully initiated, training can be initiated by importing the `RandomForestClassifier()` function from `sklearn.ensemble` and calling the function with the needed parameters, shown as follows. These parameters are randomly chosen (no `Grid Search` is done). `Grid Search` or `RandomizedSearch` can be used to determine the best parameters and optimize the algorithm:

    ```
    from sklearn.ensemble import RandomForestClassifier
    rf = RandomForestClassifier (max_depth=10, random_
    state=0, n_estimators=100)
    ```

3. The model training is done using the `fit(X_train, y_train)` function by passing the training data to it. The training dataset and parameters are logged to Azure ML and MLflow experiments as follows:

```
# initialize runs in Azureml and mlflow
run = myexperiment.start_logging()
mlflow.start_run()
# Log dataset used
run.log("dataset name", dataset.name)
run.log("dataset Version", dataset.version)
rf.fit(X_train, y_train)
# Logging training parameters to AzureML and MLFlow
experiments
run.log("max_depth", 10)
run.log("random_state", 0)
run.log("n_estimators", 100)
```

4. After training, the output is shown as follows:

```
RandomForestClassifier(bootstrap=True, class_weight=None,
criterion='gini',
max_depth=10, max_features='auto', max_leaf_nodes=None,
min_impurity_decrease=0.0, min_impurity_split=None,
min_samples_leaf=1, min_samples_split=2,
min_weight_fraction_leaf=0.0, n_estimators=100, n_
jobs=None,
oob_score=False, random_state=0, verbose=0, warm_
start=False)
```

This is the expected result when finishing training the Random Forest model. With this, you have successfully finished training the Random Forest model and, in total, two ML models: the SVM classifier and the Random Forest classifier.

After training, it is vital to test the performance of the model in terms of accuracy and other metrics to know whether the model is fit enough for the production or testing environment.

Next, we will test the performance of the trained models on the test data that we split before training the models.

Model testing and defining metrics

In this step, we evaluate the trained model performance on a separate set of data points, named test data (which was split and versioned earlier, in the data ingestion step). The inference of the trained model is evaluated according to the selected metrics as per the use case. The output of this step is a report on the trained model performance.

To gain a comprehensive analysis of the model performance, we will measure the accuracy, precision, recall, and f-score. This is what they mean in practice in the context of the business problem:

- **Accuracy**: Number of correct predictions by the total number of predictions of data test samples.

- **Precision**: Precision measures the proportion of positives that were correctly predicted as positive. *Precision = True Positives / (True Positives + False Positives)*

- **Recall**: Recall measures the proportion of actual positives that were identified correctly. *Recall = True Positives / (True Positives + False Negatives)*

- **F-score**: Both precision and recall are taken into account in the calculation of the f-score. It is the harmonic mean (average) of precision and recall. *F1 Score = 2*(Recall * Precision) / (Recall + Precision).*

We will measure these metrics for the trained model on the validation dataset. Let's see the results for the SVM classifier and the Random Forest classifier.

Testing the SVM classifier

Using `sklearn.metrics`, we calculate the `accuracy`, `f1_score`, `precision`, and `recall` for the model performance on test data samples and log them to the Azure ML workspace and MLflow experiments using the `run.log()` function as follows.

From `sklearn.metrics`, import `accuracy_score`, `f1_score`, `precision_score`, and `recall_score`:

```
predicted_svc = svc.predict(X_test)
acc = accuracy_score(y_test, predicted_svc)
fscore = f1_score(y_test, predicted_svc, average="macro")
precision = precision_score(y_test, predicted_svc,
average="macro")
```

```
recall = recall_score(y_test, predicted_svc, average="macro")
run.log("Test_accuracy", acc)
run.log("Precision", precision)
run.log("Recall", recall)
run.log("F-Score", fscore)
run.log("Git-sha", sha)
```

The results of the test data metrics are logged in the Azure ML workspace as per the experiment. You can read these logs later after registering the model (we will register the model in *Registering models and production artifacts*).

Testing the Random Forest classifier

Similar to what we did for the SVM classifier model, using `sklearn.metrics` we calculate the `accuracy`, `f1_score`, `precision`, and `recall`:

```
acc = accuracy_score(y_test, predicted_rf)
fscore = f1_score(y_test, predicted_rf, average="macro")
precision = precision_score(y_test, predicted_rf,
average="macro")
recall = recall_score(y_test, predicted_rf, average="macro")
run.log("Test_accuracy", acc)
run.log("Precision", precision)
run.log("Recall", recall)
run.log("F-Score", fscore)
run.log("Git-sha", sha)
```

The output of the model performance metrics on test data samples are logged to the Azure ML workspace and MLflow experiments using the `run.log()` function.

Model packaging

After the trained model has been tested in the previous step, the model can be serialized into a file to be exported to the test or the production environment. Serialized files come with compatibility challenges, such as model interoperability, if not done right. Model interoperability is a challenge, especially when models are trained using different frameworks. For example, if model 1 is trained using `sklearn` and model 2 is trained using TensorFlow, then model 1 cannot be imported or exported using TensorFlow for further model fine-tuning or model inference.

To avoid this problem, ONNX offers an open standard for model interoperability. ONNX stands for Open Neural Network Exchange. It provides a serialization standard for importing and exporting models. We will use the ONNX format to serialize the models to avoid compatibility and interoperability issues.

Using ONNX, the trained model is serialized using the skl2onnx library. The model is serialized as the file svc.onnx for further exporting and importing of the model into test and production environments:

```
# Convert into SVC model into ONNX format file
from skl2onnx import convert_sklearn
from skl2onnx.common.data_types import FloatTensorType
initial_type = [('float_input', FloatTensorType([None, 6]))]
onx = convert_sklearn(svc, initial_types=initial_type)
with open("outputs/svc.onnx", "wb") as f:
    f.write(onx.SerializeToString())
```

The output of this code is a serialized svc.onnx file. Similarly, using ONNX, we will convert the Random Forest model into a serialized file named rf.onnx for further exporting and importing of the model into test and production environments:

```
# Convert into RF model into ONNX format file
from skl2onnx import convert_sklearn
from skl2onnx.common.data_types import FloatTensorType
initial_type = [('float_input', FloatTensorType([None, 6]))]
onx = convert_sklearn(rf, initial_types=initial_type)
with open("outputs/rf.onnx", "wb") as f:
    f.write(onx.SerializeToString())
```

The output of this code is a serialized rf.onnx file. Next, we will register these serialized models to the model registry.

Registering models and production artifacts

In this step, the model that has been serialized or containerized in the previous step is registered and stored in the model registry. A registered model is compiled as a logical container for one or more files that function as a model. For instance, a model made up of multiple files can be registered as a single model in the model registry. By downloading the registered model, all the files can be received. The registered model can be deployed and used for inference on demand.

Let's register our serialized models in the previous section by using the `model` `.register()` function from the Azure ML SDK. By using this function, the serialized ONNX file is registered to the workspace for further use and deploying to the test and production environment. Let's register the serialized SVM classifier model (`svc.onnx`):

```
# Register Model on AzureML WS
model = Model.register (model_path = './outputs/svc.onnx', #
this points to a local file
                          model_name = "support-vector-
classifier",
                          tags = {'dataset': dataset.name,
'version': dataset.version, 'hyparameter-C': '1', 'testdata-
accuracy': '0.9519'},
                          model_framework='pandas==0.23.4',
                          description = "Support vector classifier
to predict weather at port of Turku",
                          workspace = workspace)


print('Name:', model.name)
print('Version:', model.version)
```

The model is registered by naming and tagging the model as per the need. We can confirm the successful registering of the model by checking the registered model name and version. The output will reflect the model name you used when registering (for example, `support-vector-classifier`) and will show the model version as 1. Likewise, let's register the serialized Random Forest classifier model (`rf.onnx`):

```
# Register Model on AzureML WS
model = Model.register (model_path = './outputs/rf.onnx', #
this points to a local file
                          model_name = "random-forest-classifier",
                          tags = {'dataset': dataset.name,
'version': dataset.version, 'hyparameter-C': '1', 'testdata-
accuracy': '0.9548'},
                          model_framework='pandas==0.23.4',
                          description = "Random forest classifier
to predict weather at port of Turku",
                          workspace = workspace)

print('Name:', model.name)
print('Version:', model.version)
```

After successful registering of the model, the output of the `print` function will reflect the model name you used while registering (`random-forest-classifier`) and will show the model version as `1`. Lastly, we will register production artifacts for inference. Now you can see both models in the **Models** section of the Azure ML workspace as shown in *Figure 4.8*:

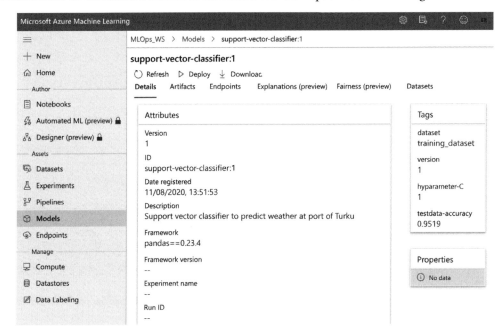

Figure 4.9 – Registered SVM model (with test metrics)

This way, you can visualize and analyze your training and testing logs for each model trained in the Azure ML workspace. It offers a bird's-eye view of training and testing the model while enabling traceability for registered models.

Registering production artifacts

For model inference in real time, a scalar is needed in order to scale the incoming data on the scale at which the data was scaled for ML training. We will use the same scaler function used for `scaling X_train` using `sc.fit_transform(X_train)` and serialize this variable into a `pickle` file. Lastly, we register this `pickle` file to the workspace for further retrieval and usage as needed (especially for model inference in the test and production environment). Using `pickle`, write the scaler variable `sc` into a `pickle` file using the `pickle.dump()` function as follows.

Import `pickle` with `open('./outputs/scaler.pkl', 'wb') as scaler_pkl:`

```
pickle.dump(sc, scaler_pkl)
```

The output of the code will save a serialized `pickle` file for the scaler with the filename `scaler.pkl`. Next, we will register this file to the model registry to later download and deploy together with our models for inference. The scaler is registered using the `model.register()` function as follows:

```
# Register Model on AzureML WS
scaler = Model.register(model_path = './outputs/scaler.pkl', #
this points to a local file
                        model_name = "scaler", # this is the
name the model is registered as
                        tags = {'dataset': dataset.name,
'version': dataset.version},
                        model_framework='pandas==0.23.4',
                        description = "Scaler used for scaling
incoming inference data",
                        workspace = workspace)

print('Name:', scaler.name)
print('Version:', scaler.version)
```

Upon saving and registering the scaler object, a registered object can be found on the Azure ML workspace. Likewise, registered models can be tracked, as shown in *Figure 4.8*:

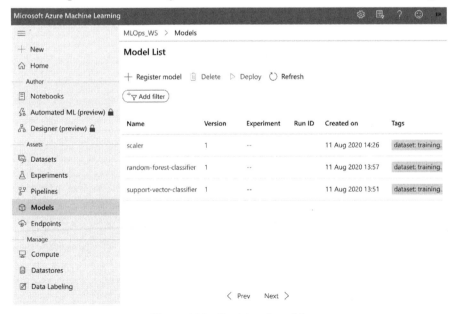

Figure 4.10 – Registered models

Congratulations! Both the SVM classifier and Random Forest classifier, along with the serialized scaler, are registered in the model registry. These models can be downloaded and deployed later. This brings us to the successful implementation of the ML pipeline!

Summary

In this chapter, we went through the theory of ML pipelines and practiced them by building ML pipelines for a business problem. We set up tools, resources, and the development environment for training these ML models. We started with the data ingestion step, followed by the model training step, testing step, and packaging step, and finally, we completed the registering step. Congrats! So far, you have implemented a critical building block of the MLOps workflow.

In the next chapter, we will look into evaluating and packaging production models.

5

Model Evaluation and Packaging

In this chapter, we will learn in detail about ML model evaluation and interpretability metrics. This will enable us to have a comprehensive understanding of the performance of ML models after training them. We will also learn how to package the models and deploy them for further use (such as in production systems). We will study in detail how we evaluated and packaged the models in the previous chapter and explore new ways of evaluating and explaining the models to ensure a comprehensive understanding of the trained models and their potential usability in production systems.

We begin this chapter by learning various ways of measuring, evaluating, and interpreting the model's performance. We look at multiple ways of testing the models for production and packaging ML models for production and inference. An in-depth study of the ML models' evaluation will be carried out as you will be presented with a framework to assess any kind of ML model and package it for production. Get ready to build a solid foundation in terms of evaluation and get ML models ready for production. For this, we are going to cover the following main topics in this chapter:

- Model evaluation and interpretability metrics
- Production testing methods
- Why package ML models?
- How to package ML models
- Inference ready models

Model evaluation and interpretability metrics

Acquiring data and training ML models is a good start toward creating business value. After training models, it is vital to measure the models' performance and understand why and how a model is predicting or performing in a certain way. Hence, model evaluation and interpretability are essential parts of the MLOps workflow. They enable us to understand and validate the ML models to determine the business value they will produce. As there are several types of ML models, there are numerous evaluation techniques as well.

Looking back at *Chapter 2, Characterizing Your Machine Learning Problem*, where we studied various types of models categorized as learning models, hybrid models, statistical models, and **HITL** (**Human-in-the-loop**) models, we will now discuss different metrics to evaluate these models. Here are some of the key model evaluation and interpretability techniques as shown in *Figure 5.1*. These have become standard in research and industry for evaluating model performance and justifying model performance:

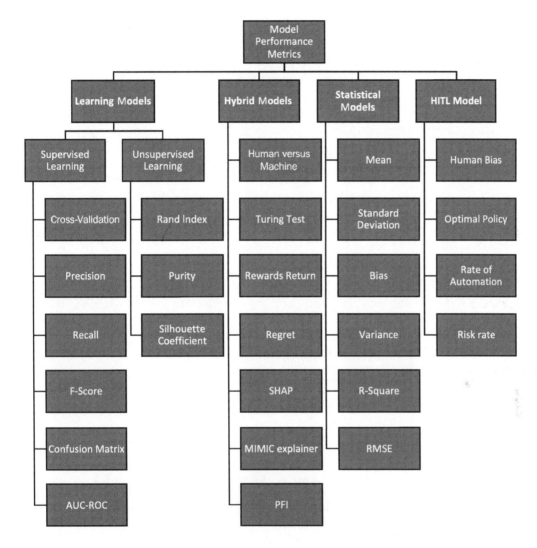

Figure 5.1 – Model evaluation and interpretation taxonomy
(The techniques in this taxonomy can be applied to almost any business problem when carefully navigated, selected, and executed.)

Learning models' metrics

Learning models are of two types – supervised learning (supervised learning models or algorithms are trained based on labeled data) and unsupervised learning (unsupervised learning models or algorithms can learn from unlabeled data).

As we have studied in previous chapters, examples of supervised learning algorithms include classification (random forest, support vector machine, and so on) and regression (linear regression, logistic regression, and so on) algorithms. On the other hand, examples of unsupervised learning include clustering (k-means, DBSCAN, Gaussian mixture models, and more) and dimensionality reduction (PCA, random forest, forward and backward feature elimination, and so on) algorithms. In order to measure these algorithms efficiently, the following are examples of some commonly used and efficient metrics.

Supervised learning models

Supervised learning models train on labeled data. In the training data, the outcome of the input is marked or known. Hence, a model is trained to learn to predict the outcome when given an input based on the labeled data. After training the model, it is important to gauge the model's potential and performance. Here are some metrics to gauge supervised models.

Cross-validation

Evaluating an ML model is vital to understanding its behaviour and this can be tricky. Normally, the dataset is split into two sub-sets: the training and the test sets. First, the training set is used to train the model, and then the test set is used to test the model. After this, the model's performance is evaluated to determine the error using metrics such as the accuracy percentage of the model on test data.

This methodology is not reliable and comprehensive because accuracy for one test set can be different from another test set. To avoid this problem, cross-validation provides a solution by fragmenting or splitting the dataset into folds and ensuring that each fold is used as a test set at some point, as shown in *Figure 5.2*:

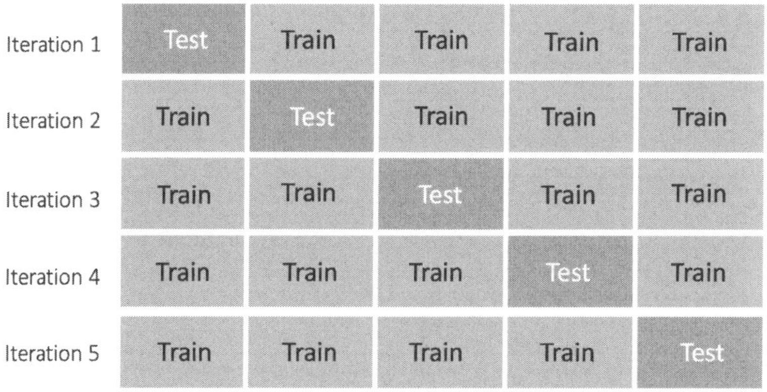

Iteration 1	Test	Train	Train	Train	Train
Iteration 2	Train	Test	Train	Train	Train
Iteration 3	Train	Train	Test	Train	Train
Iteration 4	Train	Train	Train	Test	Train
Iteration 5	Train	Train	Train	Train	Test

Figure 5.2 – K-Fold cross-validation

There are multiple cross-validation methods, including stratified cross-validation, leave-one-out cross-validation, and K-fold cross-validation. K-fold cross-validation is widely used and is worth noting as this technique involves splitting the dataset into k folds/fragments and then using each fold as a test set in successive iterations. This process is useful because each iteration has a unique test set on which accuracy is measured. Then, the accuracy for each iteration is used to find the average test results (calculated by simply taking the average of all test results).

Average accuracy acquired by cross-validation is a more reliable and comprehensive metric than the conventional accuracy measure. For example, in *Figure 5.2*, we can see five iterations. Each of these iterations has a unique test set, and upon testing accuracy for each iteration and averaging all accuracies, we get an average accuracy for the model using K-fold cross-validation. It is worth noting that K-fold is not a good choice if you have a very large training dataset or if the model requires a large amount of time, CPU, and/or GPU processing for running.

Precision

When a classifier is trained, precision can be a vital metric in quantifying positive class predictions made by the classifier that are actually true and belong to the positive class. Precision quantifies the number of correct positive predictions.

For example, let's say we have trained a classifier to predict cats and dogs from images. Upon inferring the trained model on the test images, the model is used for predicting/detecting dogs from images (in other words, dogs being the positive class). Precision, in this case, quantifies the number of correct dog predictions (positive predictions).

Precision is calculated as the ratio of correctly predicted positive examples to the total number of predicted positive examples.

Precision = TruePositives / (TruePositives + FalsePositives)

Precision focuses on minimizing false positives. High precision ranges from 0 to 1, and it relates to a low false positive rate. The higher the precision, the better it is; for example, an image classifier model that predicts whether a cancer patient requires chemotherapy treatment. If the model predicts that a patient should be submitted for chemotherapy when it is not really necessary, this can be very harmful as the effects of chemotherapy can be detrimental when not required. This case is a dangerous false positive. A high-precision score will result in fewer false positives, while having a low-precision score will result in a high number of false positives. Hence, regarding the chemotherapy treatment the prediction model should have a high-precision score.

Recall

When a classifier is trained, recall can be used to quantify the positive class predictions established from the total number of positive examples in the dataset. Recall measures the number of correct positive predictions made out of the total number of positive predictions that could have been made. Recall provides evidence of missed positive predictions, unlike precision, which only tells us the correct positive predictions out of the total number of positive predictions.

For example, take the same example discussed earlier, where we trained a classifier to predict cats and dogs from images. Upon inferring the trained model on the test images, the model is used for predicting/detecting dogs from images (in other words, dogs being the positive class). Recall, in this case, quantifies the number of missed dog predictions (positive predictions).

In this fashion, recall provides an empirical indication of the coverage of the positive class.

Recall = TruePositives / (TruePositives + FalseNegatives)

Recall focuses on minimizing false negatives. High recall relates to a low false negative rate. The higher the recall, the better it is. For example, a model that analyzes the profile data from a passenger in an airport tries to predict whether that passenger is a potential terrorist. In this case, it is more secure to have false positives than false negatives. If the models predict that an innocent person is a terrorist, this could be checked following a more in-depth investigation. But if a terrorist passes, a number of lives could be in danger. In this case, it is more secure to have false negatives than false positives as false negatives can be checked with the help of an in-depth investigation. Recall should be high to avoid false negatives. In this case, having a high recall score is prioritized over high precision.

F-score

In a case where we need to avoid both high false positives and high false negatives, f-score is a useful measure for reaching this state. F-measure provides a way to consolidate both precision and recall into single metrics that reflect both properties.

Neither precision nor recall portrays the whole story.

We can have the best precision with terrible recall, or alternatively, F-measure expresses both precision and recall. It is measured according to the following formula:

F-Measure = (2 * Precision * Recall) / (Precision + Recall)

The harmonic mean of your precision and recall is the F-measure. In most cases, you must choose between precision and recall. The harmonic mean rapidly decreases if you optimize your classifier to favor one and disfavor the other. When both precision and recall are similar, it is at its best; for example, a model that predicts cancer early by taking as input a patient's images and blood exams. In this real scenario, this could bring a lot of unnecessary costs to a hospital and possible harm to a patient's health if the model outputs a high number of false positives. On the other hand, if the model fails to detect genuine cancer patients, a number of lives would be in danger. In such cases, we need to avoid both high false positives and high false negatives and here, the f-score is a useful measure for avoiding high false positives and false negatives. F-score measures between 0 and 1. The higher the f-score, the better it is. We can expect a smaller number of false positives and false negatives with a high f-score.

Confusion matrix

The confusion matrix is a metric that reports the performance of classification models on a set of test data samples for which prediction values are pre-known. It is a metric in matrix form where a confusion matrix is an N X N matrix, and N is the number of classes being predicted. For example, let's say we have two classes to predict (binary classification), then N=2, and, as a result, we will have a 2 X 2 matrix, like the one shown here in *Figure 5.3*:

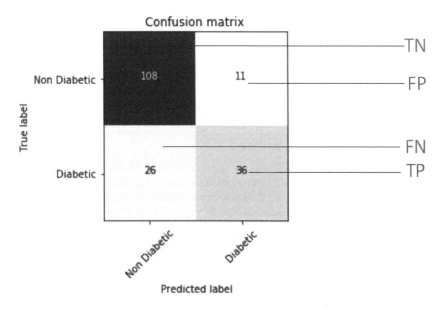

Figure 5.3 – Confusion matrix for binary classification

Figure 5.3 is an example of a confusion matrix for binary classification between diabetic and non diabetic patients. There are 181 test data samples on which predictions are made to classify patient data samples into diabetic and non diabetic categories. Using a confusion matrix, you can get critical insights to interpret the model's performance. For instance, at a glance, you will know how many predictions made are actually true and how many are false positives. Such insights are invaluable for interpreting the model's performance in many cases. Here are what these terms mean in the context of the confusion matrix:

- **True positives** (**TP**): These are cases predicted to be **yes** and are actually **yes** as per test data samples.

- **True negatives** (**TN**): These are the cases predicted to be **no** and these cases are actually **no** as per test data samples.

- **False positives** (**FP**): The model predicted **yes**, but they are **no** as per test data samples. This type of error is known as a **Type I error**.

- **False negatives** (**FN**): The model predicted **no**, but they are **yes** as per test data samples. This type of error is known as a **Type II error**.

In *Figure 5.3*, the following applies:

- The *x*-axis represents the predictions made by the ML models.

- The *y*-axis represents the actual labels.

- The first and fourth boxes in the matrix (diagonal boxes) depict the correctly predicted images.

- The second and third boxes in the matrix represent false predictions.

- In the first box, (**Non Diabetic** x **Non Diabetic**), 108 data samples (**True negatives – TN**) were predicted to be **Non Diabetic** (correct predictions).

- In the fourth box, (**Diabetes** x **Diabetes**), 36 data samples (**True positives – TP**) were predicted correctly.

- The rest of the images in the second box (**Cats** x **Dogs**) 11 images are false positives.

- The third box (**Dogs** x **Cats**), which has 26 images, contains false negatives.

The confusion matrix can provide a big picture of the predictions made on the test data samples and such insights are significant in terms of interpreting the performance of the model. The confusion matrix is the *de facto* error analysis metric for classification problems, as most other metrics are derived from this one.

AUC-ROC

A different perspective for observing model performance can enable us to interpret model performance and fine-tune it to derive better results. ROC and AUC curves can enable such insights. Let's see how the **Receiver Operating Characteristic (ROC)** curve can enable us to interpret model performance. The ROC curve is a graph exhibiting the performance of a classification model at all classification thresholds. The graph uses two parameters to depict the model's performance: **True Positive Rate (TPR**=$TP/TP+FN$) and **False Positive Rate (FPR**=$FPFP+TN$).

The following diagram shows a typical ROC curve:

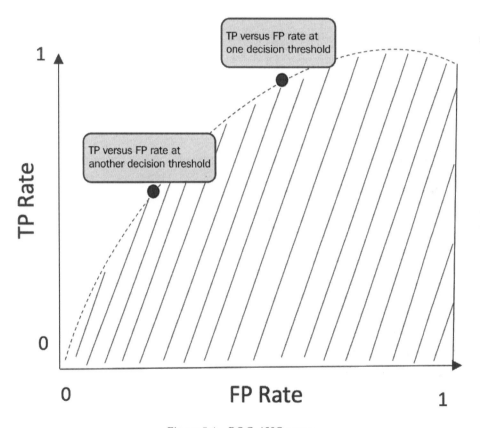

TP versus FP rate at one decision threshold

TP versus FP rate at another decision threshold

Figure 5.4 – ROC-AUC curve

An ROC curve depicts the TPR versus FPR for different thresholds for classification. Lowering the threshold for classification enables more items to be classified as positive, which in turn increases both false positives and true positives. The **Area Under the Curve (AUC)** is a metric used to quantify the effectiveness or ability of a classifier to distinguish between classes and is used to summarize the ROC curve.

The AUC value varies from 0 to 1, and the classifier is able to correctly distinguish between all the positive and negative class points if the AUC value is 1, and the classifier is unable to correctly distinguish between all the positive and negative class points if the AUC value is 0. When the AUC value is 0.5 (without manually setting a threshold), then this is a random classifier.

AUC helps us to rank predictions according to their accuracy, but it does not give us absolute values. Hence it is scale-independent. Additionally, AUC is independent of the classification threshold. The classification threshold chosen does not matter when using AUC as AUC estimates the quality of the model's predictions irrespective of what classification threshold is chosen.

The Matthew's Correlation Coefficient

Brian Matthews developed the **Matthews correlation coefficient** (**MCC**) in 1975 as a method for model evaluation. It calculates the discrepancies between real and expected values. It is an extension of confusion matrix results to measure the inefficiency of a classifier. TP, TN, FP, and FN are the four entries in a confusion matrix. These entries are factored into the coefficient:

$$MCC = \frac{TN \times TP - FN \times FP}{\sqrt{(TP + FP)(TP + FN)(TN + FP)(TN + FN)}}$$

This measure results in high scores only when a prediction returns good rates for all these four categories. The MCC score ranges from -1 to +1:

- 1 is the best agreement between actuals and predictions.
- When the score is 0, this means there is no agreement at all between actuals and predictions. The prediction is random with respect to actuals.

For example, an MCC score of 0.12 suggests that the classifier is very random. If it is 0.93, this suggests that the classifier is good. MCC is a useful metric for helping to measure the ineffectiveness of a classifier.

Unsupervised learning models

Unsupervised learning models or algorithms can learn from unlabeled data. Unsupervised learning can be used to mine insights and identify patterns from unlabeled data. Unsupervised algorithms are widely used for clustering or anomaly detection without relying on any labels. Here are some metrics for gauging the performance of unsupervised learning algorithms.

The Rand index

The Rand index is a metric for evaluating the quality of the clustering technique. It depicts the degree of similarity between the clusters. The Rand index measures the percentage of correct decisions. Decisions assign a pair of data points (for example, documents) to the same cluster.

If N data points exist, the total number of *decisions = N(N-1)/2*, which denotes the pair of data points involved in the decision.

Rand index = TP + TN / TP + FP + FN + TN

Purity

Purity is an external evaluation metric for cluster quality. To calculate purity, the clusters are labeled according to the most common class in the cluster and then the accuracy of this cluster assignment is measured by calculating the number of correctly assigned data points and dividing by N (total number of data points clustered). Good clustering has a purity value close to 1, and bad clustering has a purity value close to 0. *Figure 5.5* is a visual representation of an example of calculating *purity*, as explained below:

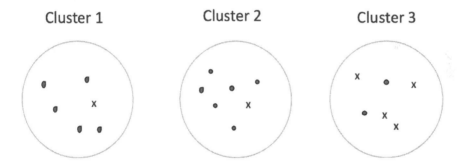

Figure 5.5 – Clusters after clustering

Purity is an external evaluation criterion regarding cluster quality. In *Figure 5.5*, the majority class and the number of members of the majority class for the three clusters are as follows: green drops x 5 (cluster 1), red dots x 5 (cluster 2), and crosses x 4 (cluster 3). Hence, purity is (1/17) x (5 + 5 + 3) = ~0.76.

The Silhouette coefficient

For clustering algorithms, determining the quality of clusters is important. To determine the quality or goodness of the clusters, the silhouette score, or silhouette coefficient, is used as a metric. Its value ranges from -1 to 1. When clusters are clearly distinguishable or well apart from one another, then the silhouette score is 1. On the contrary, -1 means clusters are wrongly allocated, and 0 means clusters are indifferent from one another. This is how the silhouette score is calculated:

Silhouette Score = (b-a)/max(a,b)

a = the average distance between each point within a cluster (average intra-cluster distance).

b = the average distance between all clusters (average inter-cluster distance).

Hybrid models' metrics

There have been rapid developments in ML by combining conventional methods to develop hybrid methods to solve diverse business and research problems. Hybrid models include semi-supervised, self-supervised, multi-instance, multi-task, reinforcement, ensemble, transfer, and federated learning models. To evaluate and validate these models, a range of metrics are used depending on the use case and model type. It is good to know these metrics to be able to use the right metrics as per the model you will develop and evaluate in the future. Here are the metrics for evaluating hybrid models:

Human versus machine test

Zeal to reach human-level performance is quite common while training and testing ML and deep learning models. In order to validate the models and conclude that the models have reached or surpassed human-level performance, human versus machine experiments are performed on tasks. The same task is implemented using an ML model and the human performance is evaluated against the ML model's performance. There are various metrics for evaluating human versus machine performance according to the context and tasks. Some examples are mentioned here:

- **Bilingual evaluation understudy** (**BLEU**) is a method for assessing the quality of text for the task of machine translation from one language to another. The quality of text generated by a machine translation algorithm is compared to the output of a human. The evaluation is done to observe how close a machine translation is to a professional human translation.

- **Recall-Oriented Understudy for Gisting Evaluation (ROUGE)** is a human versus machine performance evaluation metric used to evaluate tasks such as automatic summarization and machine translation. This metric compares an automatically generated summary or translation versus summary/translations produced by humans.

The Turing test

The Turing test was engineered by the famous Alan Turing. He referred to it as the imitation game in the 1950s. The Turing test is a test of a machine to evaluate its ability to exhibit intelligent behavior similar to that of a human. In another sense, the Turing test is also a test to evaluate the ability of a machine to fool a human into believing a task done by machine is human-like or done by a human. For instance, we can see the Turing test in operation in *Figure 5.6*, where a text-based interaction is happening between the human interrogator, X, and a computer or machine subject (Bob), and the interrogator, X, and a human subject (Alice):

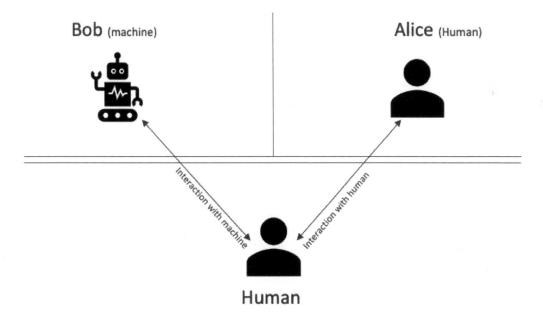

Figure 5.6 – Turing test

During the Turing test, the human interrogator, X, performs a series of interactions, both with Bob (computer) and Alice (human) with an intent to distinguish between the human and the machine correctly. The machine passes the Turing test if/when the interrogator cannot distinguish them correctly or mistakes the machine for a human (Bob for Alice).

Reward per return

Reinforcement learning models are hybrid models that involve continuous learning mechanisms between the agent and operating environment in order to achieve pre-defined goals. The agent learns based on rewards earned for efficient or optimal steps toward reaching a goal. When the goal is optimal control, you will want to measure the agent by how well it does at the task. To quantify how well the agent performs the task, the aggregate measures of reward, such as total reward per episode (otherwise known as "return") or mean reward per time step, can be used to assess and optimize control for the agent with respect to the environment and the goals.

Regret

Regret is a commonly used metric for hybrid models such as reinforcement learning models. At each time step, you calculate the difference between the reward of the optimal decision and the decision taken by your algorithm. Cumulative regret is then calculated by summing this up. The minimum regret is 0 with the optimal policy. The smaller the regret, the better an algorithm has performed.

Regret enables the actions of the agent to be assessed with respect to the best policy for the optimal performance of the agent as shown in *Figure 5.7*. The shaded region in red is the regret:

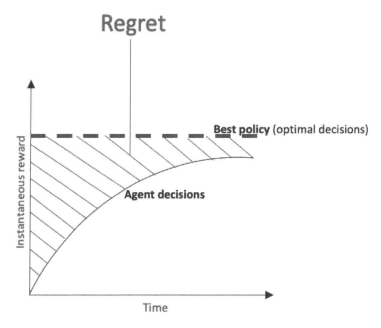

Figure 5.7 – Regret for reinforcement learning
SHapley Additive exPlanations (SHAP)

Model interpretability and explaining why the model is making certain decisions or predictions can be vital in a number of business problems or industries. Using techniques discussed earlier, we can interpret the model's performance, but there are still some gray areas, such as deep learning models, which are black-box models. It is noticeable in general that these models can be trained to achieve great results or accuracies on test data, but it is hard to say why. In such scenarios, **SHapley Additive exPlanations** (**SHAP**) can be useful to decode what is happening with the predicted results and which feature predictions correlate to the most. SHAP was proposed in this paper (at NIPS): `http://papers.nips.cc/paper/7062-a-unified-approach-to-interpreting-model-predictions`.

SHAP works both for classification and regression models. The primary goal of SHAP is to explain the model output prediction by computing the contribution of each feature. The SHAP explanation method uses Shapley values to explain the feature importance for model outputs or predictions. Shapley values are computed from cooperative game theory, and these values range from `-1` to `1`. Shapley values describe the distribution of model outputs among the features, as shown in *Figure 5.8*:

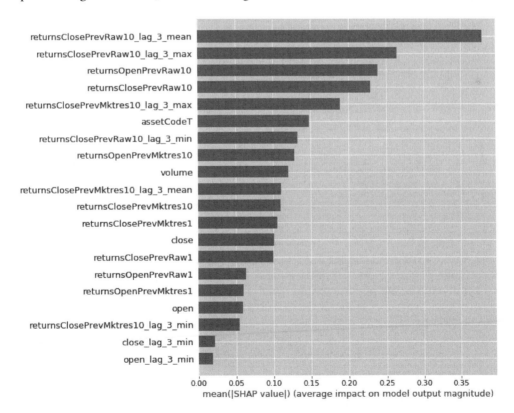

Figure 5.8 – Shapley values bar chart depicting feature importance

There are several SHAP explainer techniques, such as SHAP Tree Explainer, SHAP Deep Explainer, SHAP Linear Explainer, and SHAP Kernel Explainer. Depending on the use case, these explainers can provide useful information on model predictions and help us to understand black-box models. Read more here: `https://christophm.github.io/interpretable-ml-book/shap.html`

MIMIC explainer

Mimic explainer is an approach mimicking black-box models by training an interpretable global surrogate model. These trained global surrogate models are interpretable models that are trained to approximate the predictions of any black-box model as accurately as possible. By using the surrogate model, a black-box model can be gauged or interpreted as follows.

The following steps are implemented to train a surrogate model:

1. To train a surrogate model, start by selecting a dataset, X. This dataset can be the same as the one used for training the black-box model or it can be another dataset of similar distributions depending on the use case.

2. Get the predictions of the black-box model for the selected dataset, X.

3. Select an interpretable model type (linear model, decision tree, random forest, and so on).

4. Using the dataset, X, and its predictions, train the interpretable model.

5. Now you have a trained surrogate model. Kudos!

6. Evaluate how well the surrogate model has reproduced predictions of the black-box model, for example, using R-square or F-score.

7. Get an understanding of black-box model predictions by interpreting the surrogate model.

The following interpretable models can be used as surrogate models: **Light Gradient boosting model** (**LightGBM**), linear regression, stochastic gradient descent, or random forest and decision tree.

Surrogate models can enable ML solution developers to gauge and understand the black-box model's performance.

Permutation feature importance explainer (PFI)

Permutation Feature Importance (**PFI**) is a technique used to explain classification and regression models. This technique is useful for interpreting and understanding a feature to model output or prediction correlation. PFI is an alternative to SHAP. It works by randomly assessing one feature at a time for the entire dataset and calculating the change in performance evaluation metrics. The change in performance metric is evaluated for each feature; the more significant the change, the more important the feature is.

PFI can describe the overall behavior of any model, but does not explain individual predictions of the model. PFI is an alternative to SHAP, but is still quite different as PFI is based on the decrease in performance of the model, while SHAP is based on the magnitude of feature attributions.

Statistical models' metrics

As we learned in *Chapter 2, Characterizing Your Machine Learning Problem*, there are three types of statistical models: inductive learning, deductive learning, and transduction learning. Statistical models offer a good degree of interpretability.

Mean

The mean, or average, is the central value of the dataset. It is calculated by summing all the values and dividing the sum by the number of values:

mean = x1 + x2 + x3 +.... + xn / n

Standard deviation

The standard deviation measures the dispersion of the values in the dataset. The lower the standard deviation, the closer the data points to the mean. A widely spread dataset would have a higher standard deviation.

Bias

Bias measures the strength (or rigidity) of the mapping function between the independent (input) and dependent (output) variables. The stronger the assumptions of the model regarding the functional form of the mapping, the greater the bias.

High bias is helpful when the underlying true (but unknown) model has matching properties as the assumptions of the mapping function. However, you could get completely off-track if the underlying model does not exhibit similar properties as the functional form of the mapping. For example, the assumption that there is a linear relationship in the variables when in reality it is highly non-linear and it would lead to a bad fit:

- **Low bias**: Weak assumptions with regard to the functional form of the mapping of inputs to outputs

- **High bias**: Strong assumptions with regard to the functional form of the mapping of inputs to outputs

The bias is always a positive value. Here is an additional resource for learning more about bias in ML. This article offers a broader explanation: `https://kourentzes.com/forecasting/2014/12/17/the-bias-coefficient-a-new-metric-for-forecast-bias/`.

Variance

The variance of the model is the degree to which the model's performance changes when it is fitted on different training data. The impact of the specifics on the model is captured by the variance.

A high variance model will change a lot with even small changes in the training dataset. On the other hand, a low variance model wouldn't change much even with large changes in the training dataset. The variance is always positive.

R-squared

R-squared, also known as the coefficient of determination, measures the variation in the dependent variable that can be explained by the model. It is calculated as the explained variation divided by the total variation. In simple terms, R-squared measures how close the data points are to the fitted regression line.

The value of R-squared lies between 0 and 1. A low R-squared value indicates that most of the variation in the response variable is not explained by the model, but by other factors not included in it. In general, you should aim for a higher R-squared value because this indicates that the model better fits the data.

RMSE

The **root mean square error** (**RMSE**) measures the difference between the predicted values of the model and the observed (true) values.

Options are many, and you need to choose the right metric for real-world production scenarios to have well-justified evaluations; for example, why a data scientist or a data science team might want to select one evaluation metric over another, for instance, R-squared over mean for a regression problem. It depends on the use case and type of data.

HITL model metrics

There are two types of **HITL** models – human reinforcement learning and active learning models. In these models, human-machine collaboration fosters the algorithm to mimic human-like behaviors and outcomes. A key driver for these ML solutions is the human in the loop. Humans validate, label, and retrain the models to maintain the accuracy of the model.

Human bias

Just like the human brain, ML systems are subject to cognitive bias. Human cognitive biases are processes that disrupt your decision making and reasoning ability, ending up in the production of errors. Human bias occurrences include stereotyping, selective perception, the bandwagon effect, priming, affirmation predisposition, observational selection bias, and the speculator's false notion. In many cases, it is vital to avoid such biases for ML systems in order to make rational and optimal decisions. This will make ML systems more pragmatic than humans if we manage to deduce human bias and rectify it. This will be especially useful in HITL-based systems. Using bias testing, three types of human biases can be identified and worked upon to maintain the ML system's decision making such that it is free from human bias. These three human biases are as follows:

Interaction bias

When an ML system is fed a dataset containing entries of one particular type, an interaction bias is introduced that prevents the algorithm from recognizing any other types of entries. This type of bias can be identified in inference testing for trained models. Methods such as SHAP and PFI can be useful in identifying feature bias.

Latent bias

Latent bias is experienced when multiple examples in the training set have a characteristic that stands out. Then, the ones without that characteristic fail to be recognized by the algorithm. For example, recently, the Amazon HR algorithm for selecting people based on applications for roles within the company showed bias against women, the reason being latent bias.

Selection bias

Selection bias is introduced to an algorithm when the selection of data for analysis is not properly randomized. For example, in designing a high-performance face recognition system, it is vital to include all possible types of facial structures and shapes and from all ethnic and geographical samples, so as to avoid selection bias. Selection bias can be identified by methods such as SHAP or PFI to observe model feature bias.

Optimal policy

In the case of human reinforcement learning, the goal of the system is to maximize the rewards of the action in the current state. In order to maximize the rewards for actions, optimal policy can be used as a metric to gauge the system. The optimal policy is the policy where the action that maximizes the reward/return of the current state is chosen. The optimal policy is the metric or state that is ideal for a system to perform at its best. In a human reinforcement learning-based system, a human operator or teacher sets the optimal policy as the goal of the system is to reach human-level performance.

Rate of automation

Automation is the process of automatically producing goods or getting a task done through the use of robots or algorithms with no direct human assistance.

The level of automation of an ML system can be calculated using the rate of automation of the total tasks. It is basically the percentage of tasks fully automated by the system, and these tasks do not require any human assistance. It shows what percentage of tasks are fully automated out of all the tasks. For example, AlphaGo, by DeepMind, has achieved 100% automation to operate on its own to defeat human world champion players.

Risk rate

The probability of an ML model performing errors is known as the error rate. The error rate is calculated based on the model's performance for production systems. The lower the error rate, the better it is for an ML system. The goal of a human in the loop is to reduce the error rate and teach the ML model to function at its most optimal.

Production testing methods

As there are various businesses in operation, so are different types of production systems serving these businesses. In this section, we look into the different types of production systems or setups commonly used and how to test them.

Batch testing

Batch testing validates your model by performing testing in an environment that is different from its training environment. Batch testing is carried out on a set of samples of data to test model inference using metrics of choice, such as accuracy, RMSE, or f1-score. Batch testing can be done in various types of computes, for example, in the cloud, or on a remote server or a test server. The model is usually served as a serialized file, and the file is loaded as an object and inferred on test data.

A/B testing

You will surely have come across A/B testing. It is often used in service design (websites, mobile apps, and so on) and for assessing marketing campaigns. For instance, it is used to evaluate whether a specific change in the design or tailoring content to a specific audience positively affects business metrics such as user engagement, the click-through rate, or the sales rate. A similar technique is applied in testing ML models using A/B testing. When models are tested using A/B testing, thc test will answer important questions such as the following:

- Does the new model B work better in production than the current model A?

- Which of the two models' nominees work better in production to drive positive business metrics?

To evaluate the results of A/B testing, statistical techniques are used based on the business or operations to determine which model will perform better in production. A/B testing is usually conducted in this manner, and real-time or live data is fragmented or split into two sets, Set A and Set B. Set A data is routed to the old model, and Set B data is routed to the new model. In order to evaluate whether the new model (model B) performs better than the old model (model A), various statistical techniques can be used to evaluate model performance (for example, accuracy, precision, recall, f-score, and RMSE), depending on the business use case or operations. Depending on a statistical analysis of model performance in correlation to business metrics (a positive change in business metrics), a decision is made to replace the new model with the old one or determine which model is better.

A/B testing is performed methodically using statistical hypothesis testing, and this hypothesis validates two sides of a coin – the null hypothesis and the alternate hypothesis. The null hypothesis asserts that the new model does not increase the average value of the monitoring business metrics. The alternate hypothesis asserts that the new model improves the average value of the monitoring business metrics. Ultimately, A/B testing is used to evaluate whether *the new model drives a significant boost in specific business metrics*. There are various types of A/B testing, depending on business use cases and operations, for example, `Z-test`, `G-test` (I recommend knowing about these and others), and others. Choosing the right A/B test and metrics to evaluate can be a win-win for your business and ML operations.

Stage test or shadow test

Before deploying a model for production, which would then lead to making business decisions, it can be valuable to replicate a production-like environment (staging environment) to test the model's performance. This is especially important for testing the robustness of the model and assessing its performance on real-time data. It could be facilitated by deploying the develop branch or a model to be tested on a staging server and inferring the same data as the production pipeline. The only shortcoming here will be that end users will not see the results of the develop branch or business decisions will not be made in the staging server. The results of the staging environment will statistically be evaluated using suitable metrics (for example, accuracy, precision, recall, f-score, and RMSE) to determine the robustness and performance of the model in correlation to business metrics.

Testing in CI/CD

Implementing testing as part of CI/CD pipelines can be rewarding in terms of automating and evaluating (based on set criteria) the model's performance. CI/CD pipelines can be set up in multiple ways depending on the operations and architecture in place, for instance:

- Upon a successful run of an ML pipeline, CI/CD pipelines can trigger a new model's A/B test in the staging environment.

- When a new model is trained, it is beneficial to set up a dataset separate from the test set to measure its performance against suitable metrics, and this step can be fully automated.

- CI/CD pipelines can periodically trigger ML pipelines at a set time in a day to train a new model, which uses live or real-time data to train a new model or fine-tune an existing model.

- CI/CD pipelines can monitor the ML model's performance of the deployed model in production, and this can be triggered or managed using time-based triggers or manual triggers (initiated by team members responsible for quality assurance).

- CI/CD pipelines can provision two or more staging environments to perform A/B testing on unique datasets to perform more diverse and comprehensive testing.

These are a variety of scenarios, and depending on requirements, CI/CD pipelines offer various workflows and operations tailored to the needs of the business and tech requirements. Selecting an efficient architecture and CI/CD process can augment tech operations and team performance overall. CI/CD testing can augment and automate testing to great lengths.

Why package ML models?

MLOps enables a systematic approach to train and evaluate models. After models are trained and evaluated, the next steps are to bring them to production. As we know, ML doesn't work like traditional software engineering, which is deterministic in nature and where a piece of code or module is imported into the existing system and it works. Engineering ML solutions is non-deterministic and involves serving ML models to make predictions or analyze data.

In order to serve the models, they need to be packed into software artifacts to be shipped to the testing or production environments. Usually, these software artifacts are packaged into a file or a bunch of files or containers. This allows the software to be environment- and deployment-agnostic. ML models need to be packaged for the following reasons:

Portability

Packaging ML models into software artifacts enables them to be shipped or transported from one environment to another. This can be done by shipping a file or bunch of files or a container. Either way, we can transport the artifacts and replicate the model in various setups. For example, a packaged model can be deployed in a virtual machine or serverless setup.

Inference

ML inference is a process that involves processing real-time data using ML models to calculate an output, for example, a prediction or numerical score. The purpose of packaging ML models is to be able to serve the ML models in real time for ML inference. Effective ML model packaging (for example, a serialized model or container) can facilitate deployment and serve the model to make predictions and analyze data in real time or in batches.

Interoperability

ML model interoperability is the ability of two or more models or components to exchange information and to use exchanged information in order to learn or fine-tune from each other and perform operations with efficiency. Exchanged information can be in the form of data or software artifacts or model parameters. Such information enables models to fine-tune, retrain, or adapt to various environments from the experience of other software artifacts in order to perform and be efficient. Packaging ML models is the foundation for enabling ML model interoperability.

Deployment agnosticity

Packaging ML models into software artifacts such as serialized files or containers enables the models to be shipped and deployed in various runtime environments, such as in a virtual machine, a container serverless environment, a streaming service, microservices, or batch services. It opens opportunities for portability and deployment agnosticity using the same software artifacts that an ML model is packaged in.

How to package ML models

ML models can be packaged in various ways depending on business and tech requirements and as per operations for ML. ML models can be packaged and shipped in three ways, as discussed in the following sub-sections.

Serialized files

Serialization is a vital process for packaging an ML model as it enables model portability, interoperability, and model inference. Serialization is the method of converting an object or a data structure (for example, variables, arrays, and tuples) into a storable artefact, for example, into a file or a memory buffer that can be transported or transmitted (across computer networks). The main purpose of serialization is to reconstruct the serialized file into its previous data structure (for example, a serialized file into an ML model variable) in a different environment. This way, a newly trained ML model can be serialized into a file and exported into a new environment where it can de-serialized back into an ML model variable or data structure for ML inferencing. A serialized file does not save or include any of the previously associated methods or implementation. It only saves the data structure as it is in a storable artefact such as a file.

Here are some popular serialization formats in *figure 5.1*:

Sr. No.	Format	File extension	Framework	Quantization
1	Pickle	.pkl	scikit-learn	No
2	HD5	.h5	Keras	Yes
3	ONNX	.onnx	TensorFlow, PyTorch, scikit-learn, caffe, keras, mxnet, IoS Core ML	Yes
4	PMML	.pmml	scikit-learn	No
5	Torch Script	.pt	PyTorch	Yes
6	Apple ML model	.mlmodel	IoS core ML	Yes
7	MLeap	.zip	PySpark	No
8	Protobuf	.pb	TensorFlow	Yes

Table 5.1 – Popular ML model serialization formats

All these serialized formats (except ONNX) have one problem in common, the problem of interoperability. To address that, ONNX is developed as an open source project supported by Microsoft, Baidu, Amazon, and other big companies. This enables a model to be trained using one framework (for example, in scikit-learn) and then retrained again using TensorFlow. This has become a game changer for industrialized AI as models can be rendered interoperable and framework-independent.

ONNX has unlocked new avenues, such as federated learning and transfer learning. Serialized models enable portability and also batch inferencing (batch inference, or offline inference, is the method of generating predictions on a batch of data points or samples) in different environments.

Packetizing or containerizing

We often encounter diverse environments for production systems. Every environment possesses different challenges when it comes to deploying ML models, in terms of compatibility, robustness, and scalability. These challenges can be avoided by standardizing some processes or modules and containers are a great way to standardize ML models and software modules.

A container is a standard unit of software made up of code and all its dependencies. It enables the quick and reliable operation of applications from one computing environment to another. It enables the software to be environment- and deployment-agnostic. Containers are managed and orchestrated by Docker. Docker has become an industry standard at developing and orchestrating containers.

Docker is an open source (`https://opensource.com/resources/what-open-source`) tool. It has been developed to make it convenient to build, deploy, and run applications by using containers. By using containers, a developer can package an application with its components and modules, such as files, libraries, and other dependencies, and deploy it as one package. Containers are a reliable way to run applications using a Linux OS with customized settings. Docker containers are built using Dockerfiles, which are used to containerize an application. After building a Docker image, a Docker container is built. A Docker container is an application running with custom settings as orchestrated by the developer. *Figure 5.8* shows the process of building and running a Docker container from a Dockerfile. A Dockerfile is built into a Docker image, which is then run as a Docker container:

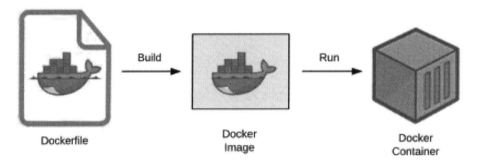

Figure 5.9 – Docker artifacts

A Dockerfile, Docker image, and a Docker container are foundational components for building and running containers. These are each described here:

- **Dockerfile**: A Dockerfile is a text document containing a set of Docker commands ordered by the developer to build a Docker image. Docker is able to read the Dockerfile and build a Docker image.

- **Docker image**: This is a sequential collection of execution parameters to use within a collection of root filesystems within a container during runtime. Docker images are like a snapshot of containers. Containers are constructed from Docker images.

- **Docker container**: Containers are constructed from Docker images. A container is a runtime instance of a Docker image.

ML models can be served in Docker containers for robustness, scalability, and deployment agnosticity. In later chapters, we will deploy ML models using Docker for the purpose of hands-on experience, hence, it is good to have a general understanding of this tool.

Microservice generation and deployment

Microservices enable the collection of services that are independently deployable. Each of these services is highly maintainable, testable, and loosely coupled. Microservices are orchestrated by architecture that is organized around business capabilities to enable a system to serve business needs. For example, Spotify has transitioned from a monolithic complex system to a microservices-based system. It was done by splitting the complex system into fragmented services, with specific goals such as a search engine, content tagging, content classification, user behavioral analytics for a recommendation engine, and autogenerated playlists. Fragmented microservices are now developed by a dedicated team. Each microservice is isolated and less dependent on one another. This way, it is easier to develop and maintain. The company can be consistent with customer service and continuously improve without putting the service down.

Typically, a microservice is generated by tailoring serialized files into a containerized Docker image. These Docker images can then be deployed and orchestrated into any Docker - supported environment. Deploying and managing Docker images can be performed using container management tools, such as Kubernetes. Docker enables extreme portability and interoperability, Docker images can be easily deployed to any popular cloud service, such as Google Cloud, Azure, or AWS. Docker images can be deployed and managed to any Docker corporate server or data center or real-time environment as long as it supports Docker.

Microservices can be served in a REST API format, and this is a popular way to serve ML models. Some Python frameworks, such as Flask, Django, and FastAPI, have become popular in enabling ML models to serve as REST API microservices. To facilitate robust and scalable system operations, software developers can sync with Dockerized microservices via a REST API. To orchestrate Docker-based microservice deployments on Kubernetes-supported infrastructure, Kubeflow is a good option. It is cloud-agnostic and can be run on-premises or on local machines. Besides that, Kubeflow is based on Kubernetes, but keeps the Kubernetes details and difficulties inside a box. Kubeflow is a robust way of serving a model. This is a tool worth exploring: `https://www.kubeflow.org/docs/started/kubeflow-overview/`.

Inference ready models

We have previously worked on a business problem to predict the weather at a port. To build a solution for this business problem, data processing and ML model training were performed, followed by serializing models. Now, in this section, we explore how inference is done on the serialized model. This section's code is available from the attached Jupyter notebook in the chapter's corresponding folder in the book's GitHub repository. Here are the instructions for running the code:

1. Log in to the Azure portal again.

2. From **Recent Resources**, select the `MLOps_WS` workspace, and then click on the **Launch Studio** button. This will direct you to the `MLOps_WS` workspace.

3. In the **Manage** section, click on the **Compute** section, and then select the machine created in *Chapter 4, Machine Learning Pipelines*. Click on the **Start** button to start the instance. When the VM is ready, click on the JupyterLab link.

4. Now, in JupyterLab, navigate to the chapter's corresponding folder (`05_model_evaluation_packaging`) and open the notebook (`model_evaluation_packaging.ipynb`).

Connecting to the workspace and importing model artifacts

First, we import the requisite packages, connect to the ML workspace using the `Workspace()` function, and then download the serialized scaler and model to perform predictions. `Scaler` will be used to scale input data into the same scale of data that was used for model training. The `Model` file is serialized in ONNX format. Both the `Scaler` and `Model` files are imported using the `Model()` function:

```
import pandas as pd
import numpy as np
import warnings
import pickle
from math import sqrt
warnings.filterwarnings('ignore')
from azureml.core.run import Run
from azureml.core.experiment import Experiment
from azureml.core.workspace import Workspace
from azureml.core.model import Model
# Connect to Workspace
ws = Workspace.from_config()
print(ws)
# Load Scaler and model to test
scaler = Model(ws,'scaler').download(exist_ok=True)
svc_model = Model(ws,'support-vector-classifier').
download(exist_ok=True)
```

After running this code, you will see new files downloaded in the left panel in the JupyterLab window.

Loading model artifacts for inference

We open and load the `Scaler` and `Model` files into variables that can be used for ML model inference. `Scaler` is read and loaded into a variable using pickle, and the ONNX runtime is used to load the ONNX file using `InferenceSession()` for making ML model predictions as follows:

```
with open('scaler.pkl', 'rb') as file:
    scaler = pickle.load(file)
# Compute the prediction with ONNX Runtime
```

```
import onnxruntime as rt
import numpy
sess = rt.InferenceSession("svc.onnx")
input_name = sess.get_inputs()[0].name
label_name = sess.get_outputs()[0].name
```

ML model inference

To perform ML model inference, scale the test data and set it up for inference using the `fit_transform()` method. Now, perform inference on the test data by using the ONNX session and run `sess.run()` by passing the input data, `test_data`, in `float 32` format. Lastly, print the results of model inference:

```
test_data = np.array([34.927778, 0.24, 7.3899, 83, 16.1000, 1])
test_data = scaler.fit_transform(test_data.reshape(1, 6))
# Inference
pred_onx = sess.run([label_name], {input_name: test_data.
astype(numpy.float32)})[0]
print(pred_onx[0])
```

With these steps, we have successfully downloaded the serialized model, loaded it to a variable, and performed inference on a test data sample. The expected result of the block code is the value 1.

Summary

In this chapter, we have explored the various methods to evaluate and interpret ML models. We have learned about production testing methods and the importance of packaging models, why and how to package models, and the various practicalities and tools for packaging models for ML model inference in production. Lastly, to understand the workings of packaging and de-packaging serialized models for inference, we performed the hands-on implementation of ML model inference using serialized models on test data.

In the next chapter, we will learn more about deploying your ML models. Fasten your seatbelts and get ready to deploy your models to production!

Section 2: Deploying Machine Learning Models at Scale

This section will explain the options, methods, and landscape of machine learning model deployment. We will deep dive into some of the fundamental aspects of production deployments enabled by continuous integration, delivery, and deployment methods. You will also get insights into designing and developing robust and scalable microservices and APIs to serve your machine learning solutions.

This section comprises the following chapters:

- *Chapter 6, Key Principles for Deploying Your ML System*

- *Chapter 7, Building Robust CI and CD Pipelines*

- *Chapter 8, APIs and Microservice Management*

- *Chapter 9, Testing and Securing Your ML Solution*

- *Chapter 10, Essentials of Production Release*

6
Key Principles for Deploying Your ML System

In this chapter, you will learn the fundamental principles for deploying **machine learning** (**ML**) models in production and implement the hands-on deployment of ML models for the business problem we have been working on. To get a comprehensive understanding and first-hand experience, we will deploy ML models that were trained and packaged previously (in *Chapter 4*, *Machine Learning Pipelines*, and *Chapter 5*, *Model Evaluation and Packaging*) using the Azure ML service on two different deployment targets: an Azure container instance and a Kubernetes cluster.

We will also learn how to deploy ML models using an open source framework called MLflow that we have already worked with. This will enable you to get an understanding of deploying ML models as REST API endpoints on diverse deployment targets using two different tools (the Azure ML service and MLflow). This will equip you with the skills required to deploy ML models for any given scenario on the cloud.

In this chapter, we start by looking at how ML is different in research and production and continue exploring the following topics:

- ML in research versus production

- Understanding the types of ML inference in production

- Going through the mapping infrastructure for your solution

- Hands-on deployment (for the business problem)

- Understanding the need for continuous integration and continuous deployment

ML in research versus production

ML in research is implemented with specific goals and priorities to improve the state of the art in the field, whereas the aim of ML in production is to optimize, automate, or augment a scenario or a business.

In order to understand the deployment of ML models, let's start by comparing how ML is implemented in research versus production (in the industry). Multiple factors, such as performance, priority, data, fairness, and interpretability, as listed in *Table 6.1*, depict how deployments and ML work differently in research and production:

	Research	Production
Data	Static	Dynamic (constantly changing)
Fairness	Recommended	Necessary
Interpretability	Recommended	Necessary
Performance	State of the art	Better than simpler models
Priority	Fast training	Fast inference

Table 6.1 – ML in research and production

Data

In general, data in research projects is static because data scientists or statisticians are working on a set dataset and trying to beat the current state-of-the-art models. For example, recently, many breakthroughs in natural language processing models have been witnessed, for instance, with BERT from Google or XLNet from Baidu. To train these models, data was scraped and compiled into a static dataset. In the research world, to evaluate or benchmark the performance of the models, static datasets are used to evaluate the performance, as shown in *Table 6.2* (source: https://arxiv.org/abs/1906.08237):

Model	SQuAD1.1	SQuAD2.0	RACE	MNLI	QNLI	QQP	RTE	SST-2	MRPC	CoLA	STS-B
BERT-Large (Best of 3)	86.7/92.8	82.8/85.5	75.1	87.3	93.0	91.4	74.0	94.0	88.7	63.7	90.2
XLNet-Large-wikibooks	88.2/94.0	85.1/87.8	77.4	88.4	93.9	91.8	81.2	94.4	90.0	65.2	91.1

Table 6.2 – BERT versus XLNet performance (in research)

For instance, we can compare the performance of two models by comparing their performance on a popular dataset called SQUAD (10,000+ QnA) version 1.1, on which BERT performs with 92.8% accuracy and XLNET with 94.0% accuracy. Likewise, data used in research for training and evaluating models is static, whereas data in production or in industrial use cases is dynamic and constantly changing as per the environment, operations, business, or users.

Fairness

In real life, biased models can be costly. Unfair or biased decisions will lead to poor choices for business and operations. For ML models in production, it is important that decisions made are as fair as possible. It can be costly for the business if the models in production are not fair. For example, recently, Amazon made HR screening software that screens applicants based on their suitability for the job they applied for. ML specialists at Amazon discovered that male candidates were favored over female candidates (source: https://www.businessinsider.com/amazon-ai-biased-against-women-no-surprise-sandra-wachter-2018-10). This kind of system bias can be costly because, in Amazon's case, you can miss out on some amazing talent as a result of bias. Hence having fair models in production is critical and should be monitored constantly. In research, fair models are important as well but not as critical as in production or real life, and fairness is not critically monitored as in production. The goal in research is to beat the state of the art, and model fairness is a secondary goal.

Interpretability

Model interpretability is critical in production in order to understand the correlation or causality between the ML model's decisions and its impact on the operations or business to optimize, augment, or automate a business or task at hand. This is not the case in research, where the goal is to challenge or beat the state-of-the-art results, and here the priority is better performance (such as accuracy, or other metrics). In the case of research, ML model interpretability is good to have but not mandatory. Typically, ML projects are more concerned with predicting outcomes than with understanding causality. ML models are great at finding correlations in data, but not causation. We strive not to fall into the pit of equating association with the cause in our ventures. Our ability to rely on ML is severely hampered as a result of this issue. This problem severely limits our ability to use ML to make decisions. We need resources that can understand the causal relationships between data and build ML solutions that can generalize well from a business viewpoint. Having the right model interpretability mechanisms can enhance our understanding of causality and enable us to craft ML solutions that generalize well and are able to handle previously unseen data. As a result, we can make more reliable and transparent decisions using ML.

In the case of production (in a business use case), a lack of interpretability is not recommended at all. Let us look at a hypothetical case. Let's assume you have cancer and have to choose a surgeon to perform your surgery. Two surgeons are available, one is human (with an 80% cure rate) and another is an AI black-box model (with a 90% cure rate) that cannot be interpreted or explain how it works, but it has a high cure rate. What would you choose? AI or a surgeon to cure cancer? It would be easier to replace the surgeon with AI if the model was not a black-box model. Though the AI is better than the surgeon, without understanding the model, decision, trust and compliance is an issue. Model interpretability is essential to make legal decisions. Hence, it is vital to have model interpretability for ML in production. We will learn more about this in later chapters.

Performance

When it comes to the performance of the ML models, the focus in research is to improve on the state-of-the-art models, whereas in production the focus is to build better models than simpler models that serve the business needs (**state-of-the-art** models are not the focus).

Priority

In research, training the models faster and better is the priority, whereas in production faster inference is the priority as the focus is to make decisions and serve the business needs in real time.

Understanding the types of ML inference in production

In the previous section, we saw the priorities of ML in research and production. To serve the business needs in production, ML models are inferred using various deployment targets, depending on the need. Predicting or making a decision using an ML model is called ML model inference. Let's explore ways of deploying ML models on different deployment targets to facilitate ML inference as per the business needs.

Deployment targets

In this section, we will look at different types of deployment targets and why and how we serve ML models for inference in these deployment targets. Let's start by looking at a virtual machine or an on-premises server.

Virtual machines

Virtual machines can be on the cloud or on-premises, depending on the IT setup of a business or an organization. Serving ML models on virtual machines is quite common. ML models are served on virtual machines in the form of web services. The web service running on a virtual machine receives a user request (as an HTTP request) containing the input data. The web service, upon receiving the input data, preprocesses it in the required format to infer the ML model, which is part of the web service. After the ML model makes the prediction or performs the task, the output is transformed and presented in a user-readable format. Commonly into **JavaScript Object Notation (JSON)** or **Extensible Markup language string (XML)**. Usually, a web service is served in the form of a REST API. REST API web services can be developed using multiple tools; for instance, FLASK or FAST API web application tools can be used to develop REST API web services using Python or Spring Boot in Java, or Plumber in R, depending on the need. A combination of virtual machines is used in parallel to scale and maintain the robustness of the web services.

In order to orchestrate the traffic and to scale the machines, a load balancer is used to dispatch incoming requests to the virtual machines for ML model inference. This way, ML models are deployed on virtual machines on the cloud or on-premises to serve the business needs, as shown in the following diagram:

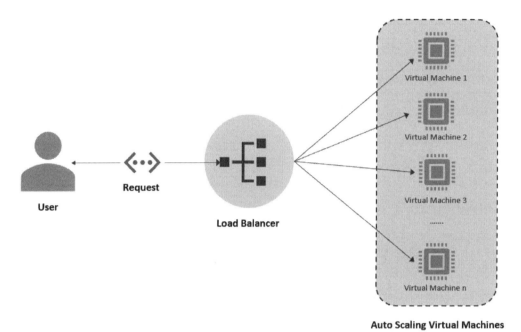

Figure 6.1 – Deployment on virtual machines

Containers

Containers are a reliable way to run applications using the Linux OS with customized settings. A container is an application running with a custom setting orchestrated by the developer. Containers are an alternative and more resource-efficient way of serving models than virtual machines. They operate like virtual machines as they have their own runtime environment, which is isolated and confined to memory, the filesystem, and processes.

Containers can be customized by developers to confine them to required resources such as memory, the filesystem, and processes, and the virtual machines are limited to such customizations. They are more flexible and operate in a modular way and hence provide more resource efficiency and optimization. They allow the possibility to scale to zero, as containers can be reduced to zero replicas and run a backup on request. This way, lower computation power consumption is possible compared to running web services on virtual machines. As a result of this lower computation power consumption, cost-saving on the cloud is possible.

Containers present many advantages; however, one disadvantage can be the complexity required to work with containers, as it requires expertise.

There are some differences in the way containers and virtual machines operate. For example, there can be multiple containers running inside a virtual machine that share the operating system and resources with the virtual machine, but the virtual machine runs its own resources and operating system. Containers can operate modularly, but virtual machines operate as single units. Docker is used to build and deploy containers; however, there are alternatives, such as Mesos and CoreOS rkt. A container is typically packaged with the ML model and web service to facilitate the ML inference, similar to how we serve the ML model wrapped in a web service in the virtual machine. Containers need to be orchestrated to be consumed by users. The orchestration of containers means the automation of the deployment, management, scaling, and networking of containers. Containers are orchestrated using a container orchestration system such as Kubernetes. In the following diagram, we can see container orchestration with auto-scaling (based on the traffic of requests):

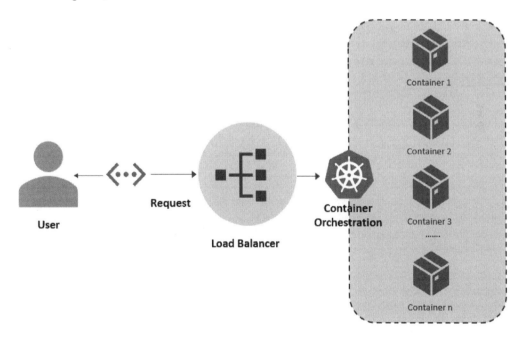

Figure 6.2 – Deployment on containers

Serverless

Serverless computing, as the name suggests, does not involve a virtual machine or container. It eliminates infrastructure management tasks such as OS management, server management, capacity provisioning, and disk management. Serverless computing enables developers and organizations to focus on their core product instead of mundane tasks such as managing and operating servers, either on the cloud or on-premises. Serverless computing is facilitated by using cloud-native services.

For instance, Microsoft Azure uses Azure Functions, and AWS uses Lambda functions to deploy serverless applications. The deployment for serverless applications involves submitting a collection of files (in the form of `.zip` files) to run ML applications. The .zip archive typically has a file with a particular function or method to execute. The zip archive is uploaded to the cloud platform using cloud services and deployed as a serverless application. The deployed application serves as an API endpoint to submit input to the serverless application serving the ML model.

Deploying ML models using serverless applications can have many advantages: there's no need to install or upgrade dependencies, or maintain or upgrade systems. Serverless applications auto-scale on demand and are robust in overall performance. Synchronous (execution happens one after another in a single series, A->B->C->D) and asynchronous (execution happens in parallel or on a priority basis, not in order: A->C->D->B or A and B together in parallel and C and D in parallel) operations are both supported by serverless functions. However, there are some disadvantages, such as cloud resource availability such as RAM or disk space or GPU unavailability, which can be crucial requirements for running heavy models such as deep learning or reinforcement learning models. For example, we can hit the wall of resource limitation if we have deployed a model without using serverless operations. The model or application deployed will not auto-scale and thus limit the available computation power. If more users infer the model or application than the limit, we will hit the resource unavailability blocker. In the following diagram, we can see how traditional applications and serverless applications are developed:

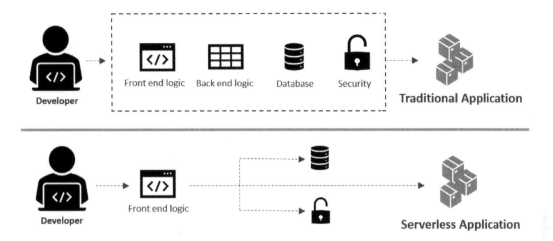

Figure 6.3: Traditional versus serverless deployments

To develop serverless applications, the developer only has to focus on the application's logic and not worry about backend or security code, which is taken care of by the cloud services upon deploying serverless applications.

Model streaming

Model streaming is a method of serving models for handling streaming data. There is no beginning or end of streaming data. Every second, data is produced from thousands of sources and must be processed and analyzed as soon as possible. For example, Google Search results must be processed in real time. Model streaming is another way of deploying ML models. It has two main advantages over other model serving techniques, such as REST APIs or batch processing approaches. The first advantage is asynchronicity (serving multiple requests at a time). REST API ML applications are robust and scalable but have the limitation of being synchronous (they process requests from the client on a first come, first serve basis), which can lead to high latency and resource utilization. To cope with this limitation, stream processing is available. It is inherently asynchronous as the user or client does not have to coordinate or wait for the system to process the request.

Stream processing is able to process asynchronously and serve the users on the go. In order to do so, stream processing uses a message broker to receive messages from the users or clients. The message broker allows the data as it comes and spreads the processing over time. The message broker decouples the incoming requests and facilitates communication between the users or clients and the service without being aware of each other's operations, as shown in figure 5.4. There are a couple of options for message streaming brokers, such as Apace Storm, Apache Kafka, Apache Spark, Apache Flint, Amazon Kinesis, and StreamSQL. The tool you choose is dependent on the IT setup and architecture.

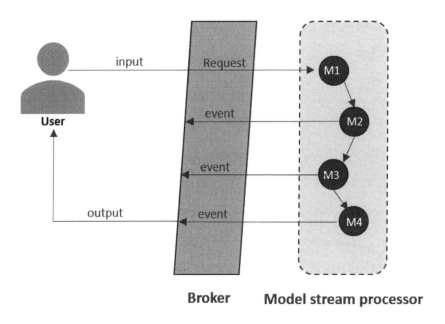

Figure 6.4 – Model streaming process

The second advantage of stream processing is when multiple models are being inferred in an ML system. REST APIs are great for single-model or dual-model processing, but they manage to produce latency and use high amounts of computation of resources when multiple models need to be inferred, and on top of this they are limited to synchronous inference.

In the case of multiple models, stream processing is a good option as all models and artifacts (code and files) needed to run the ML system can be packaged together and deployed on a stream processing engine (it runs on its own cluster of machines and manages resource allocation for distributing data processing).

For example, let's look at the use case of an intelligent email assistant tasked to automate customer service, as shown in *Figure 5.4*. In order to automate replies to serve its users, the email assistant system performs multiple predictions using multiple models:

- Predict the class of the email, such as spam or accounts or renewal
- Intent recognition
- Sentiment prediction
- Answer/text generation

These four models deployed on REST API endpoints will generate high latency and maintenance costs, whereas a streaming service is a good alternative as it can package and serve multiple models as one process and continuously serve user requests in the form of a stream. Hence in such cases, streaming is recommended over REST API endpoints.

Mapping the infrastructure for our solution

In this section, we map infrastructural needs and deployment targets needed to address diverse business needs, as seen in *Table 6.3*:

Business Need	Solution	Deployment Target
A business needs to infer a single ML model now and then as per the demand	ML models served as a REST API	Virtual machines
A business needs to infer one or two models on demand and auto-scale when requests from the users increase in quantity	ML models served as a REST API	Containers
A business needs a robust and scalable ML model service to predict their business operations	Collection of model artifacts (files and code) such as a zip file	Serverless application
A business needs to handle continuous requests from the user for multiple ML models and scale as per the quantity of the users to serve their requests	Collection of ML models served as a streaming service	Model streaming

Table 6.3 – Mapping the infrastructure for ML solutions

Depending on your use case, it is recommended to select suitable infrastructure and deployment targets to serve ML models to generate business or operational impact.

Hands-on deployment (for the business problem)

In this section, we will learn how to deploy solutions for the business problem we have been working on. So far, we have done data processing, ML model training, serialized models, and registered them to the Azure ML workspace. In this section, we will explore how inference is performed on the serialized model on a container and an auto-scaling cluster. These deployments will give you a broad understanding and will prepare you well for your future assignments.

We will use Python as the primary programming language, and Docker and Kubernetes for building and deploying containers. We will start with deploying a REST API service on an Azure container instance using Azure ML. Next, we will deploy a REST API service on an auto-scaling cluster using Kubernetes (for container orchestration) using Azure ML, and lastly, we will deploy on an Azure container instance using MLflow and an open source ML framework; this way, we will learn how to use multiple tools and deploy ML models on the cloud (Azure). Let's get started with deployment on **Azure Container Instances** (**ACI**).

Deploying the model on ACI

To get started with deployment, go to the GitHub repository cloned on Azure DevOps previously (in *Chapter 3*, *Code Meets Data*), access the folder named 06_ ModelDeployment, and follow the implementation steps in the 01_Deploy_model_ ACI.ipynb notebook:

1. We start by importing the required packages and check for the version of the Azure ML SDK, as shown in the following code:

    ```
    %matplotlib inline
    import numpy as np
    import matplotlib.pyplot as plt
    import azureml.core
    from azureml.core import Workspace
    from azureml.core.model import Model


    # display the core SDK version number
    print("Azure ML SDK Version: ", azureml.core.VERSION)
    ```

    The preceding code will print the Azure ML SDK version (for example, 1.10.0; your version may be different).

2. Next, using the `workspace` function from the Azure ML SDK, we connect to the ML workspace and download the required serialized files and model trained earlier using the `Model` function from the workspace. The serialized `scaler` and `model` are used to perform inference or prediction. `Scaler` will be used to shrink the input data to the same scale of data that was used for model training, and the `model` file is used to make predictions on the incoming data:

```
ws = Workspace.from_config()
print(ws.name, ws.resource_group, ws.location, sep =
'\n')
scaler = Model(ws,'scaler').download(exist_ok=True)
model = Model(ws,'support-vector-classifier').
download(exist_ok=True)
```

3. After the `scaler` and the `model` files are downloaded, the next step is to prepare the `scoring` file. The `scoring` file is used to infer the ML models in the containers deployed with the ML service in the Azure container instance and Kubernetes cluster. The `scoring` script takes input passed by the user and infers the ML model for prediction and then serves the output with the prediction to the user. It contains two primary functions, `init()` and `run()`. We start by importing the required libraries and then define the `init()` and `run()` functions:

```
%%writefile score.py
import json
import numpy as np
import os
import pickle
import joblib
import onnxruntime
import time
from azureml.core.model import Model
```

`%%writefile score.py` writes this code into a file named `score.py`, which is later packed as part of the ML service in the container for performing ML model inference.

4. We define the `init()` function; it downloads the required models and deserializes them into variables to be used for the predictions:

```
def init():
    global model, scaler, input_name, label_name
```

```
    scaler_path = os.path.join(os.getenv('AZUREML_MODEL_
DIR'), 'scaler/2/scaler.pkl')
    # deserialize the scalar file back into a variable to
be used for inference
    scaler = joblib.load(scaler_path)


model_onnx = os.path.join(os.getenv('AZUREML_MODEL_DIR'),
'support-vector-classifier/2/svc.onnx')
# deserialize support vector classifer model
    model = onnxruntime.InferenceSession(model_onnx,
None)
    input_name = model.get_inputs()[0].name
    label_name = model.get_outputs()[0].name
```

Using onnxruntime we can deserialize the support vector classifier model. The InferenceSession() function is used for deserializing and serving the model for inference, and the input_name and label_name variables are loaded from the deserialized model.

5. In a nutshell, the init() function loads files (model and scaler) and deserializes and serves the model and artifact files needed for making predictions, which are used by the run() function as follows:

```
def run(raw_data):
            try:
                data = np.array(json.loads(raw_data)
['data']).astype('float32')
                data = scaler.fit_transform(data.
                reshape(1, 7))
                # make prediction


                model_prediction = model.run([label_
name], {input_name: data.astype(np.float32)})[0]


# you can return any data type as long as it is JSON-
serializable


            except Exception as e:
                model_prediction = 'error'
```

```
return model_prediction
```

The `run()` function takes raw incoming data as the argument, performs ML model inference, and returns the predicted result as the output. When called, the `run()` function receives the incoming data, which is sanitized and loaded into a variable for scaling. The incoming data is scaled using the scaler loaded previously in the `init()` function. Next, the model inference step, which is the key step, is performed by inferencing scaled data to the model, as shown previously. The prediction inferred from the model is then returned as the output. This way, the scoring file is written into `score.py` to be used for deployment.

6. Next, we will proceed to the crucial part of deploying the service on an Azure container instance. For this, we define a deployment environment by creating an environment **YAML (Yet Another Markup Language)** file called `myenv.yml`, as shown in the following code. Using the `CondaDependencies()` function, we mention all the `pip` packages that need to be installed inside the Docker container that will be deployed as the ML service. Packages such as `numpy`, `onnxruntime`, `joblib`, `azureml-core`, `azureml-defaults`, and `scikit-learn` are installed inside the container upon triggering the environment file:

```
from azureml.core.conda_dependencies import
CondaDependencies

myenv = CondaDependencies.create(pip_packages=["numpy",
"onnxruntime", "joblib", "azureml-core", "azureml-
defaults", "scikit-learn==0.20.3"])


with open("myenv.yml","w") as f:
    f.write(myenv.serialize_to_string())
```

7. Next, we define the inference configuration by using the `InferenceConfig()` function, which takes `score.py` and the environment file as the arguments upon being called. Next, we call the `AciWebservice()` function to initiate the compute configuration (`cpu_cores` and `memory`) in the `aciconfig` variable as follows:

```
from azureml.core.model import InferenceConfig
from azureml.core.environment import Environment
myenv = Environment.from_conda_specification(name="myenv",
file_path="myenv.yml")
inference_config = InferenceConfig(entry_script="score.
py", environment=myenv)
from azureml.core.webservice import AciWebservice
```

```
aciconfig = AciWebservice.deploy_configuration(cpu_
cores=1,
memory_gb=1,
tags={"data": "weather"},
description='weather-prediction')
```

8. Now we are all set to deploy the ML or web service on the ACI. We will use `score.
    py`, the environment file (`myenv.yml`), `inference_config`, and `aci_config`
    to deploy the ML or web service. We will need to point to the models or artifacts to
    deploy. For this, we use the `Model()` function to load the `scaler` and `model` files
    from the workspace and get them ready for deployment:

```
%%time
from azureml.core.webservice import Webservice
from azureml.core.model import InferenceConfig
from azureml.core.environment import Environment
from azureml.core import Workspace
from azureml.core.model import Model

ws = Workspace.from_config()
model1 = Model(ws, 'support-vector-classifier')
model2 = Model(ws, 'scaler')
service = Model.deploy(workspace=ws,
                        name='weatherprediction',
                        models=[model1, model2],
                        inference_config=inference_config,
                        deployment_config=aciconfig)
service.wait_for_deployment(show_output=True)
```

9. After the models are mounted into variables, `model1` and `model2`, we proceed with deploying them as a web service. We use the `deploy()` function to deploy the mounted models as a web service on the ACI, as shown in the preceding code. This process will take around 8 minutes, so grab your popcorn and enjoy the service being deployed. You will see a message like this:

```
Running.............................................
...........................
Succeeded
ACI service creation operation finished, operation
"Succeeded"
CPU times: user 610 ms, sys: 103 ms, total: 713 ms
Wall time: 7min 57s
```

Congratulations! You have successfully deployed your first ML service using MLOps.

10. Let's check out the workings and robustness of the deployed service. Check out the service URL and Swagger URL, as shown in the following code. You can use these URLs to perform ML model inference for input data of your choice in real time:

```
print(service.scoring_uri)
print(service.swagger_uri)
```

11. Check for the deployed service in the Azure ML workspace.

12. Now, we can test the service using the Azure ML SDK `service.run()` function by passing some input data as follows:

```
import json
test_sample = json.dumps({'data': [[34.927778, 0.24,
7.3899, 83, 16.1000, 1016.51, 1]]})
test_sample = bytes(test_sample,encoding = 'utf8')
prediction = service.run (input_data=test_sample)
```

The features in the input data are in this order: `Temperature_C`, `Humidity`, `Wind_speed_kmph`, `Wind_bearing_degrees`, `Visibility_km`, `Pressure_millibars`, and `Current_weather_condition`. Encode the input data in UTF-8 for smooth inference. Upon inferring the model using `service.run()`, the model returns a prediction of `0` or `1`. `0` means a clear sky and `1` means it will rain. Using this service, we can make weather predictions at the port of Turku as tasked in the business problem.

13. The service we have deployed is a REST API web service that we can infer with an HTTP request as follows:

```
import requests

headers = {'Content-Type': 'application/json', 'Accept':
'application/json'}

if service.auth_enabled:
    headers['Authorization'] = 'Bearer '+ service.get_
keys()[0]

elif service.token_auth_enabled:
    headers['Authorization'] = 'Bearer '+ service.get_
token()[0]


scoring_uri = service.scoring_uri

print(scoring_uri)

response = requests.post(scoring_uri, data=test_sample,
headers=headers)

print(response.status_code)

print(response.elapsed)

print(response.json())
```

When a `POST` request is made by passing input data, the service returns the model prediction in the form of `0` or `1`. When you get such a prediction, your service is working and is robust enough to serve production needs.

Next, we will deploy the service on an auto-scaling cluster; this is ideal for production scenarios as the deployed service can auto-scale and serve user needs.

Deploying the model on Azure Kubernetes Service (AKS)

To get started with the deployment, go to the Git repository cloned on Azure DevOps in *Chapter 3, Code Meets Data*, access the `06_ModelDeployment` folder, and follow the implementation steps in the `02_Deploy_model_AKS.ipynb` notebook:

1. As we did in the previous section, start by importing the required packages, such as `matplotlib`, `numpy`, and `azureml.core`, and the required functions, such as `Workspace` and `Model`, from `azureml.core`, as shown in the following code block:

```
%matplotlib inline
import numpy as np
import matplotlib.pyplot as plt


import azureml.core
from azureml.core import Workspace
from azureml.core.model import Model


# display the core SDK version number
print("Azure ML SDK Version: ", azureml.core.VERSION)
```

2. Print the version of the Azure ML SDK and check for the version (it will print, for example, `1.10.0`; your version may be different). Use the config file and `Workspace` function connect to your workspace, as shown in the following code block:

```
ws = Workspace.from_config()
print(ws.name, ws.resource_group, ws.location, sep =
'\n')
scaler = Model(ws,'scaler').download(exist_ok=True)
model = Model(ws,'support-vector-classifier').
download(exist_ok=True)
```

3. Download the `model` and `scaler` files as we did previously. After the `model` and the `scaler` files are downloaded, the next step is to prepare the `scoring` file, which is used to infer the ML models in the containers deployed with the ML service. The `scoring` script takes an input passed by the user, infers the ML model for prediction, and then serves the output with the prediction to the user. We will start by importing the required libraries, as shown in the following code block:

```
%%writefile score.py
import json
import numpy as np
import os
import pickle
import joblib
import onnxruntime
import time
from azureml.core.model import Model
```

4. As we made `score.py` previously for ACI deployment, we will use the same file. It contains two primary functions, `init()` and `run()`. We define the `init()` function; it downloads the required models and deserializes them into variables to be used for predictions:

```
def init():
    global model, scaler, input_name, label_name
    scaler_path = os.path.join(os.getenv('AZUREML_MODEL_
DIR'), 'scaler/2/scaler.pkl')
    # deserialize the model file back into a sklearn
model
    scaler = joblib.load(scaler_path)

    model_onnx = os.path.join(os.getenv('AZUREML_MODEL_
DIR'), 'support-vector-classifier/2/svc.onnx')
    model = onnxruntime.InferenceSession(model_onnx,
None)
    input_name = model.get_inputs()[0].name
    label_name = model.get_outputs()[0].name
```

5. As we did in the previous section on ACI deployment, by using `onnxruntime` package functions we can deserialize the support vector classifier model. The `InferenceSession()` function is used to deserialize and serve the model for inference, and the `input_name` and `label_name` variables are loaded from the deserialized model. In a nutshell, the `init()` function loads files (`model` and `scaler`), and deserializes and serves the model and artifact files needed for making predictions that are used by the `run()` function:

```python
def run(raw_data):
    try:
        data = np.array(json.loads(raw_data)
['data']).astype('float32')
        data = scaler.fit_transform(data.
reshape(1, 7))
        # make prediction
        model_prediction = model.run([label_
name], {input_name: data.astype(np.float32)})[0]
        # you can return any data type as
long as it is JSON-serializable

    except Exception as e:
        model_prediction = 'error'

    return model_prediction
```

We will use the same `run()` function previously used in the section *Deploying the model on ACI* for the AKS deployment. With this we can proceed to deploying the service on AKS.

6. Next, we will proceed to the crucial part of deploying the service on **Azure Kubernetes Service**. Create an environment in which your model will be deployed using the CondaDependencies() function. We will mention all the required pip and conda packages to be installed inside the Docker container that will be deployed as the ML service. Packages such as numpy, onnxruntime, joblib, azureml-core, azureml-defaults, and scikit-learn are installed inside the container upon triggering the environment file. Next, use the publicly available container in the Microsoft Container Registry without any authentication. This container will install your environment and will be configured for deployment to your target AKS:

```
from azureml.core import Environment
from azureml.core.conda_dependencies import
CondaDependencies


conda_deps = CondaDependencies.create(conda_
packages=['numpy','scikit-learn==0.19.1','scipy'], pip_
packages=["numpy", "onnxruntime", "joblib", "azureml-
core", "azureml-defaults", "scikit-learn==0.20.3"])
myenv = Environment(name='myenv')
myenv.python.conda_dependencies = conda_deps


# use an image available in public Container Registry
without authentication
myenv.docker.base_image = "mcr.microsoft.com/azureml/
o16n-sample-user-base/ubuntu-miniconda"
```

7. Now, define the inference configuration by using the InferenceConfig() function, which takes score.py and the environment variable as the arguments upon being called:

```
from azureml.core.model import InferenceConfig
inf_config = InferenceConfig(entry_script='score.py',
environment=myenv)
```

8. Now we are all set to deploy the ML or web service on Azure Kubernetes Service (auto-scaling cluster). In order to do so, we will need to create an AKS cluster and attach it to the Azure ML workspace. Choose a name for your cluster and check if it exists using the `ComputeTarget()` function. If not, a cluster will be created or provisioned using the `ComputeTarget.create()` function. It takes a workspace object, `ws`; a service name; and a provisioning config to create the cluster. We use the default parameters for the provisioning config to create a default cluster:

```
%%time
from azureml.core.compute import ComputeTarget
from azureml.core.compute_target import
ComputeTargetException
from azureml.core.compute import AksCompute,
ComputeTarget


# Choose a name for your AKS cluster
aks_name = 'port-aks'


# Verify that cluster does not exist already
try:
    aks_target = ComputeTarget(workspace=ws, name=aks_
name)
    print('Found existing cluster, use it.')
except ComputeTargetException:
    # Use the default configuration (can also provide
parameters to customize)
    prov_config = AksCompute.provisioning_configuration()

    # Create the cluster
    aks_target = ComputeTarget.create(workspace = ws,
                                      name = aks_name,
provisioning_configuration = prov_config)


if aks_target.get_status() != "Succeeded":
aks_target.wait_for_completion(show_output=True)
```

After creating a cluster, you will get the following message:

```
Creating......................................................
.....................
SucceededProvisioning operation finished, operation
"Succeeded"
```

Congrats, you have successfully created a cluster!

> **Note**
>
> If a cluster with the same AKS cluster name (aks_name = port-aks)
> already exists, a new cluster will not be created. Rather, the existing cluster
> (named port-aks here) will be attached to the workspace for further
> deployments.

9. Next, we proceed to the critical task of deploying the ML service in the Kubernetes
    cluster. In order to deploy, we need some prerequisites, such as mounting the
    models to deploy. We mount the models using the Model() function to load the
    scaler and model files from the workspace and get them ready for deployment,
    as shown in the following code:

```
from azureml.core.webservice import Webservice,
AksWebservice
# Set the web service configuration (using default here)
aks_config = AksWebservice.deploy_configuration()
%%time
from azureml.core.webservice import Webservice
from azureml.core.model import InferenceConfig
from azureml.core.environment import Environment
from azureml.core import Workspace
from azureml.core.model import Model

ws = Workspace.from_config()
model1 = Model(ws, 'support-vector-classifier')
model2 = Model(ws, 'scaler')
```

10. Now we are all set to deploy the service on AKS. We deploy the service with the help of the `Model.deploy()` function from the Azure ML SDK, which takes the workspace object, `ws`; `service_name`; `models`; `inference_config`; `deployment_config`; and `deployment_target` as arguments upon being called:

```
%%time
aks_service_name ='weatherpred-aks'


aks_service = Model.deploy (workspace=ws,
                             name=aks_service_name,
                             models=[model1, model2],
                             inference_config=inf_config,
                             deployment_config=aks_config,
                             deployment_target=aks_target)


aks_service.wait_for_deployment(show_output = True)
print(aks_service.state)
```

Deploying the service will take approximately around 10 mins. After deploying the ML service, you will get a message like the following:

```
Running...................... Succeeded AKS service
creation operation finished, operation "Succeeded"
```

Congratulations! Now you have deployed an ML service on AKS. Let's test it using the Azure ML SDK.

11. We use the `service.run()` function to pass data to the service and get the predictions, as follows:

```
import json


test_sample = json.dumps({'data': [[34.927778, 0.24,
7.3899, 83, 16.1000, 1016.51, 1]]})
test_sample = bytes(test_sample,encoding = 'utf8')
prediction = service.run(input_data=test_sample)
```

12. The deployed service is a REST API web service that can be accessed with an HTTP request as follows:

```
import requests

headers = {'Content-Type': 'application/json', 'Accept':
'application/json'}

if service.auth_enabled:
    headers['Authorization'] = 'Bearer '+ service.get_
keys()[0]
elif service.token_auth_enabled:
    headers['Authorization'] = 'Bearer '+ service.get_
token()[0]

scoring_uri = service.scoring_uri
print(scoring_uri)
response = requests.post(scoring_uri, data=test_sample,
headers=headers)
print(response.status_code)
print(response.elapsed)
print(response.json())
```

When a POST request is made by passing input data, the service returns the model prediction in the form of 0 or 1. When you get such a prediction, your service is working and is robust to serve production needs. The service scales from 0 to the needed number of container replicas based on the user's request traffic.

Deploying the service using MLflow

Lastly, let's do the deployment of an ML service on the deployment target (ACI) using MLflow to get hands-on experience with an open source framework. To get started, go to the Git repository cloned on Azure DevOps previously (in *Chapter 3, Code Meets Data*), access the folder named 06_ModelDeployment, and follow the implementation steps in the 02_Deploy_model_MLflow.ipynb notebook. Before implementing, it is recommended to read this documentation to understand the concepts behind the mlflow.azureml SDK: https://docs.microsoft.com/en-us/azure/machine-learning/how-to-use-mlflow#deploy-and-register-mlflow-models.

1. We start by importing the required packages and check for the version of the Azure ML SDK, as shown in the following code block:

    ```
    import numpy as np
    import mlflow.azureml
    import azureml.core
    # display the core SDK version number
    print("Azure ML SDK Version: ", azureml.core.VERSION)
    ```

2. Next, using the workspace function from the Azure ML SDK, we connect to the ML workspace and set the tracking URI for the workspace using set_tracking_uri:

    ```
    from azureml.core import Workspace
    from azureml.core.model import Model

    ws = Workspace.from_config()
    print(ws.name, ws.resource_group, ws.location, sep = '\n')
    mlflow.set_tracking_uri(ws.get_mlflow_tracking_uri())
    ```

3. Now go to the workspace and fetch the path to the mlflow model from the models or experiments section and set the path:

    ```
    from azureml.core.webservice import AciWebservice, Webservice
    # Set the model path to the model folder created by your run
    model_path = "model path"
    ```

4. Now we are all set to deploy to the ACI using `mlflow` and the `azureml` SDK. Configure the ACI deployment target using the `deploy_configuration` function and deploy to the ACI using the `mlflow.azureml.deploy` function. The `deploy` function takes `model_uri`, `workspace`, `model_name`, `service_name`, `deployment_config`, and custom tags as arguments upon being called:

```
# Configure
aci_config = AciWebservice.deploy_configuration
(cpu_cores=1,
memory_gb=1,
tags={'method' : 'mlflow'},
description='weather pred model',
location='eastus2')

# Deploy on ACI
(webservice,model) = mlflow.azureml.deploy(model_uri=
'runs:/{}/{}'.format(run.id, model_path), workspace=ws,
model_name='svc-mlflow', service_name='port-weather-
pred', deployment_config=aci_config, tags=None, mlflow_
home=None, synchronous=True)
webservice.wait_for_deployment(show_output=True)
```

You will get a deployment succeeded message upon successful deployment. For more clarity on MLflow deployment, follow these examples: https://docs.microsoft.com/en-us/azure/machine-learning/how-to-use-mlflow#deploy-and-register-mlflow-models.

Congratulations! You have deployed ML models on diverse deployment targets such as ACI and AKS using `azureml` and `mlflow`.

Next, we will focus on bringing the full capabilities of MLOps to the table using continuous integration and continuous deployment to have a robust and dynamically developing system in production.

Understanding the need for continuous integration and continuous deployment

Continuous integration (**CI**) and **continuous deployment** (**CD**) enable continuous delivery to the ML service. The goal is to maintain and version the source code used for model training, enable triggers to perform necessary jobs in parallel, build artifacts, and release them for deployment to the ML service. Several cloud vendors enable DevOps services that can be used for monitoring ML services, ML models in production, and orchestration with other services in the cloud.

Using CI and CD, we can enable continuous learning, which is critical for the success of an ML system. Without continuous learning, an ML system is destined to end up as a failed **PoC** (**Proof of Concept**). We will delve into the concepts of CI/CD and implement hands-on CI and CD pipelines to see MLOps in play in the next chapter.

Summary

In this chapter, we have learned the key principles of deploying ML models in production. We explored the various deployment methods and targets and their needs. For a comprehensive understanding and hands-on experience, we implemented the deployment to learn how ML models are deployed on a diverse range of deployment targets such as virtual machines, containers, and in an auto-scaling cluster. With this, you are ready to handle any type of deployment challenge that comes your way.

In the next chapter, we will delve into the secrets to building, deploying, and maintaining robust ML services enabled by CI and CD. This will enable the potential of MLOps! Let's delve into it.

7
Building Robust CI/CD Pipelines

In this chapter, you will learn about continuous operations in the MLOps pipeline. The principles you will learn in this chapter are key to driving continuous deployments in a business context. To get a comprehensive understanding and first-hand experience, we will go through the concepts and hands-on implementation simultaneously. We will set up a CI/CD pipeline for the test environment while learning about components of **continuous integration** (**CI**) and **continuous deployment** (**CD**), pipeline testing, and releases and types of triggers. This will equip you with the skills to automate the deployment pipelines of **machine learning** (**ML**) models for any given scenario on the cloud with continual learning abilities in tune with business. Let's start by looking at why we need CI/CD in MLOps after all. We will continue by exploring the other topics as follows:

- Continuous integration, delivery, and deployment in MLOps

- Setting up a CI/CD pipeline and test environment (using Azure DevOps)

- Pipeline execution and testing

- Pipeline execution triggers

Continuous integration, delivery, and deployment in MLOps

Automation is the primary reason for CI/CD in the MLOps workflow. The goal of enabling continuous delivery to the ML service is to maintain data and source code versions of the models, enable triggers to perform necessary jobs in parallel, build artifacts, and release deployments for production. Several cloud vendors are promoting DevOps services to monitor ML services and models in production, as well as orchestrate with other services on the cloud. Using CI and CD, we can enable continual learning, which is critical for a ML system's success. Without continual learning, a ML system is deemed to end up as a failed **Proof of Concept (PoC)**.

> *Only a model deployed with continual learning capabilities can bring business value.*

In order to learn to deploy a model in production with continual learning capabilities, we will explore CI, CD, and continuous delivery methods.

As you can see in *Figure 7.1*, CI is key to CD and continuous delivery. Let's see how these three are interconnected:

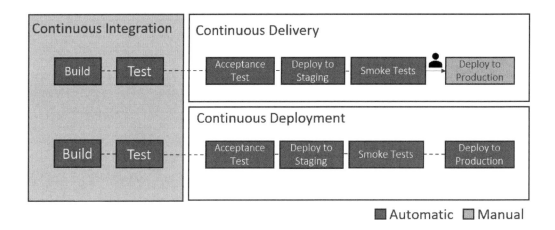

Figure 7.1 – Continuous integration, delivery, and deployment pipelines

Continuous integration

CI aims to synchronize the application (ML pipeline and application) with the developer in real time. The developer's changes in commits or merges are validated by creating an application build on the go and by performing automated tests against the build. CI emphasizes automated testing with a focus on checking the application's robustness (if it is not broken or bugged) when new commits are merged to the master or main branch. Whenever a new commit is made to the master branch, a new build is created that is tested for robustness using automated testing. By automating this process, we can avoid delayed delivery of software and other integration challenges that can keep users waiting for days for the release. Automation and testing are at the heart of CI.

Continuous delivery

Continuous delivery extends from CI to ensure that the new changes or releases are deployed and efficiently brought to users; this is facilitated by automating testing and release processes. Automating testing and release processes enable developers and product managers to deploy the changes with one click of a button, enabling seamless control and supervision capabilities at any phase of the process. In the continuous delivery process, quite often, a human agent (from the QA team) is involved in approving a build (pass or fail) before deploying it in production (as shown in *Figure 7.1* in a continuous delivery pipeline). In a typical continuous delivery pipeline, a build goes through preliminary acceptance tests before getting deployed on the staging phase where a human agent supervises the performance using smoke tests and other suitable tests.

Once the smoke tests have been passed, the human agent passes the build to be deployed in production. Automating the build and release process and having a human agent involved in the process ensures great quality as regards production and we can avoid some pitfalls that may go unnoticed with a fully automated pipeline. Using continuous delivery, a business can have full control over its release process and release a new build in small batches (easy to troubleshoot in the case of blockers or errors) or have a full release within a requisite time frame (daily, weekly, or monthly).

Continuous deployment

CD enables full automation and goes one step further than continuous delivery. All stages of build and release to your production are completely automated without any human intervention, unlike in continuous delivery. In such an automated pipeline, only a failed test can stop a new change from being deployed to production. Continuous deployment takes the pressure off the team to maintain the release pipeline and accelerates deployment straight to the customers enabling continual learning via feedback loops with customers.

With such automation, there is no longer a release day for developers. It takes the pressure off them and they can just focus on building the software without worrying about tests and release management. Developers can build, test, and deploy the software at their convenience and can go live within minutes instead of waiting for release days or for human approval, which can delay the release of software to users by days and sometimes weeks. Continuous deployment ensures full automation to deploy and serve robust and scalable software to users.

Setting up a CI/CD pipeline and the test environment (using Azure DevOps)

In the previous section, we went through the theory of CI, continuous delivery, and continuous deployment, and now it is time to see it in practice. Using Azure DevOps, we will set up a simple CI/CD pipeline of our own for the business problem (weather prediction), which we have been working on previously (in *Chapter 6, Key Principles for Deploying Your ML System*, in the Hands-on deployment section (for the business problem)).

Azure DevOps is a service provided by Microsoft that facilitates source code management (version control), project management, CI, continuous delivery, and continuous deployment (automated builds, testing, and release capabilities). It also enables life cycle management for software applications. We will use Azure DevOps for hands-on training as it comes with seamless integration with the Azure ML service, which we have been using previously in *Chapter 6*. You will experience the integration and syncing of both services to make deployments with ease. Let's get started.

Go to your Azure DevOps project, `Learn_MLOps`. Go to the cloned repository and access the `07_CICD_Pipeline` folder. We will use these files (in the folder named `07_CICD_Pipeline`) as drivers to build a release pipeline:

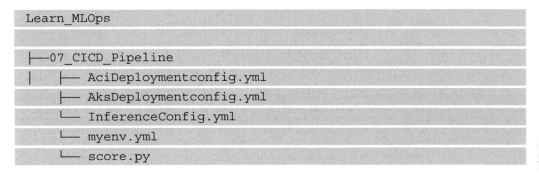

```
Learn_MLOps


├──07_CICD_Pipeline
│       ├── AciDeploymentconfig.yml
│       ├── AksDeploymentconfig.yml
│       └── InferenceConfig.yml
│       └── myenv.yml
│       └── score.py
```

We will deploy previously trained ML models (from *Chapter 4*, *Machine Learning Pipelines*) on two deployment targets: one is **Azure Container Instances** (**ACI**) for the test environment, and the second is an **Azure Kubernetes Service** (**AKS**) cluster for the production environment. The `AciDeployment.yml` file contains the configuration for the ACI deployment target, and the `AksDeployment.yml` file contains the configuration for the AKS cluster. `InferenceConfig.yml` points to inference artifacts such as `score.py` and `myenv.yml`.

The functions defined in `score.py` will be used to pre-process the incoming data and infer the pre-processed data with the ML model to make predictions. The `myenv.yml` file is a configuration for the inference environment, for example, the Python version and packages to install within the environment. These files will be used as drivers to facilitate the release pipeline. Now that you have familiarized yourself with these files, let's begin by connecting the Azure ML service and the Azure DevOps project using a service principal.

Creating a service principal

We need to sync Azure ML services and Azure DevOps in order to facilitate CI between both the services. Previously (in *Chapter 4*, *Machine Learning Pipelines*) we had developed and managed our ML models using Azure ML service, and we used the `Learn_MLOps` workspace. Now, we will connect the Azure ML workspace (named `Learn_MLOps`) with the Azure DevOps project (named `Learn_MLOps`) using a service principal.

A service principal is an identity created for inter-application communication; it is a connection automation tool to access Azure resources. Service principal also takes care of the networking and connectivity aspects of your applications. Perform the following steps to set up a service principal for the pipelines:

1. Go to **Project Settings** (on the bottom left of your screen) and select **Service connections**. Click the **New service connection** option/button to reveal the New service connection window, as shown in *Figure 7.2*:

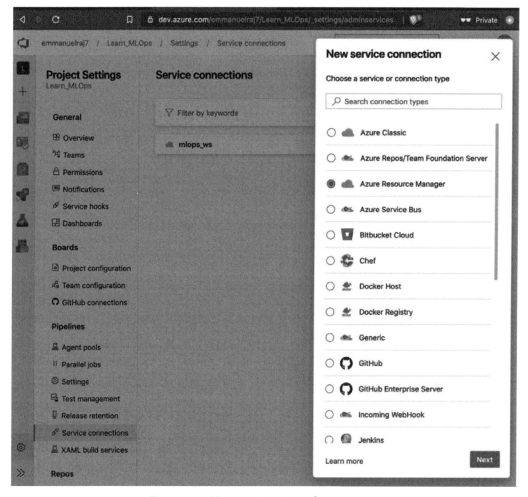

Figure 7.2 – New service principal connection

2. Select **Azure Resource Manager** for the connection type and proceed by clicking **Next**. Select **Service principal (automatic)** and proceed to the final step of creating a service principal.

3. You will be prompted to create a new service connection. Set the scope as **Machine Learning Workspace** and point to the **Subscription, Resource group** and **Machine Learning Workspace** as shown in *Figure 7.3*:

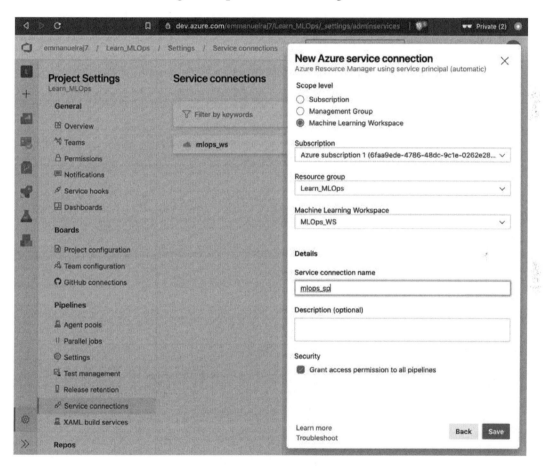

Figure 7.3 – Final step in creating a service principal

4. Name the service principal in the **Service connection name** input box (e.g. mlops_sp as shown in *Figure 7.3*). Lastly, tick the checkbox (**Grant access permission to all pipelines**) and click **Save** to create the service principal.

With this, your service principal with the given name (for example, `mlops_sp`) is ready to be used for orchestrating CI/CD pipelines. Next, we will install the extension used for the pipelines.

Installing the extension to connect to the Azure ML workspace

Microsoft has developed an extension called **Machine Learning**. It is available in the Azure DevOps Marketplace. It is used to orchestrate models and artifacts from our desired Azure ML workspace. It lets us deploy models from the workspace to our desired deployment targets such as ACI or AKS. We will install the ML extension and use it to orchestrate the CI/CD pipeline. Perform the following steps to install the extension:

1. Go to the Marketplace to look for the **Machine Learning** extension. To go to the Marketplace, click on the bag icon in the top right of your screen, as shown in *Figure 7.4*:

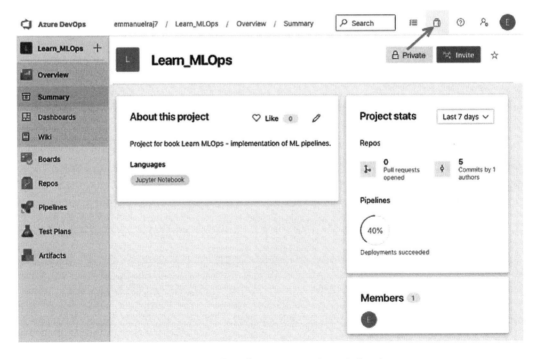

Figure 7.4 – Finding the Azure DevOps Marketplace

After entering the Marketplace, you will be presented with multiple extensions to add to your Azure DevOps project. Next, we will search for the **Machine Learning** extension.

2. Search for the **Machine Learning** extension and install the extension for free. Click the **Get it free** button to install the extension as shown in *Figure 7.5*:

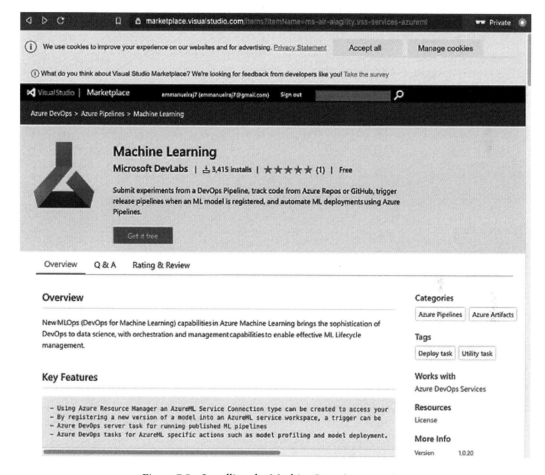

Figure 7.5 – Installing the Machine Learning extension

The **Machine Learning** extension will be installed upon clicking the **Get it free** button. After successful installation, you can use the **Machine Learning** extension to orchestrate jobs in the CI/CD pipeline. With these prerequisites, you are set to configure the continuous deployment or continuous delivery pipeline.

Setting up a continuous integration and deployment pipeline for the test environment

In this section, we will configure the CI/CD pipeline for the staging environment (also called the test environment). We will use this pipeline to facilitate continual learning and automate deployments. Let's get started by going to **Pipelines** >> **Releases**, as shown in *Figure 7.6*:

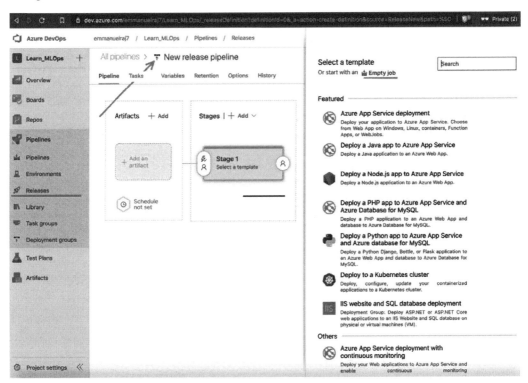

Figure 7.6 – Setting up your CI/CD pipeline

Create a new pipeline in the **Release** section. Name your pipeline as you wish. For the demo, the pipeline has been named `Port Weather ML Pipeline`. Next, we will start connecting the requisite artifacts to enable the pipeline, such as the repository containing the code and the Azure ML workspace containing the models to deploy.

Connecting artifacts to the pipeline

Connect to your Azure DevOps repository. The Azure DevOps repository serves as the central code repository to orchestrate deployments and operations on Azure DevOps. Hence, let's connect the repository (Learn_MLOps) to the release pipeline:

1. As shown in *Figure 7.7*, go to the **Artifacts** section, click **Add**, select **Azure Repository**, and then select the repository (for example, **Learn_MLOps**) to connect with the release pipeline:

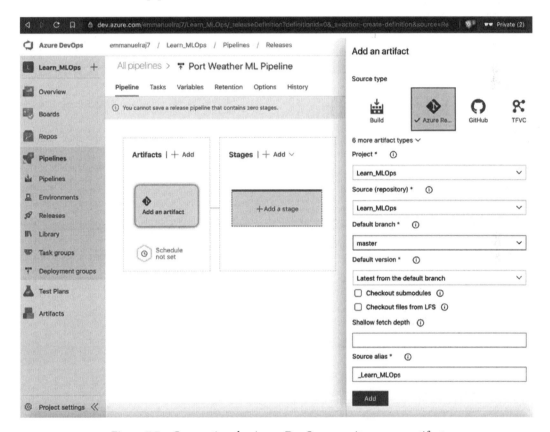

Figure 7.7 – Connecting the Azure DevOps repository as an artifact

2. Select the default branch (for example, **master**) and finally, click the **Add** button at the bottom of the screen to connect the repository to the release pipeline. After adding the repository, you will be able to see the repository name (**Learn_MLOps**) and icon in the **Artifacts** section.

3. Connect to your Azure ML workspace. To connect your Azure ML workspace to the release pipeline, go to the **Artifacts** section, click the **Add** button, and select **Azure ML Model Artifact** for the artifact type, as shown in *Figure 7.8*. Select the **Service Endpoint** (your Azure ML workspace, for example, **mlops_ws**) and the models to deploy. Let's select **model-scaler** as the model. We will use the `scaler` artifact previously registered in *Chapter 4, Machine Learning Pipelines,* to scale the incoming data using the standard:

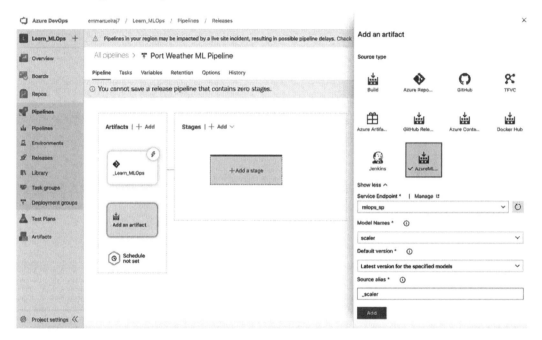

Figure 7.8 – Connecting the scaler as an artifact

4. After selecting the `model_scaler` artifact, add the artifact to the release pipeline by clicking the **Add** button. After adding the `model_scaler` artifact, you will be able to see the model's name (`model_scaler`) and a model icon in the **Artifacts** section, as shown in *Figure 7.9*.

In the same way, connect the **support_vector_classifier** model to the release pipeline artifacts. Start by clicking the **Add** button on **Artifacts**, select **Azure ML Model Artifact**, point to the service endpoint (the service principal connected to your Azure ML workspace, for example: `mlops_sp`) and select the **support_vector_classifier** model trained previously in *Chapter 4, Machine Learning Pipelines*. Add the model artifact to the pipeline by hitting the **Add** button:

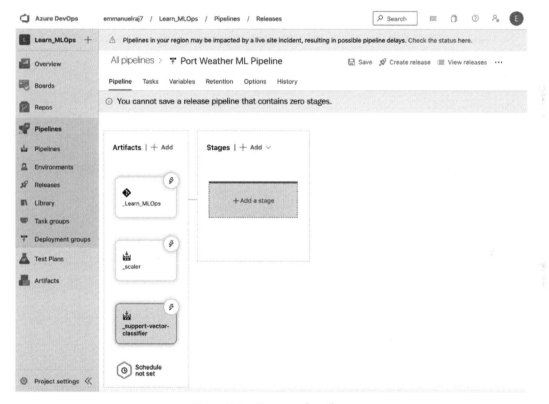

Figure 7.9 – Connected artifacts

After adding the **support_vector_classifier** model, you will be able to see the model's name (**support_vector_classifier**) and a model icon in the **Artifacts** section, as shown in *Figure 7.9*.

Congratulations! We have all three desired artifacts (`Learn_MLOps`, `scaler`, and **support_vector_classifier**) connected to the release pipeline. We can use these artifacts to orchestrate the deployments in the pipeline. Next, get ready to configure the Staging/TEST environment!

Setting up a test environment

Let's set up a continuous integration and continuous deployment pipeline for the TEST environment in the pipeline. In this stage, we test the robustness of the service and perform various tests to validate the service readiness for production:

1. To get started, click on the **Add a stage** box in the **Stages** section and add an empty job (as shown in *Figure 7.6*) with the name DEV TEST. We will name the stage DEV TEST as this will be our development and testing environment. Ideally, both DEV and TEST are different stages, but for simplicity and avoiding repetitive implementation, we will merge them both. See the following *Figure 7.10*:

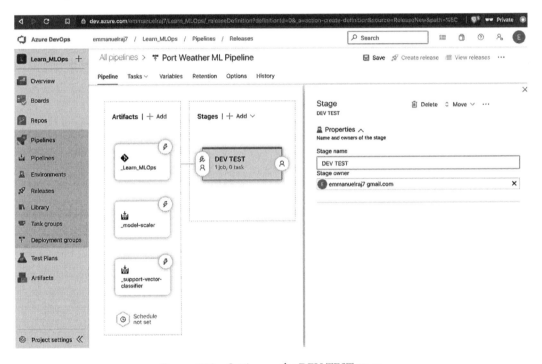

Figure 7.10 – Setting up the DEV TEST stage

2. After naming the stage, save the stage by clicking the **Save** button at the top. Every stage is a composition of a series of steps or jobs to check the robustness of the stage. Next, we will configure the jobs within the **DEV TEST** stage. A CI/CD job, in simple terms, is a process or script to execute or test deployments (for example, a job to deploy a model on the Kubernetes cluster). To configure jobs, click on the **1 job, 0 task** link in the **DEV TEST** stage, as shown in *Figure 7.11*:

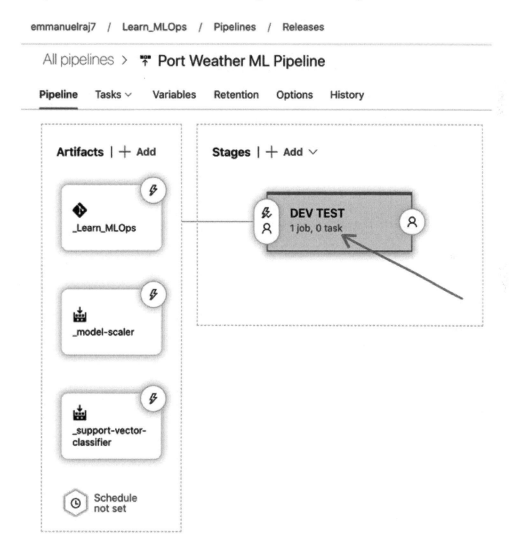

Figure 7.11 – Configuring DEV TEST jobs

Upon clicking the **1 job, 0 task** link in the **DEV TEST** stage, you will have to add agent jobs.

3. Add a task to the agent job by clicking + in the **Agent job** tab. We will use a pre-made template job named **AzureML Model Deploy**. Search and add AzureML model deploy, as shown in *Figure 7.12*:

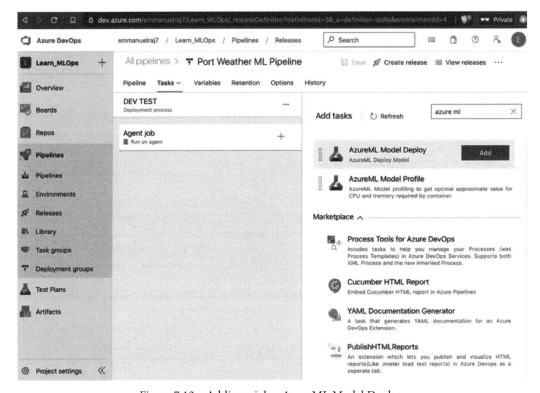

Figure 7.12 – Adding a job – AzureML Model Deploy

Upon adding the **AzureML Model Deploy** job, you will be prompted to connect to your Azure ML workspace and the inferenceconfig file.

4. Next, you will be prompted to enter the deployment information. As shown in *Figure 7.13*, point to your Azure ML workspace (for example, **mlops_ws**) and set the **Model Source** option to **Model Artifact** (as we are using the model artifacts generated previously when training and packaging models):

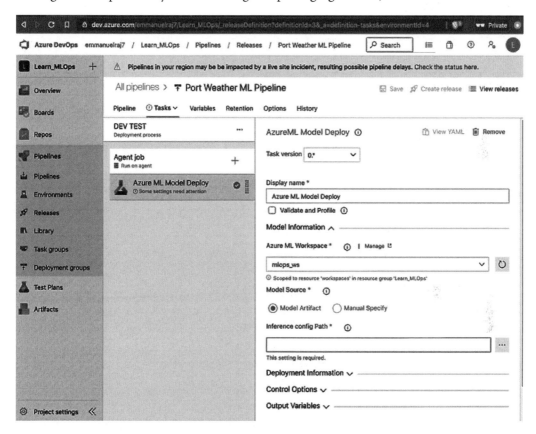

Figure 7.13 – Adding a job – Azure ML Model Deploy

Next, we will look at the `inferenceConfig` file and its functionality. The following snippet is taken from `inferenceConfig.yml` (in the repository). Here is a snapshot of `inferenceConfig.yml`:

`inferenceConfig.yml`

```
entryScript: score.py
runtime: python
condaFile: myenv.yml
```

It is a representation of the settings for a custom environment in which we will deploy our models. It points to the `score.py` file (previously created in *Chapter 6, Key Principles for Deploying Your ML System*) and the `conda` file `myenv.yml`, which defines the `conda` environment (packages and dependencies to install). Here is a snapshot of `myenv.yml`:

`myenv.yml`

```
name: project_environment
dependencies:
    # The python interpreter version.
    # Currently Azure ML only supports 3.5.2 and later.
- python=3.6.2

- pip:
    - numpy
    - onnxruntime
    - joblib
    - azureml-core~=1.10.0
    - azureml-defaults~=1.10.0
    - scikit-learn==0.20.3
    - inference-schema
    - inference-schema[numpy-support]
    - azureml-monitoring

channels:
- anaconda
- conda-forge
```

Both the `score.py` and `myenv.yml` files are tied up in the `inferenceConfig.yml` file to facilitate the deployment and inference of ML models. Proceed by selecting your inference configuration file (`inferenceConfig.yml`), as shown in *Figure 7.14*:

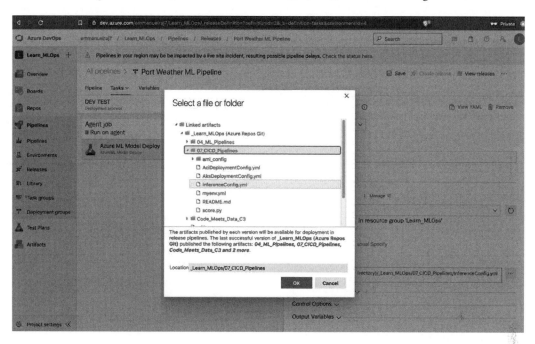

Figure 7.14 – Selecting your inference configuration file

After pointing to the `inferenceConfig.yml` file in your Azure DevOps repository, your basic configuration is done for the deployment. Lastly, we will configure the deployment information by pointing to the **Model Deployment** target, naming the deployment (web service), and pointing to the deployment configuration file (the deployment configuration file has configurations for deployment, with parameters such as computer type, autoscaler configurations, and other enablers for infrastructure definition). For the test environment, we will deploy the ML web service or endpoint in ACI. Here is a snapshot of the deployment config file (`AciDeploymentConfig.yml`) for ACI:

`AciDeploymentConfig.yml`

```
computeType: ACI
containerResourceRequirements:
    cpu: 1
    memoryInGB: 1
authEnabled: False
sslEnabled: False
appInsightsEnabled: True
```

It contains the infrastructural definition for provisioning the requisite compute for deployment, such as CPU units, memory in GB, and other authentication or security definitions. Let's select this deployment configuration file to set up the release pipeline for the staging environment, as shown in *Figure 7.15*:

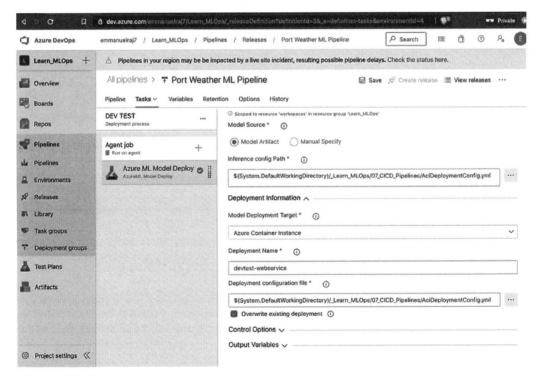

Figure 7.15 – Adding deployment information

After adding the deployment configuration file, save the job by clicking the **Save** button in the top right of the screen and then go to **Pipelines** >> **Releases** (on the left of your screen) to see your pipeline successfully set up. Let's continue from here to test the pipeline.

Pipeline execution and testing

Now, it is time to test your pipeline and for that we will create a release and validate whether the pipeline release has executed successfully. The following steps will help you to test your pipeline:

1. Click on the **Create release** button to execute jobs configured on your pipeline. A popup will appear on the right of your screen (as shown in *Figure 7.16*) to view and select artifacts to deploy in your staging environment.

2. Select the artifacts (`_scaler` and `_support-vector-classifier`) and select their versions. For simplicity, version 1 is recommended for both.

    If you want to choose another version of your model or scaler make sure to change the path of your model and scaler in the `score.py` file (that is, insert the appropriate version number in the `scaler` and `model` paths `model-scaler/{version number}/modelscaler.pkl` and `support-vector-classifier/{version number}/svc.onnx`. If you choose version 1, you don't have to worry about changing the code in `score.py` file as the paths contain version 1.

3. After selecting artifacts and needed versions (version 1 is recommended), click on the **Create** button to create the release for your selected artifacts:

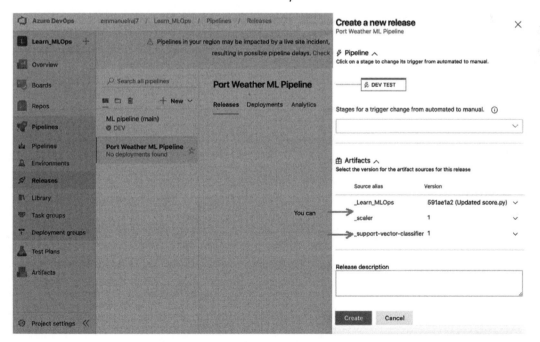

Figure 7.16 – Creating a release

4. Now the release pipeline (the CI/CD pipeline) is triggered to execute. All the steps defined in the pipeline will execute, such as downloading the artifacts, provisioning the ACI compute instance for deployment, and deploying the web service. Upon successful execution, you'll be notified with a green tick-mark on your release, as shown in *Figure 7.17*:

Figure 7.17 – Monitoring releases

5. You can monitor all your releases in the **Releases** section and manage the deployed web services from the Azure ML service. A successful release means all the steps in the jobs have been executed successfully and your artifacts (`scaler` and `_support-vector-classifier`) have been deployed as a web service on ACI, as shown in *Figure 7.18*:

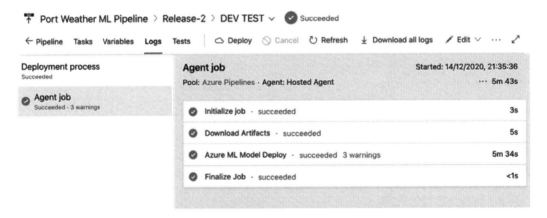

Figure 7.18 – Successful jobs in a release (test environment)

6. Finally, go and check your Azure ML workspace (from the **Endpoints** section) to view the deployed web service, as shown in *Figure 7.19*:

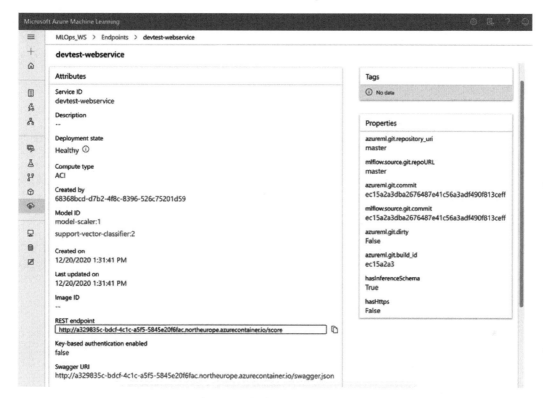

Figure 7.19 – Web service deployed on the Azure ML workspace

We have successfully deployed a web service in the test environment. We can see the REST endpoint and the service name **devtest-webservice**. This brings us to the successful conclusion of the building and testing of the CI/CD pipeline for the test environment. Pipelines can be driven using triggers, and in the next section, we will look at what the triggers are and how we can use them to build optimal CI/CD pipelines.

Pipeline execution triggers

In an effective CI/CD pipeline, process execution should be possible by means of multiple events or triggers. Having the option to trigger the pipeline by only regular events, such as code repository or push-or-pull requests, might be a handicap or limitation for the system. Having the option to trigger the pipeline process using multiple events enhances the flexibility and functionality of the CI/CD pipeline. Let's look at some types of triggers that can add value to the CI/CD pipeline process:

- **Artifactory triggers**

  Artifacts are generated at different stages in the pipeline and development process. Generated artifacts, such as a trained model, metadata, uploaded Docker images, or any file that has been uploaded, can be triggered to execute a certain process in the CI/CD pipeline. Having such options can enable great flexibility and functionality for the CI/CD pipeline.

- **Docker Hub triggers**

  Every time you push a new Docker image to a Docker Hub repository of your choice, a trigger in the CI/CD pipeline can be executed as per requirements. For example, when you upload a new Docker image to Docker Hub (or Azure Container Registry), the pipeline is triggered to deploy the Docker image as a web service.

- **Schedule triggers**

  The pipeline process can be triggered following a specific time schedule. This type of trigger is very useful for a scheduled clean-up or cron jobs or any other workflow that needs to be run following a time interval; for example, a trigger for ML model retraining at 12:00 every day.

- **API triggers**

  The purpose of API triggers is to integrate with external services (or any other application or service you have). This can be set up so your pipeline process is triggered based on an event on another system. For example, when the system admin comments `retrain` on a developer's platform, the pipeline can be triggered to retrain the existing deployed model. These triggers are facilitated using API calls.

- **Git triggers**

  Git triggers are commonly used to trigger pipeline executions, for instance when new code is committed to a branch or a new pull request is made. When changes are made to a repository, then certain processes can be triggered in the pipeline as per requirements.

Azure DevOps provides multiple trigger options (all of the above). Now, let's set up a Git trigger, based on the Git commit made to the repository:

1. Go to **Pipelines >> Releases** and click **Edit** (in the top right of your screen) to edit the existing pipeline.

2. Click on the repository artifact (named **_Learn_MLOps**), as shown in *Figure 7.20*, and enable (by clicking on the toggle switch) the continuous deployment trigger.

3. Add a branch filter by including the develop branch. This will trigger the pipeline to execute when changes or commits are made to the develop branch of the repository. For the test or staging stage, configure a Git trigger for the develop branch only (not the master or another branch). For production we can configure a Git trigger for the master branch. This way, we can separate the Git trigger branches for the test and production stages:

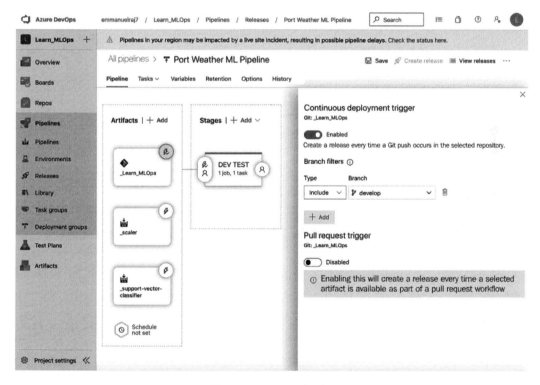

Figure 7.20 – Enabling a Git trigger for the test environment

4. Click on the **Save** button at the top to configure the Git trigger. Congratulations! You have successfully set up a continuous deployment Git trigger for your test environment. Whenever there are changes to the develop branch of the repository, the pipeline will be triggered to deploy a web service in the test (**DEV TEST**) environment.

Summary

In this chapter, we have learned the key principles of continuous operations in MLOps, primarily, continuous integration, delivery, and deployment. We have learned this by performing a hands-on implementation of setting up a CI/CD pipeline and test environment using Azure DevOps. We have tested the pipeline for execution robustness and finally looked into some triggers to enhance the functionality of the pipeline and also set up a Git trigger for the test environment. This chapter serves as the foundation for continual operations in MLOps and equips you with the skills to automate the deployment pipelines of ML models for any given scenario on the cloud, with continual learning abilities in tune with your business.

In the next chapter, we will look into APIs, microservices, and what they have to offer for MLOps-based solutions.

8
APIs and Microservice Management

In this chapter, you will learn about APIs and microservice management. So far, we have deployed ML applications that are served as APIs. Now we will look into how to develop, organize, manage, and serve APIs. You will learn the principles of API and microservice design for ML inference so that you can design your own custom ML solutions.

In this chapter, we will learn by doing as we build a microservice using FastAPI and Docker and serve it as an API. For this, we will go through the fundamentals of designing an API and microservice for an ML model trained previously (in *Chapter 4, Machine Learning Pipelines*). Lastly, we will reflect on some key principles, challenges, and tips to design a robust and scalable microservice and API for test and production environments. The following topics will be covered in this chapter:

- Introduction to APIs and microservices
- The need for microservices for ML
- Old is gold – REST API-based microservices
- Hands-on implementation of serving an ML model as an API

- Developing a microservice using Docker
- Testing the API service

Introduction to APIs and microservices

APIs and microservices are powerful tools that help to enable your **ML** (**ML**) models to become useful in production or legacy systems for serving the models or communicating with other components of the system. Using APIs and microservices, you can design a robust and scalable ML solution to cater to your business needs. Let's take a look at what APIs and microservices are and how they realize your model's potential in the real world.

What is an Application Programming Interface (API)?

An **API** is the gateway that enables developers to communicate with an application. APIs enable two things:

- Access to an application's data
- The use of an application's functionality

By accessing and communicating with application data and functionalities, APIs have enabled the world's electronics, applications, and web pages to communicate with each other in order to work together to accomplish business or operations-centric tasks.

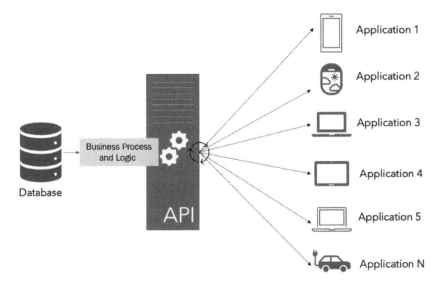

Figure 8.1 – Workings of an API

In *Figure 8.1*, we can see the role of an API as it enables access to application data (from the database) and communication with third parties or other applications such as mobile applications (for mobile users), weather applications (on mobile or the web), electric cars, and so on. APIs have been in operation since the dawn of computers, intending to enable inter-application communication. Over time, we have seen developers come to a consensus with protocols such as **Simple Object Access Protocol** (**SOAP**) and **Representational State Transfer** (**REST**) in the early 2000s. In recent years, a generation of new types of API protocols have been developed, such as **Remote Procedure Call** (**RPC**) and GraphQL as seen in the following table:

API Protocol	Release Year	Formatting Type	Key Strength
SOAP	1990's	XML	Widely used and established
REST	2000	XML, JSON, and others	Flexible data formatting
JSON-RPC	2005	JSON	Easy implementation
Thrift	2007	JSON or binary	Adaptability to many use cases
gRPC	2015	JSON and others	Ability to define any type of function
GraphQL	2015	JSON	Flexible data structuring

Table 8.1 – API protocols comparison

It is valuable to understand the mainstream API protocols if you are a developer of applications (hosted on the cloud or communicating with other services). It helps you design your APIs as per your business or functionality needs. As a programmer, count yourself fortunate to have many API protocols at your disposal, as 20 years ago, only SOAP and REST were available. Now a variety of choices are at your disposal depending on your needs, for example, GraphQL, Thrift, and JSON-RPC. These protocols have various advantages and drawbacks, making it easy to find the best suited to your situation.

Microservices

Microservices are a modern way of designing and deploying apps to run a service. Microservices enable distributed applications rather than one big monolithic application where functionalities are broken up into smaller fragments (called microservices). A microservice is an individual application in a microservice architecture. This is contrary to centralized or monolithic architectures, where all functionalities are tied up together in one big app. Microservices have grown in popularity due to **Service-Oriented Architecture** (**SOA**), an alternative to developing traditional monolithic (singular and self-sufficient applications).

Microservices gained massive adoption as they enable developers to develop, integrate, and maintain applications with ease. Eventually, this comes down to the fact that individual functionalities are treated independently, at first permitting you to develop an individual functionality of a service step by step. Lastly, it allows you to work on each functionality independently while integrating the whole system to orchestrate the service. This way, you can add, improve, or fix it without risking breaking the entire application. Microservices are valuable for bigger companies since they allow teams to work on isolated things without any complicated organization. In *Figure 8.2*, we can see the difference between monoliths and microservices. Microservices enable distributed applications compared to monoliths, which are non-distributed applications:

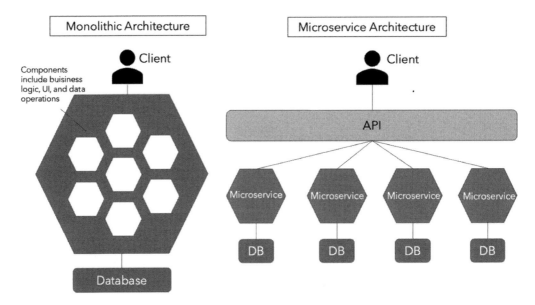

Figure 8.2 – Microservices versus monoliths

Software development teams are empowered to work independently and within well-understood service responsibilities. Microservices-based architecture encourages software development teams to take ownership of their services or modules. One possible downside to microservices-based architecture is if you break an application up into parts, there is a severe need for those parts to communicate effectively in order to keep the service running.

The relationship between APIs and microservices is fascinating as it has two sides. As a result of microservices-based architecture, an API is a direct outcome of implementing that architecture in your application. Whereas at the same time, an API is an essential tool for communicating between services in a microservices-based architecture to function efficiently. Let's have a look at the next section, where we will glance through some examples of ML applications.

The need for microservices for ML

To understand the need for microservices-based architecture for ML applications, let's look at a hypothetical use case and go through various phases of developing a ML application for the use case.

Hypothetical use case

A large car repair facility needs a solution to estimate the number of cars in the facility and their accurate positions. A bunch of IP cameras is installed in the repair stations for monitoring the facility. Design an ML system to monitor and manage the car repair facility.

Stage 1 – Proof of concept (a monolith)

A quick PoC is developed in a typical case using available data points and applying ML to showcase and validate the use case and prove to the business stakeholders that ML can solve their problems or improve their business.

In our hypothetical use case, a monolith Python app is developed that does the following:

- Fetches streams from all cameras
- Determines the positions of cars (head or tail) from each camera
- Aggregates all estimations into a facility state estimator

We can see in *Figure 8.3*, the app is dockerized and deployed to the server:

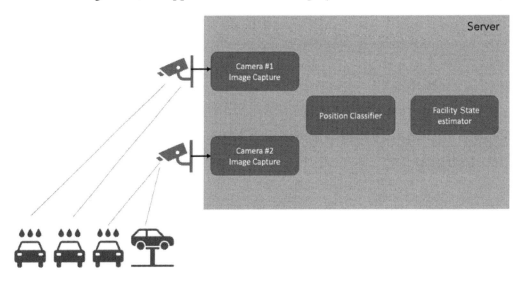

Figure 8.3 – Monolith ML application (PoC for hypothetical use case)

All cameras are connected to this server via the local network. The algorithms for car position estimation and the facility state estimator work but need further improvements, and overall the PoC works. This monolith app is highly prone to crashing due to the instability of the cameras, the local network, and other errors. Such instabilities can be handled better by microservices. Let's see this in practice in stage 2.

Stage 2 – Production (microservices)

In this stage, an application that is less prone to crashing is essential to run the car repair facility's monitoring operations continuously. For this reason, a monolith application is replaced with microservices-based architecture as shown in *Figure 8.4*:

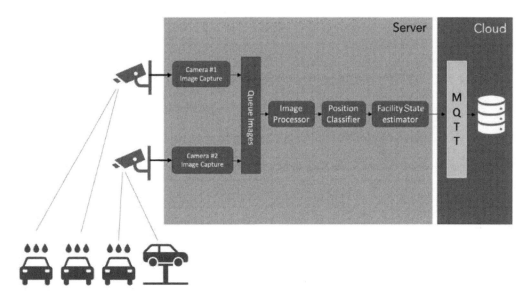

Figure 8.4 – Microservices (production-ready application for hypothetical use case)

The application is fragmented into multiple services in the following manner:

- Video stream collector.

- **Image processor**: This aggregates images – it receives, processes, and caches images, and generates packets for further processing.

- **Position classifier**: Estimates a car's position (head or tail) parked in the repair facility.

- **Facility setup estimator**: This asynchronously receives car position estimations and calibrates the facility setup and sends real-time data to the cloud.

- The cloud collects and stores data using MQTT (a standard lightweight, publish-subscribe network protocol that transports messages between devices). The data is portrayed on a dashboard for the car facility operators to analyze operations.

All of the communication between each microservice is facilitated using APIs. The advantages of microservice architecture are that if any of the services crash or errors take place, that particular microservice is spawned to replace the failed one to keep the whole service running. Secondly, each microservice can be maintained and improved continuously by a dedicated team (of data scientists, developers, and DevOps engineers), unlike coordinating teams, to work on a monolithic system.

Old is gold – REST API-based microservices

Old is gold. Plus, it's better to start somewhere where there are various API protocols. The **Representational State Transfer** (**REST**) protocol has become a gold standard for many applications over the years, and it's not so very different for ML applications today. The majority of companies prefer developing their ML applications based on the REST API protocol.

A REST API or RESTful API is based on REST, an architectural method used to communicate mainly in web services development.

RESTful APIs are widely used; companies such as Amazon, Google, LinkedIn, and Twitter use them. Serving our ML models via RESTful APIs has many benefits, such as the following:

- Serve predictions on the fly to multiple users.

- Add more instances to scale up the application behind a load balancer.

- Possibly combine multiple models using different API endpoints.

- Separate our model operating environment from the user-facing environment.

- Enable microservices-based architecture. Hence, teams can work independently to develop and enhance the services.

A RESTful API uses existing HTTP methodologies that are defined by the RFC 2616 protocol. *Table 8.2* summarizes the HTTP methods in combination with their CRUD operations and purpose in ML applications.

HTTP Method	CRUD	Purpose in ML applications
GET	READ	A GET request is used to read or retrieve a resource representation and returns a representation in XML or JSON. In ML applications, a GET request is used for model inference.
POST	CREATE	A POST request is often used to create new resources. For ML applications, it is used to infer predictive ML models.
PUT	Update/ Replace	To update or replace a resource, which can be an object, file, or block. In ML applications, it is often used to send a file for ML inference, for example, a JPEG image file to classify.
PATCH	Update/ Modify	To update or modify a resource, which can be a file, object, or block.
DELETE	Delete	To delete a resource. In ML applications, it can be used to delete a microservice or files (data or models).

Table 8.2 – REST API HTTP methods

The fundamental HTTP methods are GET, POST, PUT, PATCH, and DELETE. These methods correspond to **CRUD** operations such as create, read, update, and delete. Using these methods, we can develop RESTful APIs to serve ML models. RESTful APIs have gained significant adoption due to drivers such as OpenAPI. The OpenAPI Specification is a standardized REST API description format. It has become a standardized format for humans and machines; it enables REST API understandability and provides extended tooling such as API validation, testing, and an interactive documentation generator. In practice, the OpenAPI file enables you to describe an entire API with critical information such as the following:

- Available endpoints (/names) and operations on each endpoint (GET /names, POST /names)

- Input and output for each operation (operation parameters)

- Authentication methods

- Developer documentation

- Terms of use, license, and other information

You can find more about OpenAPI on this site: https://swagger.io/specification/.

In the next section, we will develop a RESTful API to serve an ML model and test it using an OpenAPI based interface called Swagger UI.

Hands-on implementation of serving an ML model as an API

In this section, we will apply the principles of APIs and microservices that we have learned previously (in the section *Introduction to APIs and microservices*) and develop a RESTful API service to serve the ML model. The ML model we'll serve will be for the business problem (weather prediction using ML) we worked on previously. We will use the FastAPI framework to serve the model as an API and Docker to containerize the API service into a microservice.

FastAPI is a framework for deploying ML models. It is easy and fast to code and enables high performance with features such as asynchronous calls and data integrity checks. FastAPI is easy to use and follows the OpenAPI Specification, making it easy to test and validate APIs. Find out more about FastAPI here: https://fastapi.tiangolo.com/.

API design and development

We will develop the API service and run it on a local computer. (This could also be developed on the VM we created earlier in the Azure Machine learning workspace. For learning, it is recommended to practice it locally for ease.)

To get started, clone the book repository on your PC or laptop and go to the `08_API_Microservices` folder. We will use these files to build the API service:

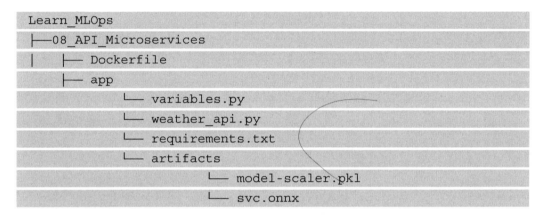

```
Learn_MLOps
├──08_API_Microservices
│    ├── Dockerfile
├── app
            └── variables.py
            └── weather_api.py
            └── requirements.txt
            └── artifacts
                        └── model-scaler.pkl
                └── svc.onnx
```

The files listed in the directory tree for the folder `08_API_Microservices` include a Dockerfile (used to build a Docker image and container from the `FASTAPI` service) and a folder named app. The app folder contains the files `weather_api.py` (contains the code for API endpoint definitions), `variables.py` (contains the input variables definition), and `requirements.txt` (contains Python packages needed for running the API service), and a folder with model artifacts such as a model scaler (used to scale incoming data) and a serialized model file (`svc.onnx`).

The model was serialized previously, in the model training and evaluation stage, as seen in *Chapter 5, Model Evaluation and Packaging*. The model is downloaded and placed in the folder from the model registry in the Azure Machine learning workspace (`Learn_MLOps`) as shown in *Figure 8.3*:

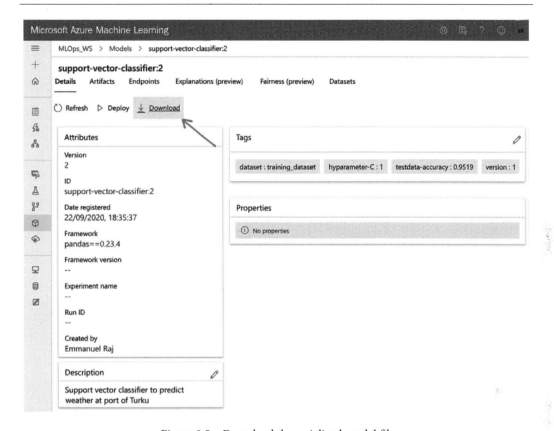

Figure 8.5 – Download the serialized model file

You can replace the `svc.onnx` and `model-scalar.pkl` files with the files you have trained in your Azure Machine learning workspace or else just continue using these files for quick experimentation. Now we will look into the code of each file. Let's start with `variables.py`.

variables.py

We use only one package for defining input variables. The package we use is called `pydantic`; it is a data validation and settings management package using Python-type annotations. Using `pydantic`, we will define input variables in the class named `WeatherVariables` used for the `fastAPI` service:

```
from pydantic import BaseModel


class WeatherVariables(BaseModel):
                temp_c: float
```

```
humidity: float
wind_speed_kmph: float
wind_bearing_degree: float
visibility_km: float
pressure_millibars: float
current_weather_condition: float
```

In the WeatherVariables class, define variables and their types as shown in the preceding code. The same variables that were used for training the model in *Chapter 4, Machine Learning Pipelines*, will be used for inference. We define those input variables here as temp_c, humidity, wind_speed_kmph, wind_bearing_degree, visibility_km, pressure_millibars, and current_weather_condition. Data types for these variables are defined as float. We will import the WeatherVariables class and use the defined input variables in the fastAPI service. Let's look at how we can use the variables defined in the WeatherVariables class in the fastAPI service using the Weather_api.py file.

Weather_api.py

This file is used to define the fastAPI service. The needed model artifacts are imported and used to serve API endpoints to infer the model for making predictions in real time or in production:

1. We start by importing the required packages as follows:

```
import uvicorn
from fastapi import FastAPI
from variables import WeatherVariables
import numpy
import pickle
import pandas as pd
import onnxruntime as rt
```

We imported the required packages, such as uvicorn (an ASGI server implementation package), fastapi, numpy, pickle, pandas, and onnxruntime (used to deserialize and infer onnx models).

> **Note**
>
> We imported the `WeatherVariables` class previously created in the `variables.py` file. We will use the variables defined in this file for procuring input data for the `fastAPI` service.

2. Next, we create an `app` object. You will notice some syntactic similarities of `fastAPI` with the Flask web framework (if you have ever used Flask).

    For instance, in the next step, we create the `app` object using the function `FastAPI()` to create the `app` object. Creating an `app` object is similar to how we do it via the `Flask` example: from Flask, import `Flask` and then we use the `Flask` function to create the `app` object in the manner `app = Flask ()`. You will notice such similarities as we build API endpoints using `fastAPI`:

```
app = FastAPI()


# Load model scalar
pickle_in = open("artifacts/model-scaler.pkl", "rb")
scaler = pickle.load(pickle_in)


# Load the model
sess = rt.InferenceSession("artifacts/svc.onnx")
input_name = sess.get_inputs()[0].name
label_name = sess.get_outputs()[0].name
```

3. After creating the `app` object, we will import the necessary model artifacts for inference in the endpoints. `Pickle` is used to deserialize the data scaler file `model-scaler.pkl`. This file was used to train the model (in *Chapter 4, Machine Learning Pipelines*), and now we'll use it to scale the incoming data before model inference. We will use the previously trained support vector classifier model, which was serialized into the file named `scv.onnx` (we can access and download the file as shown in *Figure 8.3*).

4. ONNX Runtime is used to load the serialized model into inference sessions (`input_name` and `label_name`) for making ML model predictions. Next, we can move to the core part of defining the API endpoints to infer the ML model. To begin, we make a GET request to the index route using the wrapper function `@app.get('/')`:

```
@app.get('/')
def index():
    return {'Hello': 'Welcome to weather prediction
service, access the api    docs and test the API at
http://0.0.0.0/docs.'}
```

A function named `index()` is defined for the index route. It returns the welcome message, pointing to the docs link. This message is geared toward guiding the users to the docs link to access and test the API endpoints.

5. Next, we will define the core API endpoint, `/predict`, which is used to infer the ML model. A wrapper function, `@app.post('/predict')`, is used to make a POST request:

```
@app.post('/predict')
def predict_weather(data: WeatherVariables):
    data = data.dict()

    # fetch input data using data varaibles
    temp_c = data['temp_c']
    humidity = data['humidity']
    wind_speed_kmph = data['wind_speed_kmph']
    wind_bearing_degree = data['wind_bearing_degree']
    visibility_km = data['visibility_km']
    pressure_millibars = data['pressure_millibars']
    current_weather_condition = data['current_weather_
condition']
```

A function named `predict_weather()` is initiated for the endpoint `/predict`. Inside the function, we have created a variable called `data` that will capture the input data; this variable captures the JSON data we are getting through the POST request and points to `WeatherVariables`. As soon as we do the POST request, all the variables in the incoming data will be mapped to variables in the `WeatherVariables` class from the `variables.py` file.

6. Next, we convert the data into a dictionary, fetch each input variable from the dictionary, and compress them into a `numpy` array variable, `data_to_pred`. We will use this variable to scale the data and infer the ML model:

```
    data_to_pred = numpy.array([[temp_c, humidity, wind_speed_kmph,
    wind_bearing_degree,visibility_km, pressure_millibars,
    current_weather_condition]])

    # Scale input data
    data_to_pred = scaler.fit_transform(data_to_pred.reshape(1, 7))

    # Model inference
    prediction = sess.run(
        [label_name], {input_name: data_to_pred.astype(numpy.float32)})[0]
```

The data (`data_to_pred`) is reshaped and scaled using the scaler loaded previously using the `fit_transform()` function.

7. Next, the model inference step, which is the key step, is performed by inferencing scaled data to the model, as shown in the preceding code. The prediction inferred from the model is then returned as the output to the `prediction` variable:

```
    if(prediction[0] > 0.5):
        prediction = "Rain"
    else:
        prediction = "No_Rain"
    return {
        'prediction': prediction
    }
```

Lastly, we will convert the model inference into a human-readable format by suggesting `rain` or `no_rain` based on the ML model's predictions and return the `prediction` for the `POST` call to the `/predict` endpoint. This brings us to the end of the `weather_api.py` file. When a `POST` request is made by passing input data, the service returns the model prediction in the form of `0` or `1`. The service will return `rain` or `not_rain` based on the model prediction. When you get such a prediction, your service is working and is robust enough to serve production needs.

Requirement.txt

This text file contains all the packages needed to run the `fastAPI` service:

```
numpy
fastapi
uvicorn
scikit-learn==0.20.3
pandas
onnx
onnxruntime
```

These packages should be installed in the environment where you would like to run the API service. We will use `numpy`, `fastapi` (an ML framework for creating robust APIs), `uvicorn` (an AGSI server), `scikit-learn`, `pandas`, `onnx`, and `onnxruntime` (to deserialize and infer `onnx` models) to run the FastAPI service. To deploy and run the API service in a standardized way, we will use Docker to run the FastAPI service in a Docker container.

Next, let's look at how to create a Dockerfile for the service.

Developing a microservice using Docker

In this section, we will package the FastAPI service in a standardized way using Docker. This way, we can deploy the Docker image or container on the deployment target of your choice within around 5 minutes.

Docker has several advantages, such as replicability, security, development simplicity, and so on. We can use the official Docker image of `fastAPI` (`tiangolo/uvicorn-gunicorn-fastapi`) from Docker Hub. Here is a snippet of the Dockerfile:

```
FROM tiangolo/uvicorn-gunicorn-fastapi:python3.7
COPY ./app /app
```

```
RUN pip install -r requirements.txt
EXPOSE 80
CMD ["uvicorn", "weather_api:app", "--host", "0.0.0.0",
"--port", "80"]
```

Firstly, we use an official `fastAPI` Docker image from Docker Hub by using the `FROM` command and pointing to the image – `tiangolo/uvicorn-gunicorn-fastapi:python3.7`. The image uses Python 3.7, which is compatible with `fastAPI`. Next, we copy the `app` folder into a directory named `app` inside `docker image/container`. After the folder `app` is copied inside the Docker image/container, we will install the necessary packages listed in the file `requirements.txt` by using the `RUN` command.

As the `uvicorn` server (AGSI server) for `fastAPI` uses port `80` by default, we will `EXPOSE` port `80` for the Docker image/container. Lastly, we will spin up the server inside the Docker image/container using the command `CMD "uvicorn weather_api:app –host 0.0.0.0 –port 80"`. This command points to the `weather_api.py` file to access the `fastAPI` app object for the service and host it on port `80` of the image/container.

Congrats, you are almost there. Now we will test the microservice for readiness and see whether and how it works.

Testing the API

To test the API for readiness, we will perform the following steps:

1. Let's start by building the Docker image. For this, a prerequisite is to have Docker installed. Go to your terminal or Command Prompt and clone the repository to your desired location and access the folder `08_API_Microservices`. Execute the following Docker command to build the Docker image:

```
docker build -t fastapi .
```

Execution of the `build` command will start building the Docker image following the steps listed in the Dockerfile. The image is tagged with the name `fastapi`. After successful execution of the `build` command, you can validate whether the image is built and tagged successfully or not using the `docker images` command. It will output the information as follows, after successfully building the image:

```
(base) user ~ docker images
REPOSITORY     TAG       IMAGE ID       CREATED
SIZE
fastapi        latest    1745e964f57f   56 seconds ago
1.31GB
```

2. Run a Docker container locally. Now, we can spawn a running Docker container from the Docker image created previously. To run a Docker container, we use the RUN command:

```
docker run -d –name weathercontainer -p 80:80 fastapi
```

A Docker container is spawned from the `fastapi` Docker image. The name of the running container is `weathercontainer` and its port 80 is mapped to port 80 of the local computer. The container will run in the background as we have used `-d` in the RUN command. Upon successfully running a container, a container ID is output on the terminal, for example, `2729ff7a385b0a255c63cf03ec9b0e1411ce4426c9c49e8db 4883e0cf0fde567`.

3. Test the API service using sample data. We will check whether the container is running successfully or not. To check this, use the following command:

```
docker container ps
```

This will list all the running containers as follows:

```
(base) user ~ docker container ps
CONTAINER ID     IMAGE     COMMAND                        CREATED
STATUS           PORTS                     NAMES
2729ff7a385b     fastapi     "uvicorn weather_api…"
18 seconds ago   Up 17 seconds    0.0.0.0:80->80/tcp
weathercontainer
```

We can see that the container from the image `fastapi` is mapped and successfully running on port `80` of the local machine. We can access the service and test it from the browser on our local machine at the address `0.0.0.0:80`.

> **Note**
>
> If you have no response or errors when you run or test your API service, you may have to disable CORS validation from browsers such as Chrome, Firefox, and Brave or add an extension (for example, go to the Chrome Web Store and search for one) that will disable CORS validation for running and testing APIs locally. By default, you don't need to disable CORS; do it only if required.

You will see the message that follows:

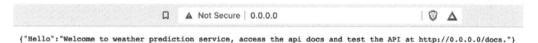

Figure 8.6 – FastAPI service running on local port 80

FastAPI uses the OpenAPI (read more: `https://www.openapis.org/`, `https://swagger.io/specification/`) Specification to serve the model. The **OpenAPI Specification (OAS)** is a standard, language-agnostic interface for RESTful APIs. Using OpenAPI features, we can access API documentation and get a broad overview of the API. You can access the API docs and test the API at `0.0.0.0:80/docs` and it will direct you to a Swagger-based UI (it uses the OAS) to test your API.

4. Now, test the `/predict` endpoint (by selecting the endpoint and clicking the **Try it out** button) using input data of your choice, as shown in *Figure 8.6*:

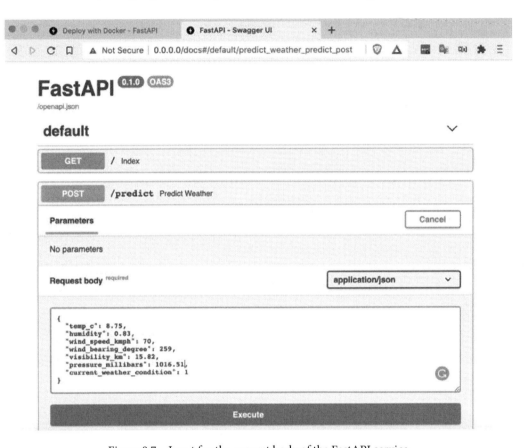

Figure 8.7 – Input for the request body of the FastAPI service

5. Click **Execute** to make a `POST` call and test the endpoint. The input is inferred with the model in the service and the model prediction `Rain` or `No_Rain` is the output of the `POST` call, as shown in *Figure 8.7*:

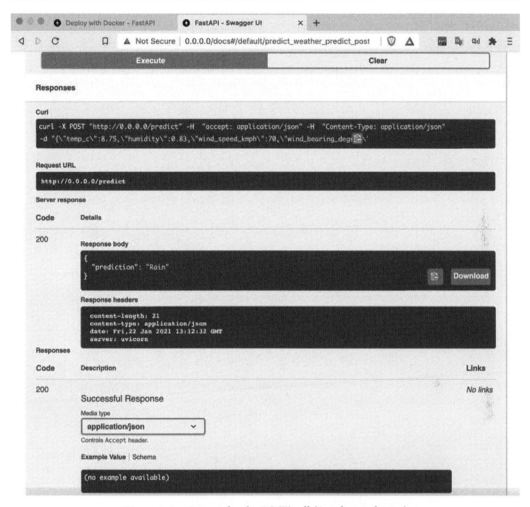

Figure 8.8 – Output for the POST call (/predict endpoint)

The successful execution of the POST call for the /predict API will result in the output model prediction as shown in *Figure 8.6*. The model running in the Docker container outputs the weather condition as Rain for the POST call. Congratulations, you have successfully spawned a fastAPI container and tested it. This exercise should have equipped you with the skills to build, deploy, and test ML-based API services for your use cases.

Summary

In this chapter, we have learned the key principles of API design and microservice deployment in production. We touched upon the basics of API design methods and learned about FastAPI. For our business problem, we have learned by doing a practical implementation of developing an API service in the *Hands-on implementation of serving an ML model as an API* section using FastAPI and Docker. Using the practical knowledge gained in this chapter, you can design and develop robust API services to serve your ML models. Developing API services for ML models is a stepping stone to take ML models to production.

In the next chapter, we will delve into the concepts of testing and security. We will implement a testing method to test the robustness of an API service using Locust. Let's go!

9
Testing and Securing Your ML Solution

In this chapter, we will delve into **Machine Learning** (**ML**) solution testing and security aspects. You can expect to get a primer on various types of tests to test the robustness and scalability of your ML solution, as well as the knowledge required to secure your ML solution. We will look into multiple attacks on ML solutions and ways to defend your ML solution.

In this chapter, we will be learning with examples as we perform load testing and security testing for the business use case of weather prediction we have been previously working on. We will start by reflecting on the need for testing and securing your ML solution and go on to explore the other following topics in the chapter:

- Understanding the need for testing and securing your ML application
- Testing your ML solution by design
- Securing your ML solution by design

Understanding the need for testing and securing your ML application

The growing adoption of data-driven and ML-based solutions is causing businesses to have to handle growing workloads, exposing them to extra levels of complexities and vulnerabilities.

Cybersecurity is the most alarming risk for AI developers and adopters. According to a survey released by Deloitte (`https://www2.deloitte.com/us/en/insights/ focus/cognitive-technologies/state-of-ai-and-intelligent- automation-in-business-survey.html`), in July 2020, 62% of adopters saw cybersecurity risks as a significant or extreme threat, but only 39% said they felt prepared to address those risks.

In this section, we will look into the need for securing ML-based systems and solutions. We will reflect on some of the broader challenges of ML systems such as bias, ethics, and explainability. We will also study some of the challenges present at each stage of the ML life cycle relating to confidentiality, integrity, and availability using the guidelines for ML testing and security by design.

Testing your ML solution by design

On top of performing regular software development tests, such as unit tests, integration tests, system testing, and acceptance testing, ML solutions need additional tests because data and ML models are involved. Both the data and models change dynamically over time. Here are some concepts for testing by design; applying them to your use cases can ensure robust ML solutions are produced as a result.

Data testing

The goal of testing data is to ensure that the data is of a high enough quality for ML model training. The better the quality of the data, the better the models trained for the given tasks. So how do we assess the quality of data? It can be done by inspecting the following five factors of the data:

- Accuracy
- Completeness (no missing values)
- Consistency (in terms of expected data format and volume)
- Relevance (data should meet the intended need and requirements)
- Timeliness (the latest or up-to-date data)

Based on these factors, if a company can manage each dataset's data quality when received or created, the data quality is guaranteed. Here are some steps that your team or company can use as quality assurance measures for your data:

1. **Meticulous data cataloging and control of incoming data**: A combination of data cataloging (to document and store data in the required format or pattern) and control functions can ensure a high quality of incoming data. Data cataloging and control can be done by monitoring data factors such as data formats and patterns, value distributions and anomalies, completeness, and consistency can help to provide good incoming data quality.

2. **Curating data pipelines carefully to avoid duplicate data**: When duplicated data is manufactured from the same data source and using the same logic by different people, it can get complicated to manage lineages, authenticity, and data integrity. This can produce cascading effects throughout multiple systems or databases. It is better to avoid duplicating data as much as possible.

3. **Data governance with enforced integrity**: In today's world, maintaining data integrity has become crucial. Not having the mindset of enforcing data integrity can be costly for an organization. The data could eventually become incomplete, delayed, or out of date, leading to serious data quality issues.

4. **Maintaining end-to-end traceability and lineage**: Data lineage and traceability can be achieved by the smart use of metadata and the data itself. Using both, we can document critical information such as unique keys for each dataset, adding a timestamp to each record, and logging data changes. Making sure data lineage and end-to-end traceability is enabled can give us the possibility to reproduce models and debug errors and pipelines.

Model testing

Model tests need to cover server issues such as the following:

- Evaluating the accuracy or key metric of the ML model
- Testing on random data points
- Testing for acceptable loss or performance on your task
- Unit tests for model robustness using real data

These tests can be orchestrated in two phases: pre-training and post-training. Having these tests facilitated in the workflow can produce robust models for production. Let's look at what pre-train and post-train tests can be done by design.

Pre-training tests

Tests can be performed to catch flaws before we proceed to the training stage. These flaws could be in the data, pipelines, or parameters. *Figure 9.1* suggests running pre-training and post-training tests as part of a proposed workflow for developing high-quality models:

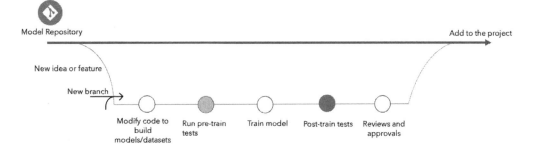

Figure 9.1 – Proposed workflow for developing high-quality models

Here are some ways to detect and avoid pre-training flaws using pre-training tests:

- Eliminating data pipeline debt by handling any data leakage, edge cases, and optimizing to make the pipeline time- and resource-efficient

- Making sure the shape of your model output matches the labels in your dataset

- Examining the output ranges to make sure they match our expectations (such as checking that the output of a classification model is a distribution with class probabilities that sum to 1)

- Examining your training and validation datasets for label leakage

- Making sure the ETL pipeline outputs or fetches data in the required format

Pre-training tests do not need parameters to run, but they can be quite useful in catching bugs before running the model training.

Post-training tests

Post-training tests enable us to investigate model performance and the logic behind model predictions and foresee any possible flaws in the model before deploying the model to production. Post-training tests enable us to detect flaws in model performance and functionality. Post-training tests involve a model performance evaluation test, invariance test, and minimum functionality test. Here is a recommended read for more insights on post-training tests: *Beyond Accuracy: Behavioral Testing of NLP Models with CheckList* (https://homes.cs.washington.edu/~marcotcr/acl20_checklist.pdf)

Deployment and inference testing

Deployment testing involves testing **Continuous Integration/Continuous Delivery (CI/CD)** pipeline delivery, integration tests, and testing that deployment is successful. It is critical to test the deployed model and that is where inference testing comes in to stress- or load-test the deployed model and test its performance on real-time data.

In the next section, we will load test a previously deployed model (for a use case).

Hands-on deployment and inference testing (a business use case)

When you have your service (either API or ML) ready and you are about to serve it to the users but you don't have any clue about how many users it can actually handle and how it will react when many users access it simultaneously, that's where load testing is useful to benchmark how many users your service can serve and to validate whether the service can cater to the business requirements.

We will perform load testing for the service we deployed previously (in *Chapter 7, Building Robust CI and CD Pipelines*). Locust.io will be used for load testing. locust.io is an open source load-testing tool. For this, we will install locust (using pip) and curate a Python script using the locust.io SDK to test an endpoint. Let's get started by installing locust:

1. Install locust: Go to your terminal and execute the following command:

    ```
    pip install locust
    ```

    Using pip, locust will be installed – it takes around a minute to install. After installation is successful it's time to curate the Python script using the locust.io SDK to test an endpoint.

2. Curate the load_test.py script: Go to your favorite IDE and start curating the script or follow the steps in the premade script. To access the premade script go to the *Engineering MLOps* repository cloned previously, access the 09_Testing_Security folder, and go to the load_test.py file. Let's demystify the code in load_test.py – firstly, the needed libraries are imported as follows:

    ```
    import time
    import json
    from locust import HttpUser, task, between
    ```

We imported the `time`, `json`, and `locust` libraries, and then from `locust` we import the following required functions: `HttpUser` (a user agent that can visit different endpoints), `task`, and `between`.

3. Create a `test_data` variable with sample test data to infer the ML model during the load test. Define `headers` we will use for the API calls in our load test:

```
test_data = json.dumps({"data": [[8.75, 0.83, 70, 259,
15.82, 1016.51, 1.0]]})
headers = {'Content-Type': 'application/json'}
```

4. Next, we will implement the core functionality of the load test as part of the `MLServiceUser` class (you can name it whatever you want) by extending `HttpUser`. `HttpUser` is the user agent that can visit different endpoints:

```
class MLServiceUser(HttpUser):
    wait_time = between(1, 5)


    @task
    def test_weather_predictions(self):
        self.client.post("", data=test_data,
headers=headers)
```

We created a `wait_time` variable using the `between()` function, which specifies the time it takes between finishing testing one endpoint and switching to test the next endpoint. So, we specify `wait_time` as 1 to 5 seconds in the `between(1,5)` function. The next part is the crux of defining a task that tests an endpoint.

For this, we use a `@task` wrapper or decorator to start defining our task to test an endpoint of our choice using a custom function. Define a custom function, `def test_weather_predictions()`, and make a `post` request to the endpoint using `test_data` and the headers defined previously. Now, we are set to run the load testing!

5. Run the `locust.io` server: Go to your terminal and change to the location where you have the `load_test.py` file (such as in the `09_Testing_Security` folder of the cloned repository used in this book), then run the following command to spin up a `locust.io` server:

```
Locust -f load_test-py
```

The execution of the previous command will spin up the `locust` server at port `8089`. We can perform load tests on the web interface rendered by `locust.io`. To access the web service, open a browser of your choice and go to the following web address: `http://0.0.0.0:8089/`, as shown in *Figure 9.2*:

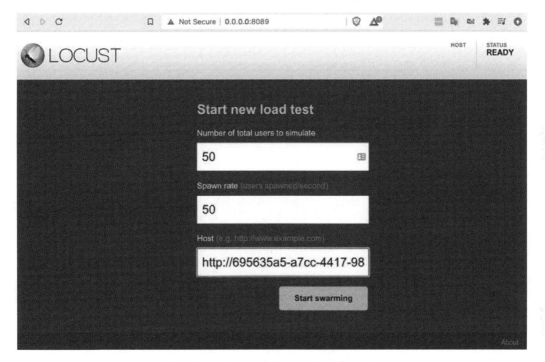

Figure 9.2 – Access the Locust.io web service

6. Run the load test: Opening the web service will prompt you to specify options such as the number of users, spawn rate, and host (the endpoint to test). Specify the number of users to simulate, and the spawn rate (how many users will be spawned per second) as per your requirements, to validate whether your endpoint is capable of serving your business/user needs, for example, 50 users and a spawn rate of 50.

7. Lastly, enter the endpoint or host you would like to load test and hit **Start swarming** to start performing the load test. In *Chapter 7*, *Building Robust CI and CD Pipelines*, we deployed an endpoint. It is recommended to test the deployed endpoint.

8. Go to your Azure ML workspace, access the **Endpoints** section, access the deployed endpoint named **dev-webservice**, and copy and paste the endpoint web address into the host textbox.

9. Next, click **Start swarming** to start load testing the endpoint. This will start the load test and open a new page where you can monitor your load tests in real time as shown in *Figure 9.3*:

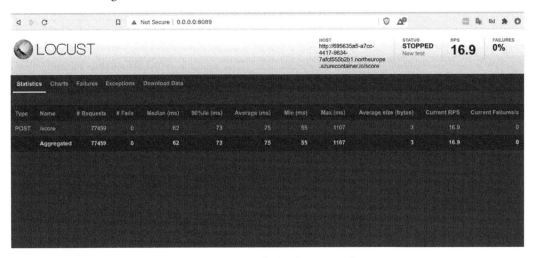

Figure 9.3 – Monitor the load test in real time

10. Analyzing load testing results: You can monitor statistics, charts, failures, and exceptions in real time. For instance, in *Figure 9.3* we are monitoring the load test for the **/score** endpoint, which is inferred using a POST request with test data. The number of requests made (**77459**), the number of fails (**0**), the average response time (**75ms**), and other information can be monitored. It is important to check that there are no failures and that the average response time is within the range to serve your business/user needs with efficiency or no major speed breaker.

If you have no failed requests and the average response time is within the range required, then your endpoint has passed the load test and is ready to be served to users. After or during the load testing, you can view charts of the load-testing performance with critical information such as total requests per second, response times, and the number of users with the progression of time. We can view this information in real time as shown in *Figure 9.4* and *Figure 9.5*:

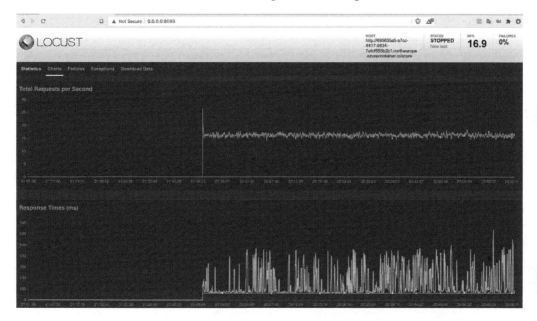

Figure 9.4 – Charts showing the total requests per second and response times

In *Figure 9.4* we can notice that the number of requests per second is in the range of 18-22 as the simulated users of locust.io make requests, and the response time in milliseconds varies from 70 to 500 in some cases, with a 430ms variance between the minimum and maximum. The average request time is 75ms (as seen in *Figure 9.3*).

Please note that this kind of performance may or may not be ideal for a given use case, depending on your business or user needs. A more stable response time is desirable; for instance, a response time variance of no more than 50ms between the minimum and maximum response times may be preferable for a stable performance. To achieve such performance it is recommended to deploy your models on higher-end infrastructure as appropriate, for example, a GPU or a high-end CPU, unlike the deployment on a CPU in an Azure container instance. Similarly, in *Figure 9.5* we can see the response times versus the number of users:

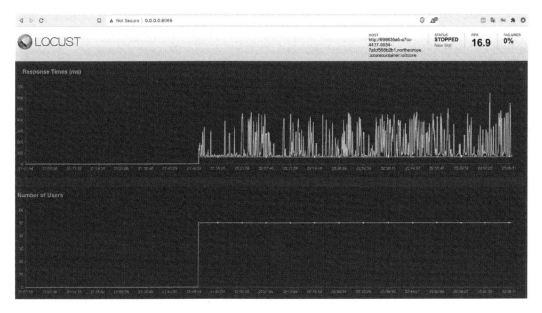

Figure 9.5 – Charts showing the total requests per second and the number of users

We can see that the number of users spawned per second is 50, as mentioned (in *Figure 9.2*). As time progresses, the spawn rate is constant and response times vary between 70-500ms, with 75ms as the average response time.

1. Document or download results: After the load test has been executed successfully you can document or present the results of the load test to the relevant stakeholders (QA/product manager) using a test report. To download or access the test report, go to the **Download Data** section and download the required information, such as request statistics, failures, or exceptions, in the form of .csv files, as shown in *Figure 9.6*:

Figure 9.6 – Download the test results

Download the statistics or failure reports required for further inspection as per your needs, and note that you can access the full test report by clicking **Download the Report**, as shown in *Figure 9.7*:

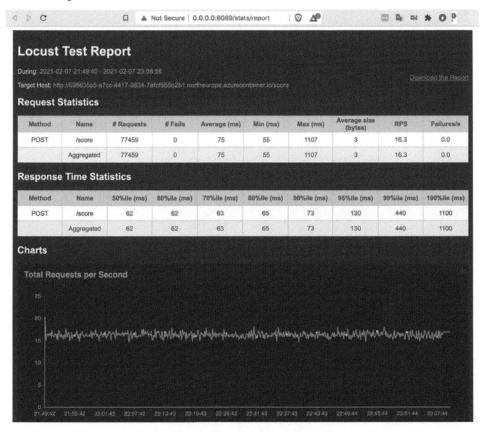

Figure 9.7 – Download the test results

A comprehensive test report is presented with critical information, such as the endpoint inferred average request time and the minimum and maximum request times, and this information is also presented in the form of visualized charts as seen in *Figure 9.7*. You can also download this full report to present to your respective stakeholders.

Congratulations, you have performed a hands-on load test to validate your endpoint and check whether your ML service is able to serve your business or user needs with efficiency.

Securing your ML solution by design

Securing your ML applications is more important than ever due to the growing adoption of AI to provide smart applications. Designing and developing ML systems without keeping security in mind can be costly in terms of exposing the system to hackers, leading to manipulation, data breaches, and non-compliance. Robustness and security play an important role in ensuring an AI system is trustworthy. To build trustworthy ML applications, keeping security in mind is vital to not leave any stones unturned.

Figure 9.8 shows a framework for creating secure ML applications by design. The framework addresses key areas in the ML life cycle, ensuring confidentiality, integrity, and availability within those specific stages. Let's reflect upon each area of the ML life cycle and address the issues of confidentiality, integrity, and availability in each area:

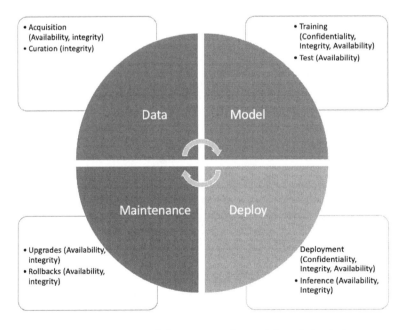

Figure 9.8 – Framework for securing the ML life cycle by design

Let's reflect upon each area of the ML life cycle and address confidentiality, integrity, and availability in each area while looking at the different types of attacks.

Types of attacks

We will explore some of the most common attacks on ML systems. At a high level, attacks by hackers can be broken down into four categories: poisoning, input attacks and evasion, reverse engineering, and backdoor attacks. Let's see how attackers manage to infiltrate ML systems via these attacks.

Poisoning

A hacker or attacker seeks to compromise an AI model in a poisoning attack. Poisoning attacks can happen at any stage (training, deployment, or real-time inference). They occur typically in training and inference. Let's see how poisoning attacks are implemented in three typical ways:

- **Dataset poisoning**: Training datasets contain the knowledge on which the model is trained. An attacker can manipulate this knowledge by infiltrating the training dataset. Here, the attacker introduces wrongly labeled or incorrect data into the training dataset, and with this the entire learning process is distorted. This is a direct way to poison a model. Training datasets can be poisoned during the data collection and curation phases, and it can be hard to notice or detect it as the training datasets can come from multiple sources, can be large, and also as the attacker can infiltrate within data distributions.

- **Algorithm poisoning** happens when an attacker meddles with the algorithm used to train the model. It can be as simple as infiltrating hyperparameters or fiddling with the architecture of the algorithm. For example, let's take federated learning (which aims to preserve the privacy of individuals' data) where model training is done on multiple subsets of private data (such as healthcare data from multiple hospitals while preserving patients' confidential information). Multiple models are derived from each subset and then combined to form a final model. During this, an attacker can manipulate any subset of the data and influence the final resulting model. The attacker can also create a fake model from fake data and concatenate it with models produced from training on multiple subsets of private data to produce a final model that deviates from performing the task efficiently, or serves the attacker's motives.

- **Model poisoning** occurs when an attacker replaces a deployed model with an alternative model. This kind of attack is identical to a typical cyber-attack where the electronic files containing the model could be modified or replaced.

Input attack and evasion

An input or evasion attack happens when the attacker modifies input to the ML system in such a manner that it causes the system to malfunction (or give a wrong prediction). These perturbations or changes can be hard to detect as these changes are very subtle or small.

For example, input attacks are popular for computer vision algorithms. This can be done by just changing a few pixels in the input image. As a result, the system might identify an image in a way that it is not supposed to or make a wrong prediction. Such small changes can effectively manipulate the prediction resulting in wrong actions being taken by the system. As a result, the ML system behaves as it should, while the output is manipulated.

ML systems are highly prone to input attacks. Hence, having an anomaly detector to monitor incoming data can be quite handy to avoid such perturbations in the incoming data. Irrespective of input data, the majority of classification models choose a valid class from their training. Another way of protecting the ML system is by preprocessing the inputs with a proxy binary model that tells you, for example, whether an input image is of a person or an animal before sending this image to the final image classifier.

Reverse engineering

For a user of an AI system, it can be a black box or opaque. It is common in AI systems to accept inputs to generate outputs without revealing what is going on inside (in terms of both the logic and algorithm). Training datasets, which effectively contain all the trained system's knowledge, are also usually kept confidential. This, in theory, makes it impossible for an outsider to predict why particular outputs are produced or what is going on inside the AI system in terms of the algorithm, training data, or logic. However, in some cases, these systems can be prone to reverse engineering. The attacker or hackers' goal in reverse engineering attacks is to replicate the original model deployed as a service and use it to their advantage.

In a paper titled *Model Extraction Attacks against Recurrent Neural Networks* (https://arxiv.org/pdf/2002.00123.pdf), published in February 2020, researchers conducted experiments on model extraction attacks against an RNN and an LSTM trained with publicly available academic datasets. The researchers effectively reproduce the functionality of an ML system via a model extraction attack. They demonstrate that a model extraction attack with high accuracy can be extracted efficiently, primarily by replicating or configuring a loss function or architecture from the target model.

In another instance, researchers from the Max Planck Institute for Informatics showed in 2018 how they were able to infer information from opaque models by using a sequence of input-output queries.

Backdoor attacks

In backdoor attacks, the attacks can embed patterns of their choice in the model in the training or inference stages and infer the deployed model using pre-curated inputs to produce unexpected outputs or triggers to the ML system. Therefore, backdoor attacks can happen both in the training and inference phases, whereas evasion and poisoning attacks can occur in a single phase during training or inference.

Poison attacks can be used as part of the attack in backdoor attacks, and in some instances, the student model can learn to hack some backdoors from the teacher model using transfer learning.

Backdoor attacks can cause integrity challenges, especially in the training stage, if the attacker manages to use a poison attack to infiltrate training data and trigger an update to the model or system. Also, backdoor attacks can be aimed to degrade performance, exhaust or redirect resources that can lead to the system's failure, or attempt to introduce peculiar behavior and outputs from the AI system.

Summary

In this chapter, we have learned the key principles of testing and security by design. We explored the various methods to test ML solutions in order to secure them. For a comprehensive understanding and hands-on experience, implementation was done to load test our previously deployed ML model (from *Chapter 7, Building Robust CI and CD Pipelines*) to predict the weather. With this, you are ready to handle the diverse testing and security scenarios that will be channeled your way.

In the next chapter, we will delve into the secrets of deploying and maintaining robust ML services in production. This will enable you to deploy robust ML solutions in production. Let's delve into it.

10
Essentials of Production Release

In this chapter, you will learn about the **continuous integration** and **continuous delivery** (**CI/CD**) pipeline, the essentials of a production environment, and how to set up a production environment to serve your previously tested and approved **machine learning** (**ML**) models to end users. We will set up the required infrastructure for the CI/CD pipeline's production environment, configure processes for production deployments, configure pipeline execution triggers for complete automation, and learn how to manage production releases. This chapter will cover the essential fundamentals of the CI/CD pipeline and production environment since *the pipeline is the product, not the model*.

By learning about the fundamentals of CI/CD pipelines, you will be able to develop, test, and configure automated CI/CD pipelines for your use cases or business. We will cover an array of topics around production deployments and then delve into a primer on monitoring ML models in production.

We are going to cover the following topics in this chapter:

- Setting up the production infrastructure
- Setting up our production environment in the CI/CD pipeline
- Testing our production-ready pipeline
- Configuring pipeline triggers for automation
- Pipeline release management
- Toward continuous monitoring the service

Let's begin by setting up the infrastructure that's required to build the CI/CD pipeline.

Setting up the production infrastructure

In this section, we will set up the required infrastructure to serve our business use case (to predict weather conditions – raining or not raining at the port of Turku to plan and optimize resources at the port). We will set up an autoscaling Kubernetes cluster to deploy our ML model in the form of a web service. Kubernetes is an open source container orchestration system for automating software application deployment, scaling, and management. Many cloud service providers offer a Kubernetes-based infrastructure as a service. Similarly, Microsoft Azure provides a Kubernetes-based infrastructure as a service called **Azure Kubernetes Service** (**AKS**). We will use AKS to orchestrate our infrastructure.

There are multiple ways to provision an autoscaling Kubernetes cluster on Azure. We will explore the following two ways to learn about the different perspectives of infrastructure provisioning:

- Azure Machine Learning workspace portal
- Azure SDK

Let's look into the easiest way first; that is, using the Azure Machine Learning workspace to provision an Azure Kubernetes cluster for production.

Azure Machine Learning workspace

In this section, we will provision an Azure Kubernetes cluster using the Azure Machine Learning workspace. Perform the following steps:

1. Go to the Azure Machine Learning workspace and then go to the **Compute** section, which presents options for creating different types of computes. Select **Inference clusters** and click **Create**, as shown in the following screenshot:

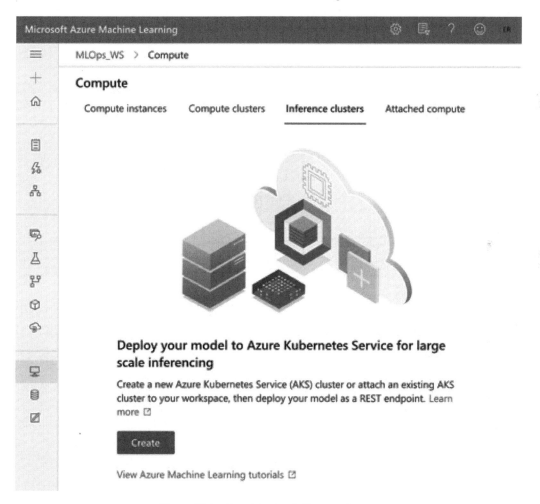

Figure 10.1 – Provisioning inference clusters

2. Clicking the **Create** button will present various compute options you can use to create a Kubernetes service. You will be prompted to select a **Region**, which is where your compute will be provisioned, and some configuration so that you can provision in terms of cores, RAM, and storage. Select a suitable option (it is recommended that you select **Standard_D2_v4** as a cost-optimal choice for this experiment), as shown in the following screenshot:

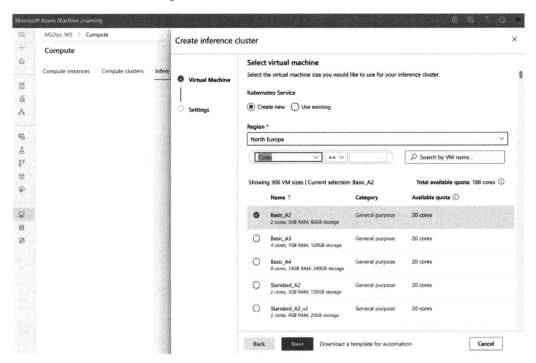

Figure 10.2 – Selecting a suitable compute option

3. After selecting a suitable compute option, you will be prompted to **Configure Settings** for the cluster, as shown in the following screenshot. Name our **Compute** (for example, `'prod-aks'` - meaning **production Azure Kubernetes Service**), set **Cluster purpose** to **Production** (as we are setting up for production), choose **Number of nodes** for the cluster, and select the **Basic** option for **Network configuration**. Omit **Enable SSL configuration** for simplicity. However, it is recommended to enable SSL connections for more security in production, as per your needs:

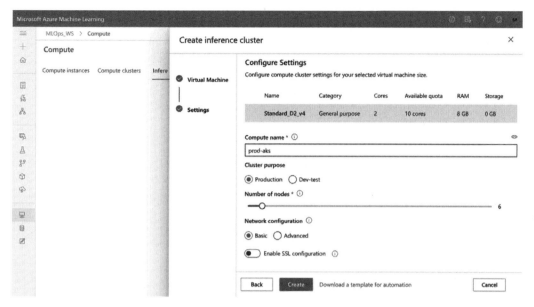

Figure 10.3 - Configure Settings

4. Click the **Create** button to provision the Kubernetes cluster for production. It will take around 15 minutes to create and provision the compute for production use:

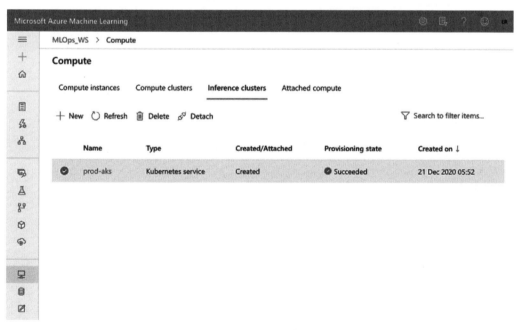

Figure 10.4 – Provisioned Kubernetes cluster

5. Once your AKS cluster has been provisioned, you will see a running Kubernetes cluster with the name you provided for the compute (for example, `prod-aks`), as shown in the preceding screenshot.

Azure Machine Learning SDK

An alternative way of creating and provisioning a Kubernetes cluster on Azure is by using the Azure Machine Learning SDK. You can use a premade script named `create_aks_cluster.py`, which can be found in the `10_Production_Release` folder. The prerequisite to running the `create_aks_cluster.py` script is the `config.json` (it can be downloaded from the Azure Machine Learning workspace) file for your Azure Machine Learning workspace, as shown in the following screenshot:

Figure 10.5 – Fetching the config file from your Azure Machine Learning workspace

Go to your Azure Machine Learning workspace and click on **Download config.json** to download your config file. After downloading it, copy or move the `config.json` file into the same directory (`10_Production_Release`) that the `create_aks_cluster.py` file is in, as shown here:

```
├──10_Production_Release
├── create_aks_cluster.py
├── config.json
```

With this, you are now set to run the script (`create_aks_cluster.py`) to create AKS compute for production deployments. Let's look at the `create_aks_cluster.py` script:

1. Import the necessary functions from the `azureml.core` SDK or library. Functions such as `Workspace`, `Model`, `ComputeTarget`, `AksCompute`, and so on will be used to provision your AKS cluster:

```
from azureml.core import Workspace
from azureml.core.model import Model
from azureml.core.compute import ComputeTarget
from azureml.core.compute_target import
ComputeTargetException
from azureml.core.compute import AksCompute,
ComputeTarget
```

2. By importing the necessary functions, you can start using them by connecting to your Azure Machine Learning workspace and creating the ws object. Do this by using the `Workspace` function and pointing it to your `config.json` file, like so:

```
ws = Workspace.from_config()
print(ws.name, ws.resource_group, ws.location, sep =
'\n')
```

3. By default, the `from_config()` function looks for the `config.json` file in same directory where you are executing the `create_aks.py` file. If your `config.json` file is in some other location, then point to the location of the file in the `from_config()` function. After successfully executing the `workspace.from_config()` function, you will see the workspace's name, resource group, and location printed out.

4. Next, we will create an AKS Kubernetes cluster for production deployments. Start by choose a name for your AKS cluster (reference it to the aks_name variable), such as prod-aks. The script will check if a cluster with the chosen name already exists. We can use the try statement to check whether the AKS target with the chosen name exists by using the ComputeTarget() function. It takes the workspace object and aks_name as parameters. If a cluster is found with the chosen name, it will print the cluster that was found and stop execution. Otherwise, a new cluster will be created using the ComputeTarget.create() function, which takes the provisioning config with the default configuration:

```
# Choose a name for your AKS cluster
aks_name = 'prod-aks'


# Verify that cluster does not exist already
try:
    aks_target = ComputeTarget(workspace=ws, name=aks_
name)
    print('Found existing cluster, use it.')
except ComputeTargetException:
    # Use the default configuration (can also provide
parameters to customize)
    prov_config = AksCompute.provisioning_configuration()


    # Create the cluster
    aks_target = ComputeTarget.create(workspace = ws,
                                name = aks_name,
provisioning_configuration = prov_config)


    if aks_target.get_status() != "Succeeded":
        aks_target.wait_for_completion(show_output=True)
```

After successfully executing the preceding code, a new cluster with the chosen name (that is, prod-aks) will be created. Usually, creating a new cluster takes around 15 minutes. Once the cluster has been created, it can be spotted in the Azure Machine Learning workspace, as we saw in *Figure 10.4*. Now that we have set up the prerequisites for enhancing the CI/CD pipeline for our production environment, let's start setting it up!

Setting up our production environment in the CI/CD pipeline

Perform the following steps to set up a production environment in the CI/CD pipeline:

1. Go to the Azure DevOps project you worked on previously and revisit the **Pipelines | Releases** section to view your **Port Weather ML Pipeline**. We will enhance this pipeline by creating a production stage.

2. Click on the **Edit** button to get started and click on **Add** under the **DEV TEST** stage, as shown in the following screenshot:

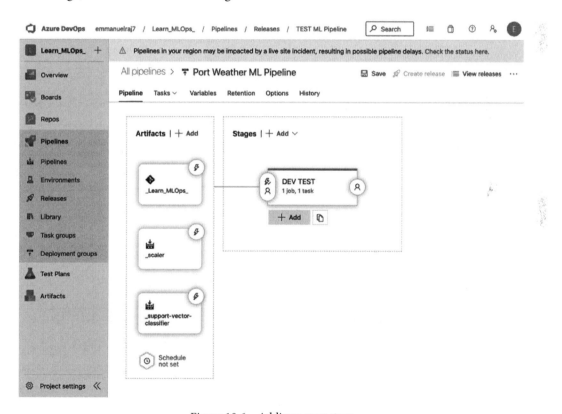

Figure 10.6 – Adding a new stage

3. Clicking the **Add** button under the **DEV TEST** stage will prompt you to select a template to create a new stage. Select **EMPTY JOB** option (under Select a template text) and name the stage `production` or `PROD` and save it, as shown in the following screenshot:

Figure 10.7 – Adding and saving the production stage (PROD)

4. A new production stage named **PROD** will be created. Now, you can configure jobs and processes at the production stage. To configure jobs for **PROD**, click on the 1 job, 0 task link (as shown in the preceding screenshot, in the **PROD** stage) in the **PROD** stage. You will be directed to the **Tasks** section, which is where you can add jobs to the **PROD** stage. In this stage, we will deploy models from our Azure Machine Learning workspace, so we will connect to it using the AzureML Model Deploy template we used previously in *Chapter 7, Building Robust CI and CD Pipelines*. Click on the + sign on the right-hand side of the **Agent job** section to add a task, as shown here:

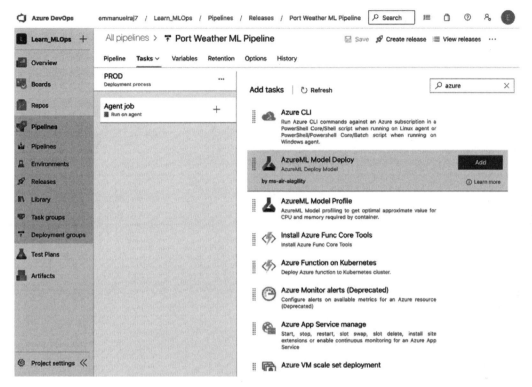

Figure 10.8 – Adding an AzureML Model Deploy task

5. Search for the **AzureML Model Deploy** template or task and add it. After adding the task, you will be prompted to configure it by connecting to your Azure Machine Learning workspace. Select your Azure Machine Learning workspace (for example, `mlops_ws`) and point to **Model Artifact** as your model source. We are doing this because we will be using the Model Artifacts we trained in *Chapter 4, Machine Learning Pipelines*.

6. Next, point to your inference configuration file from the Azure DevOps repository, as shown in the following screenshot. The inference configuration file represents the configuration settings for a custom environment that's used for deployment. We will use the same inference `Config.yml` file that we used for the **DEV TEST** environment as the environment for deployment should be the same:

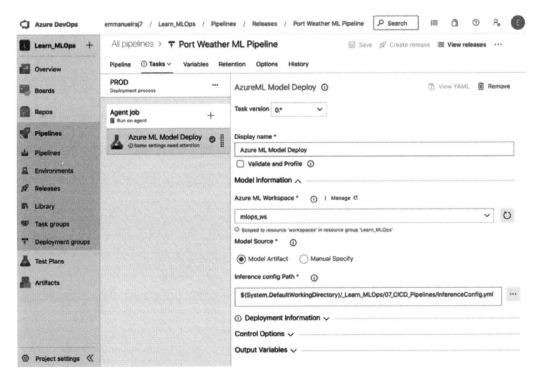

Figure 10.9 – Selecting your inference configuration

Basic configuration is done by selecting the `inferenceConfig.yml` file.

7. Next, we will configure **Deployment Information** by specifying the deployment target type as **Azure Kubernetes Service**. We're doing this because this is the production environment we will use to autoscale our Kubernetes cluster for production deployments. After selecting **Azure Kubernetes service** as your deployment target, select the AKS cluster you created previously (for example, `prod-aks`), name your deployment or web service (for example, `prod-webservice`), and select the **Deployment Configuration** file from the Azure DevOps repository that's connected to the pipeline, as shown here:

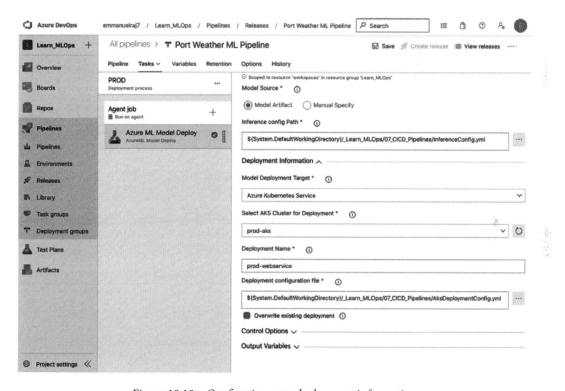

Figure 10.10 – Configuring your deployment information

The deployment configuration file we will use for the production environment is called `AksDeploymentConfig.yml`. It contains the configuration details for our deployment, including enabling autoscaling with a min and max number of replicas, authentication configuration, monitoring configuration and container resource requirements with CPU (for other situations where inference needs to be very fast or larger in-memory processing is needed, you may want to consider using a GPU resource), and memory requirements, as shown here:

```
AksDeploymentConfig.yml
computeType: AKS
autoScaler:
    autoscaleEnabled: True
    minReplicas: 1
    maxReplicas: 3
    refreshPeriodInSeconds: 10
    targetUtilization: 70
authEnabled: True
containerResourceRequirements:
    cpu: 1
    memoryInGB: 1
appInsightsEnabled: False
scoringTimeoutMs: 1000
maxConcurrentRequestsPerContainer: 2
maxQueueWaitMs: 1000
sslEnabled: False
```

8. Select the `AksDeploymentConfig.yml` file as our **Deployment Configuration** file. Now, hit the **Save** button to set up the **PROD** environment.

With that, you have successfully set up the production environment and integrated it with your CI/CD pipeline for automation. Now, let's test the pipeline by executing it.

Testing our production-ready pipeline

Congratulations on setting up the production pipeline! Next, we will test its robustness. One great way to do this is to create a new release and observe and study whether the production pipeline successfully deploys the model to production (in the production Kubernetes cluster setup containing the pipeline). Follow these steps to test the pipeline:

1. First, create a new release, go to the **Pipelines | Releases** section, select your previously created pipeline (for example, **Port Weather ML Pipeline**), and click on the **Create Release** button at the top right-hand side of the screen to initiate a new release, as shown here:

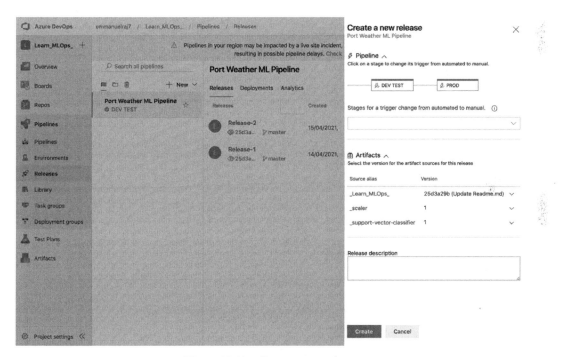

Figure 10.11 – Create a new release

2. Select the artifacts you would like to deploy in the pipeline (for example, Learn_
    MLOps repo, _scaler, and support-vector-classifier model and
    select their versions. Version 1 is recommended for testing PROD deployments
    for the first time), and click on the **Create** button at the top right-hand side of the
    screen, as shown in the preceding screenshot. Once you've done this, a new release
    is initiated, as shown in the following screenshot:

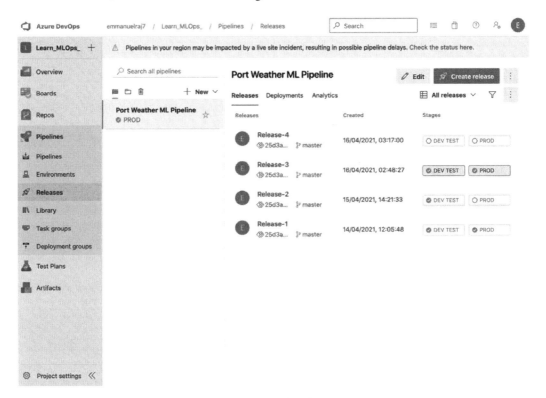

Figure 10.12 – New release's execution

3. After executing the pipeline, both the **DEV TEST** and **PROD** stages will be
    deployed (for example, **Release-5**, as shown in the preceding screenshot). You
    can check each step in each stage by monitoring the logs of each step of any stage
    (DEV TEST or PROD) while the pipeline release is in progress, until the pipeline is
    deployed successfully. You can also check the logs of previous releases.

4. Upon successfully working on a release, both the **DEV TEST** and **PROD** stages will be deployed using CI and CD. You must ensure that the pipeline is robust. Next, we can customize the pipeline further by adding custom triggers that will automate the pipeline without any human supervision. Automating CI/CD pipelines without any human supervision can be risky but may have advantages, such as real-time continuous learning (monitoring and retraining models) and faster deployments. It is good to know how to automate the CI/CD pipeline without any human supervision in the loop. Note that it is not recommended in many cases as there is a lot of room for error. In some cases, it may be useful – it really depends on your use case and ML system goals. Now, let's look at triggers for full automation.

Configuring pipeline triggers for automation

In this section, we will configure three triggers based on artifacts that we have already connected to the pipeline. The triggers we will set up are as follows:

- **Git trigger**: For making code changes to the master branch.
- **Artifactory trigger**: For when a new model or artifact is created or trained.
- **Schedule trigger**: A weekly periodic trigger.

Let's look at each of these pipeline triggers in detail.

Setting up a Git trigger

In teams, it is common to set a trigger for deployment when code changes are made to a certain branch in the repository. For example, when code changes are made to the **master** branch or the **develop** branch, CI/CD pipelines are triggered to deploy the application to the PROD or DEV TEST environments, respectively. When a pull request is made to merge code in the **master** or **develop** branch, the QA expert or product manager accepts the pull request in order to merge with the respective branch. Upon making code changes to the master or develop branch, a trigger is generated to create a new release in the pipeline. Follow these steps to create a trigger for the master branch for the experiment, as shown in the following screenshot:

1. Go to the **Pipelines | Releases** section and select your pipeline (for example, **Port Weather ML pipeline**). Then, click **Edit**:

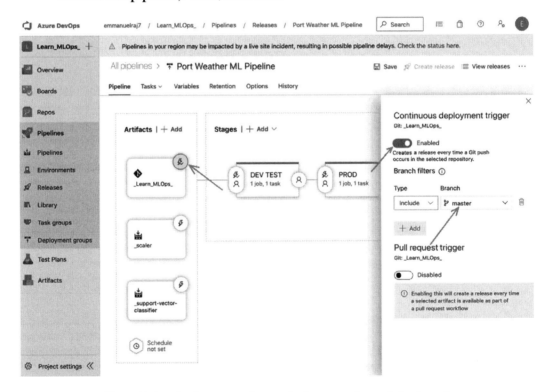

Figure 10.13 – Setting up continuous deployment triggers (git triggers)

You will be directed to a portal where you can edit your pipeline (for example, **Port Weather ML pipeline**) so that you can configure continuous deployment triggers for your artifacts.

2. To set up a Git trigger for the master branch (when changes are made to the master branch, a new release is triggered), click on the **Trigger** icon (thunder icon) and move the on/off switch button from disabled to enabled. This will enable the continuous deployment trigger.

3. Lastly, add a branch filter and point to the branch that you would like to set up a trigger for – in this case, the master branch – as shown in the preceding screenshot. Save your changes to set up the Git trigger.

By implementing these steps, you have set up a continuous deployment trigger to initiate a new release when changes are made to the master branch.

Setting up an Artifactory trigger

For ML applications, Artifactory triggers are quite useful. When new models or artifacts (files) have been trained by the Data Scientists in the team, it is useful to deploy those models to a test environment, and then eventually to production if they are promising or better than the previous models or trigger. Follow these steps to set up a continuous deployment trigger that will create a new release for the pipeline when a new model is trained, as shown in the following screenshot:

1. Go to the **Pipelines | Releases** section and select your pipeline (for example, **Port Weather ML pipeline**). Then, click **Edit**:

Figure 10.14 – Setting up CD for Artifact triggers (SVC model)

Upon clicking the **Edit** button, you will be directed to a portal where you can edit your pipeline, as shown in the preceding screenshot.

2. To set up an Artifact trigger for your model, click on your choice of model, such as **Support Vector Classifier** (**SVC**), and enable **Continuous deployment trigger**. In the preceding screenshot , a trigger has been enabled for a model (SVC). Whenever a new SVC model is trained and registered to the model registry that's connected to your Azure Machine Learning workspace, a new release will be triggered to deploy the new model via the pipeline.

3. Lastly, save your changes to set up an Artifact trigger for the SVC model. You have a continuous deployment trigger set up to initiate a new release when a new SVC model is trained and registered on your Azure Machine Learning workspace. The pipeline will fetch the new model and deploy it to the DEV TEST and PROD environments.

By implementing these steps, you have a continuous deployment trigger set up to initiate a new pipeline release when a new artifact is created or registered in your Azure Machine Learning workspace.

Setting up a Schedule trigger

Now, we will set up a time-specific Schedule trigger for the pipeline. This kind of trigger is useful for keeping the system healthy and updated via periodic new releases. Schedule triggers create new releases at set time intervals. We will set up a Schedule trigger for every week on Monday at 11:00 A.M. At this time, a new release is triggered to deploy the recent version of the SVC model to both the DEV TEST and PROD environments. Follow these steps to set up a Schedule trigger:

1. Go to the **Pipelines** | **Releases** section and select your pipeline (for example, **Port Weather ML pipeline**). Then, click **Edit**, as shown in the following screenshot:

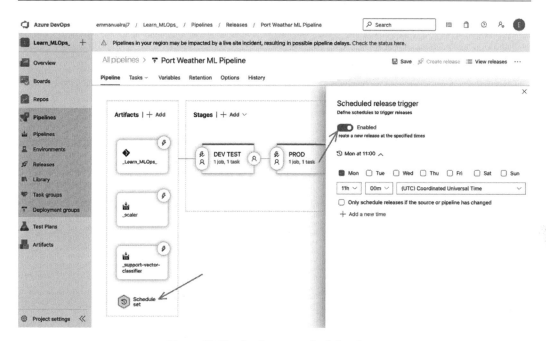

Figure 10.15 – Setting up a schedule trigger

Upon clicking the **Edit** button, you will be directed to a portal where you can edit your pipeline.

2. To set up a scheduled trigger for the pipeline, click on **Schedule Set** and enable **Scheduled release trigger**. Then, select times when you want to trigger a release. For example, in the preceding screenshot, a trigger has been enabled for every week on Monday at 11:00 A.M.

3. Lastly, save your changes to set up a set up Schedule trigger trigger for the pipeline.

By implementing these steps, you have a continuous deployment trigger set up to initiate a new pipeline release at a set time interval.

Congratulations on setting up Git, Artifact, and Schedule triggers. These triggers enable full automation for the pipeline. The pipeline has been set up and can now successfully test and deploy models. You also have the option to semi-automate the pipeline by adding a human or **Quality Assurance** (**QA**) expert to approve each stage in the pipeline. For example, after the test stage, an approval can be made by the QA expert so that you can start production deployment if everything was successful in the test stage. As a QA expert, it is vital to monitor your CI/CD pipeline. In the next section, we'll look at some best practices when it comes to managing pipeline releases.

Pipeline release management

Releases in the CI/CD pipelines allow your team to automate fully and continuously deliver software to your customers faster and with lower risk. Releases allow you to test and deliver your software in multiple stages of production or set up semi-automated processes with approvals and on-demand deployments. It is vital to monitor and manage these releases. We can manage releases by accessing the pipeline from **Pipelines | Releases** and selecting our CI/CD pipeline (for example, **Port Weather ML Pipeline**), as shown in the following screenshot:

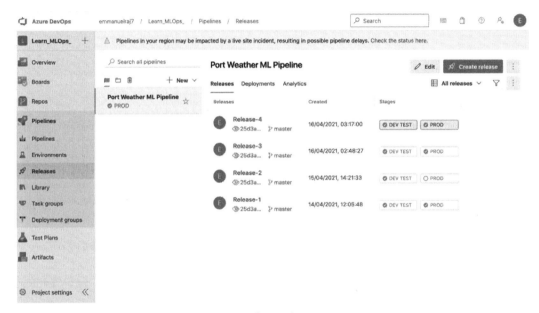

Figure 10.16 – Pipeline Release Management

Here, you can keep track of all the releases and their history and perform operations for each release, such as redeploying, abandoning, checking logs, and so on. You can see the releases shown in the following screenshot. By clicking on individual releases (for example, **Release 4**), we can check which model and artifacts were deployed in the release and how the release was triggered (manual or using automatic triggers). It provides end-to-end traceability of the pipeline. This information is crucial for the governance and compliance of the ML system:

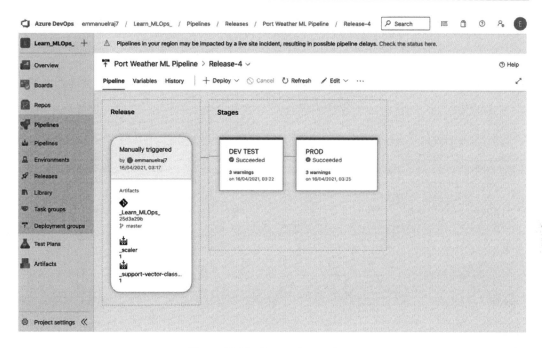

Figure 10.17 – Inspecting a release

Prevention is better than finding a cure. Just as we conduct incident reviews after a failure, it helps to prevent possible failures by conducting post-release reviews after deploying a new service or model. A thorough analysis of the release after deployment can enable us to understand answers to critical questions, such as the following:

- What works and what doesn't during a release?

- Were there any roadblocks with the release?

- Are there any unclear processes that you could solve and make more explainable for the next release?

Thoroughly understanding these questions post-release can help you improve and iterate on your strategy and develop better release management practices.

Toward continuous monitoring

With that, we have set up a fully automated and robust pipeline. So far, we have successfully implemented the deployment part or module in the MLOps workflow (as we discussed in *Chapter 1, Fundamentals of MLOps Workflow*). It is vital to monitor the deployed ML model and service in real time to understand the system's performance, as this helps maximize its business impact. One of the reasons ML projects are failing to bring value to businesses is because of the lack of trust and transparency in their decision making. Building trust into AI systems is vital these days, especially if we wish to adapt to the changing environment, regulatory frameworks, and dynamic customer needs. Continuous monitoring will enable us to monitor the ML system's performance and build trust into AIs to maximize our business value. In the next chapter, we will learn about the monitoring module in the MLOps workflow and how it facilitates continuous monitoring.

Summary

In this chapter, we covered the essential fundamentals of the CI/CD pipeline and production environment. We did some hands-on implementation to set up the production infrastructure and then set up processes in the production environment of the pipeline for production deployments. We tested the production-ready pipeline to test its robustness. To take things to the next level, we fully automated the CI/CD pipeline using various triggers. Lastly, we looked at release management practices and capabilities and discussed the need to continuous monitor the ML system. A key takeaway is that *the pipeline is the product, not the model*. It is better to focus on building a robust and efficient pipeline more than building the best model.

In the next chapter, we will explore the MLOps workflow monitoring module and learn more about the game-changing explainable monitoring framework.

Section 3: Monitoring Machine Learning Models in Production

In this part, readers will get acquainted with the principles and processes of monitoring machine learning systems in production. It will enable them to craft CI/CD pipelines to monitor deployments and equip them to set up and facilitate continuous delivery and continuous monitoring of machine learning models.

This section comprises the following chapters:

- *Chapter 11, Key Principles for Monitoring Your ML System*
- *Chapter 12, Model Serving and Monitoring*
- *Chapter 13, Governing the ML system for Continual Learning*

11
Key Principles for Monitoring Your ML System

In this chapter, we will learn about the fundamental principles that are essential for monitoring your **machine learning** (**ML**) models in production. You will learn how to build trustworthy and Explainable AI solutions using the Explainable Monitoring Framework. The Explainable Monitoring Framework can be used to build functional monitoring pipelines so that you can monitor ML models in production, analyze application and model performance, and govern ML systems. The goal of monitoring ML systems is to enable trust, transparency, and explainability in order to increase business impact. We will learn about this by looking at some real-world examples.

Understanding the principles mentioned in this chapter will equip you with the knowledge to build end-to-end monitoring systems for your use case or company. This will help you engage business, tech, and public (customers and legal) stakeholders so that you can efficiently achieve your business goals. This will also help you have the edge and have a systematic approach to governing your ML system. Using the frameworks in this chapter, you can enable trust, transparency, and explainability for your stakeholders and ML system.

We are going to cover the following main topics in this chapter:

- Understanding the key principles of monitoring an ML system
- Monitoring in the MLOps workflow
- Understanding the Explainable Monitoring Framework
- Enabling continuous monitoring for the service

Let's get started!

Understanding the key principles of monitoring an ML system

Building trust into AI systems is vital these days with the growing demands for products to be data-driven and to adjust to the changing environment and regulatory frameworks. One of the reasons ML projects are failing to bring value to businesses is due to the lack of trust and transparency in their decision making. Many black box models are good at reaching high accuracy, but they become obsolete when it comes to explaining the reasons behind the decisions that have been made. At the time of writing, news has been surfacing that raises these concerns of trust and explainability, as shown in the following figure:

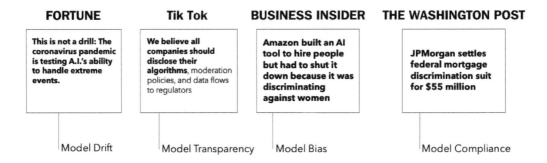

Figure 11.1 – Components of model trust and explainability

This image showcases concerns in important areas in real life. Let's look at how this translates into some key aspects of model explainability, such as model drift, model bias, model transparency, and model compliance, using some real-life examples.

Model drift

We live in a dynamically changing world. Due to this, the environment and data in which an ML model is deployed to perform a task or make predictions is continually evolving, and it is essential to consider this change. For example, the COVID-19 pandemic has presented us with an unanticipated reality. Many business operations have turned virtual, and this pandemic has presented us with a unique situation that many perceive as the **new normal**. Many small businesses have gone bankrupt, and individuals are facing extreme financial scarcity due to the rise of unemployment. These people (small business owners and individuals) have been applying for loans and financial reliefs to banks and institutions like never before (on a large scale). Fraud detection algorithms that have already been deployed and used by banks and institutions have not seen this velocity and veracity of data, in terms of loan and financial relief applications.

All these changes in features (such as the applicant's income, their credit history, the location of the applicant, the amount they've requested, and so on), due to an otherwise loan-worthy applicant who hasn't applied for any loan beforehand losing their job, may skew the model's weights/perceptive (or confuse the model). This presents an important challenge for the models. To deal with such dynamically changing environments, it is crucial to consider model drift and continually learn from it.

Drift is related to changes in the environment and refers to the degradation of predictive ML models' performance and the relationship between the variables degrading. Following are the four types of model changes with regards to models and data:

- **Data drift**: This is where properties of the independent variables change. For example, as in the previous example, data changes due to seasonality or new products or changes being added to meet the consumer's needs, as in the COVID-19 pandemic.

- **Feature drift**: This is where the properties of the feature(s) change over time. For instance, temperature changes with change in seasons. In winter the temperature is cooler compared to the temperatures in summer or autumn.

- **Model drift**: This is where properties of dependent variables change. For instance, in the preceding example, this is where the classification of fraud detection changes.

- **Upstream data changes**: This is when the data pipeline undergoes operational data changes, such as when a feature is no longer being generated, resulting in missing values. An example of this is a change of salary value for the customer (from dollar to euros), where a dollar value is no longer being generated.

For more clarity, we will learn more about drift and develop drift monitors in the next chapter (*Chapter 12, Model Serving and Monitoring*).

Model bias

Whether you like it or not, ML is already impacting many decisions in your life, such as getting shortlisted for your next job or getting mortgage approvals from banks. Even Evan law enforcement agencies are using it to drill down potential crime suspects to prevent crimes. ProPublica, a journalism organization (uses ML to predict future criminals - `https://www.propublica.org/article/machine-bias-risk-assessments-in-criminal-sentencing`). In 2016, Propublica's ML showed cases where the model was biased to predict black women as higher risk than white men, while all previous records showed otherwise. Such cases can be costly and have devastating societal impacts, so they need to be avoided. In another case, Amazon built an AI to hire people but had to shut it down as it was discriminating against women (as reported by the Washington Post). These kinds of biases can be costly and unethical. To avoid them, AI systems need to be monitored so that we can build our trust in them.

Model bias is a type of error that happens due to certain features of the dataset (used for model training) being more heavily represented and/or weighted than others. A misrepresenting or biased dataset can result in skewed outcomes for the model's use case, low accuracy levels, and analytical errors. In other words, it is the error resulting from incorrect assumptions being made by the ML algorithm. High bias can result in predictions being inaccurate and can cause a model to miss relevant relationships between the features and the target variable being predicted. An example of this is the aforementioned AI that had been built by Amazon to hire people but had a bias against women. We will learn more about model bias in the *Explainable Monitoring Framework* section, where we will explore *Bias and threat detection*.

Model transparency

AI is non-deterministic in nature. ML in particular continually evolves, updates, and retrains over its life cycle. AI is impacting almost all industries and sectors. With its increasing adoption and important decisions being made using ML, it has become vital to establish the same trust level that deterministic systems have. After all, digital systems are only useful when they can be trusted to do their jobs. There is a clear need for model transparency – many CEO and business leaders are encouraging us to understand AI's business decisions and their business impact. Recently, the CEO of TikTok made a statement stating the following:

> *"We believe all companies should disclose their algorithms, moderation policies, and data flows to regulators" (Source: TikTok).*

Such a level of openness and transparency by companies can build our trust in AI as a society and enable smoother adoption and compliance.

Model transparency is the pursuit of building trust in AI systems to ensure fairness, reduce or eliminate bias, provide accountability (auditing the end-to-end process of how the system derives results), and justify model outputs and system decisions.

Model compliance

Model compliance has become important as the cost of non-compliance with governments and society can be huge. The following headline was reported by the Washington Post:

> *"JPMorgan settles federal mortgage discrimination suit for $55 million"*

Non-compliance turned out to be a costly affair for JP Morgan. Operationalizing regulatory compliance is increasingly becoming important to avoid unnecessary fines and damage to society. Here are some drivers that enable model compliance within companies:

- **Culture of accountability**: End-to-end auditing of ML systems is essential to monitoring compliance. MLOps can play a vital role in facilitating auditing and redacting the operations and business decisions that are made using AI.

- **Ethics at the forefront**: Building responsible AI systems that bring value to society and gain our trust requires that AI predictions are inclusive, fair, and ethical. Having an ethics framework can help a company connect their customers to their values and principles, as well as ensuring AI decisions are made ethically. The European Commission has done a good job here by coming up with the *Ethics and guidelines for trustworthy AI*. You can find these guidelines here: `https://ec.europa.eu/digital-single-market/en/news/ethics-guidelines-trustworthy-ai`.

- **Compliance pipeline**: Having a compliance pipeline that satisfies both business and government regulations can be rewarding for organizations seeking to ensure real-time compliance, auditing, and redaction. MLOps can facilitate this by keeping track of all the ML models' inventory, thus giving visibility into how they work and explaining how they are working visually to stakeholders. This way of working enables humans to monitor, redact, and explain correlations to regulations, making it efficient for business stakeholders, data scientists, and regulators to work hand in hand to ensure they have transparent and explainable operations.

Explainable AI

In an ideal case, a business keeps model transparency and compliance at the forefront so that the business is dynamically adapting to the changing environment, such as model drift, and dealing with bias on the go. All this needs a framework that keeps all business stakeholders (IT and business leaders, regulators, business users, and so on) in touch with the AI model in order to understand the decisions the model is making, while focusing on increasing model transparency and compliance. Such a framework can be delivered using Explainable AI as part of MLOps. Explainable AI enables ML to be easily understood by humans.

Model transparency and explainability are two approaches that enable Explainable AI. The ML models form patterns or rules based on the data they are trained on. Explainable AI can help humans or business stakeholders understand these rules or patterns the model has discovered, and also helps validate business decisions that have been made by the ML model. Ideally, Explainable AI should be able to serve multiple business stakeholders, as shown in the following diagram:

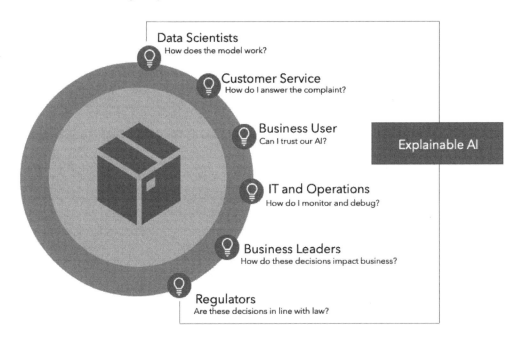

Figure 11.2 – Business-driven Explainable AI

Black box models can get high accuracy on predictions but become obsolete when they are unable to explain why they've made these decisions. Most black box models offer no visibility into model performance, no monitoring to catch potential bias or drift, and no explainability of model behavior. To address this issue, a vast amount of research and development is going on in to Explainable AI methods to offer model transparency and model explainability.

Explainable AI methods infused with MLOps can enable almost all business stakeholders to understand and validate business decisions made by the AI, and also helps explain them to the internal and external stakeholders. There is no one-stop solution for Explainable AI as every use case needs its own Explainable AI method. There are various methods that are gaining in popularity. We'll look at some examples in the following subsections.

Feature attribution methods

Feature attribution methods show how much each feature in your model has contributed to each instance's predictions. When you request explanations, you get the predictions, along with feature attribution information. Here are some feature attribution methods:

- **SHapley Additive exPlanations (SHAP)**: A method to explain the outputs of any ML model. It is based on the game theory approach, which explains the output of any ML model. In particular, it explains each feature's contribution to push the model's output.

- **Integrated Gradients**: A technique that aims to explain the relationship between a model's predictions in terms of its features. It was introduced in the paper *Axiomatic Attribution for Deep Networks*. It can explain feature importance by identifying skewed data and help with debugging model performance.

- **Local Interpretable Model-Agnostic Explanation (LIME)**: This is a model-agnostic method that's used to explain predictions. It focuses on local explanations; that is, explanations to reflect the model's behavior regarding the instance of data being predicted. For instance, LIME can suggest which factors or features were important for a model to predict an outcome. This can be seen in the following diagram:

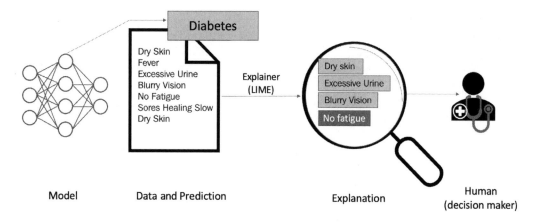

Figure 11.3 – Explaining individual predictions using LIME

In the preceding diagram, a model is predicting that a patient has diabetes. The LIME explainer highlights and implies the symptoms of diabetes, such as dry skin, excessive urine, and blurry vision, that contribute to the **Diabetes** prediction, while **No fatigue** is evidence against it. Using the explainer, a doctor can decide and draw conclusions from the model's prediction and provide the patient with the appropriate treatment.

You can learn more about AI explanations at `https://cloud.google.com/ai-platform/prediction/docs/ai-explanations/overview`.

Non-feature attribution methods

Non-feature attribution methods do not focus on how features contribute to your model's predictions. Instead, they focus on the relationship between input data and output data for your model inference. Here are some non-feature attribution methods:

- **Deeplift**: This is used to evaluate neural networks by comparing each neuron's activation to its reference activation and assigning contribution scores according to the difference. Deeplift reveals correlations and contributions. For example, let's say we are using a cat and dog image classifier to classify images between cats and dogs. Suppose the classifier predicts that the input image is a dog by using the deeplift method. Here, we can backpropagate the neurons that were activated in the image classifier's neural network to their reference activations and then assign contribution scores to each feature based on the difference.

- **Natural language explanations** (**NLE**): NLE aims to capture input-output relationships for text explanations using a fusion of techniques such as partial dependence function, gradient analysis, contextual encoding, Individual Conditional Expectation, Accumulated Local Effects, and so on. These techniques are useful for interpreting language models that classify or generate text. NLE provide easily understandable and useful reasons for users to decide whether to trust the model's decision and take action. For example, you may wish to buy a product based on a model's recommendation and explanation. Tools such as Microsoft Power BI and Qlik Sense can be used to plug and play to study NLE. These tools need to be customized as per your need or use case.

There are other methods apart from the ones mentioned in the previous list. This area is a hot topic for research in the field of AI. Many researchers and business leaders are pursuing solving Explainable AI problems to explain model decisions to internal and external stakeholders. Having an Explainable AI-driven interface provisioned for multiple business stakeholders can help them answer critical business questions. For instance, a business leader needs to be able to answer, "How do these model decisions impact business?" while for IT and Operations, it is vital to know the answer to "How do I monitor and debug?"

Answering these questions for multiple business stakeholders enables employees and businesses to adapt to AI and maximize value from it, by ensuring model transparency and model compliance while adapting to changing environments by optimizing model bias and drift.

Explainable AI = model transparency and explainability

Since ML models are becoming first-class citizens, in order to monitor a model's performance with respect to these areas, we can use Explainable Monitoring, which allows us to analyze and govern ML systems in production by monitoring and explaining their decisions using Explainable AI methods. Explainable monitoring is a hybrid of Explainable AI; it uses Explainable AI methods infused with **operations** (**Ops**) in production. Explainable monitoring is becoming an integral part of the MLOps workflow. We'll look at how Explainable Monitoring brings value to the MLOps workflow in the next section.

Monitoring in the MLOps workflow

We learned about the MLOps workflow in *Chapter 1, Fundamentals of MLOps Workflow*. As shown in the following diagram, the monitoring block is an integral part of the MLOps workflow for evaluating the ML models' performance in production and measuring the ML system's business value. We can only do both (measure the performance and business value that's been generated by the ML model) if we understand the model's decisions in terms of transparency and explainability (to explain the decisions to stakeholders and customers).

Explainable Monitoring enables both transparency and explainability to govern ML systems in order to drive the best business value:

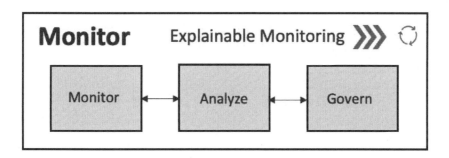

Figure 11.4 – MLOps workflow – Monitor

In practice, **Explainable Monitoring** enables us to monitor, analyze, and govern ML system, and it works in a continuous loop with other components in the MLOps workflow. It also empowers humans to engage in the loop to understand model decisions and teach the model (by labeling data and retraining the model) on the go. Explainable Monitoring enables continual learning and can be highly rewarding for a company in the long run. A continual learning pipeline with a human in the loop, enabled using Explainable Monitoring, can be seen in the following diagram:

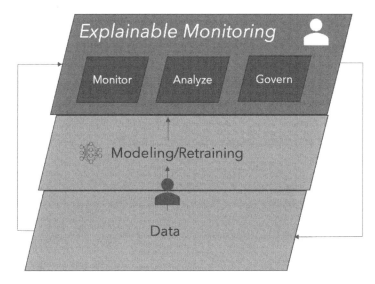

Figure 11.5 – Continual learning enabled by Explainable Monitoring

Continual learning is the system's ability to learn continuously in a changing environment while building on what had been learned previously. To facilitate continual learning, data and modeling must work hand in hand, and be assisted by humans in the loop (typically, a QA analyst or system admin, such as a data scientist or ML engineer). Explainable Monitoring plays a vital role in continual learning systems to increase revenue, stay compliant, and build ML systems responsibly. After all, only a model that's been deployed with continual learning capabilities can bring business value.

Understanding the Explainable Monitoring Framework

In this section, we will explore the Explainable Monitoring Framework (as shown in the following diagram) in detail to understand and learn how Explainable Monitoring enhances the MLOps workflow and the ML system itself:

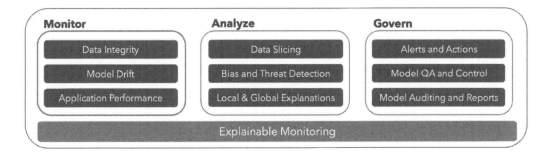

Figure 11.6 – Explainable Monitoring Framework

The Explainable Monitoring Framework is a modular framework that's used to monitor, analyze, and govern a ML system while enabling continual learning. All the modules work in sync to enable transparent and Explainable Monitoring. Let's look at how each module works to understand how they contribute and function in the framework. First, let's look at the monitor module (the first panel in the preceding diagram).

Monitor

The monitor module is dedicated to monitoring the application in production (serving the ML model). Several factors are at play in an ML system, such as application performance (telemetry data, throughput, server request time, failed requests, error handling, and so on), data integrity and model drift, and changing environments. The monitor module should capture vital information from the system logs in production to track the ML system's robustness. Let's look at the importance and functionality of three of the monitor module's functionalities: data integrity, model drift, and application performance.

Data integrity

Ensuring the data integrity of an ML application includes checking incoming (input data to the ML model) and outgoing (ML model prediction) data to ensure ML systems' integrity and robustness. The monitor module ensures data integrity by inspecting the volume, variety, veracity, and velocity of the data in order to detect outliers or anomalies. Detecting outliers or anomalies prevents ML systems from having poor performance and being susceptible to security attacks (for example, adversarial attacks). Data integrity coupled with efficient auditing can facilitate the desired performance of ML systems to derive business value.

Model drift

If model drift is not measured, the model's performance can easily become sub-par and can hamper the business with poor decision making and customer service. For example, it is hard to foresee changes or trends in data during a black swan event such as COVID-19. Here is some news that made it to the headlines:

- The accuracy of the Instacart model forecasting item's accessibility in stores fell from 93% to 61% due to a dramatic change in shopping habits (`https://fortune.com/2020/06/09/instacart-coronavirus-artificial-intelligence/`).

- Bankers doubted if credit models that have been trained for good times will respond accurately to stress scenarios (`https://www.americanbanker.com/opinion/ai-models-could-struggle-to-handle-the-market-downturn`).

- In response to market uncertainty, trading algorithms misfired. There was a 21% decline in some funds (`https://www.wired.com/story/best-ai-models-no-match-coronavirus`).

- Image classification models struggle to adapt to the "new normal" in the wake of the COVID-19 pandemic: a family at home in front of laptops can now mean "work," not "leisure." (`https://techcrunch.com/2020/08/02/ai-is-struggling-to-adjust-to-2020/`)

Hence, it is important to monitor model drift in any form, such as data drift, concept drift, or any upstream data changes, in order to adapt to the changing environments and serve businesses and customers in the most relevant way and generate the maximum business value.

Application performance

It is critical to monitor application performance to foresee and prevent any potential failures, since this ensures the robustness of ML systems. Here, we can monitor the critical system logs and telemetry data of the production deployment target (for example, Kubernetes or an on-premises server). Monitoring application performance can give us key insights in real time, such as the server's throughput, latency, server request time, number of failure requests or control flow errors, and so on. There is no hard and set way of monitoring applications and, depending on your business use case, your application performance mechanism can be curated and monitored to keep the system up and running to generate business value.

In terms of the monitor component, we monitored data integrity, model drift, and application performance. In the next section, we will analyze how to monitor the data of the model and application.

Analyze

Analyzing your ML system in production in real time is key to understanding the performance of your ML system and ensuring its robustness. Humans play a key role in analyzing model performance and detecting subtle anomalies and threats. Hence, having a human in the loop can introduce great transparency and explainability to the ML system. We can analyze model performance to detect any biases or threats and to understand why the model makes decisions in a certain pattern. We can do this by applying advanced techniques such as data slicing, adversarial attack prevention techniques, or by understanding local and global explanations. Let's see how we can do this in practice.

Data slicing

There are a great number of success stories surrounding ML in terms of improving businesses and life in general. However, there is still room to improve data tools for debugging and interpreting models. One key area of improvement is understanding why models perform poorly on certain parts or slices of data and how we can balance their overall performance. A slice is a part or a subset of a dataset. Data slicing can help us understand the model's performance on different types of sub-datasets. We can split the dataset into multiple slices or subsets and study the model's behavior on them.

For example, let's consider a hypothetical case where we have trained a random forest model to classify whether a person's income is above or below $50,000. The model has been trained on the UCI census data (`https://archive.ics.uci.edu/ml/datasets/Census-Income+%28KDD%29`). The results of the model for slices (or subsets) of data can be seen in the following table. This table suggests that the overall metrics may be considered acceptable as the overall log loss is low for all the data (see the *All* row). This is a widely used loss metric for binary classification problems and represents how close the prediction's likelihood is to the actual/true value; it is 0 or 1 in the case of binary classification. The more the predicted probability diverges from the actual value, the higher the log loss value is. However, the individual slices tell a different story:

Slice	Log Loss	Size (number of data elements in the slice)
All	0.31	31k
Sex = Male	0.44	22k
Sex = Female	0.19	11k
Occupation = Prof – specialty	0.45	5k
Education = HS – grad	0.33	10k
Education = Bachelors	0.48	5.2k
Education = Masters	0.51	1.8 k
Education = Doctorate	0.59	0.3 k

Table 11.1 – UCI census data slices

By looking at the previous table, we can conclude that the model's performance is decent. However, if we look at the performance of male versus female subjects, we can see that the model only performs well for female subjects where the log losses are less compared to the log loss for male subjects. On the other hand, if you look at the *Prof – specialty* occupation, you will see that the net performance is on par with the performance of male subjects with log losses of 0.45 and 0.41, respectively, whereas the effect size for *Prof – specialty* is considerably less. The model performs poorly for *Bachelors*, *Masters*, and *Doctorates* as the log losses are high with values of 0.44, 0.49, and 0.59, respectively. It is also important to note that if the log loss of a slice and its counterpart is below acceptable, this suggests that the model is bad overall and not just on a particular data slice.

Data slicing enables us to see subtle biases and unseen correlations to understand why a model might perform poorly on a subset of data. We can avoid these biases and improve the model's overall performance by training the model using balanced datasets that represent all the data slices (for example, using synthetic data or by undersampling, and so on) or by tuning hyperparameters of the models to reduce overall biases. Data slicing can provide an overview of model fairness and performance for an ML system, and can also help an organization optimize the data and ML models to reach optimal performance and decent fairness thresholds. Data slicing can help build trust in the AI system by offering transparency and explainability into data and model performance.

> **Note**
>
> To get a comprehensive overview of data slicing and automated data slicing methods, take a look at *Automated Data Slicing for Model Validation: A Big data - AI Integration Approach* at `https://arxiv.org/pdf/1807.06068.pdf`.

Bias and threat detection

To ensure that robust and ethical decisions are made using ML models, we need to make sure that the models are fair and secure. Any biases and threats need to be monitored and mitigated, to avoid unethical or partial decisions that benefit any particular party in order to comply with business values and the law.

There are different types of bias, such as selection bias (data that's used for training models is not representative of the population, such as minorities), framing bias (questions or a survey that's used to collect data is framed in a point of view or slant), systematic bias (repetitive or consistent error), response bias (data in which participants respond incorrectly by following their conscious bias), or confirmation bias (collecting data to validate your own preconceptions). To avoid these biases and mitigate them, techniques such as data slicing, slice-based learning, or balancing the bias-variance tradeoff can be applied, depending on the use case.

An ML system is exposed to security threats that need monitoring and mitigation. We have discussed some common threats and threat-prevention techniques involving adversarial attacks, poison attacks, privacy attacks or backdoor attacks, and so on, in *Chapter 9, Testing and Securing Your ML Solution*.

Local and global explanations

Local and global explanations offer different perspectives on model performance. Local explanations offer justification for model prediction for a specific or individual input, whereas global explanations provide insights into the model's predictive process, independent of any particular input. For example, let's take a look at a hypothetical case of a **recurrent neural network** (**RNN**) model being used to perform sentiment analysis for customer reviews. The following diagram shows the global explanation (the process as a whole) for the RNN model's sentiment analysis using the RNNVis tool:

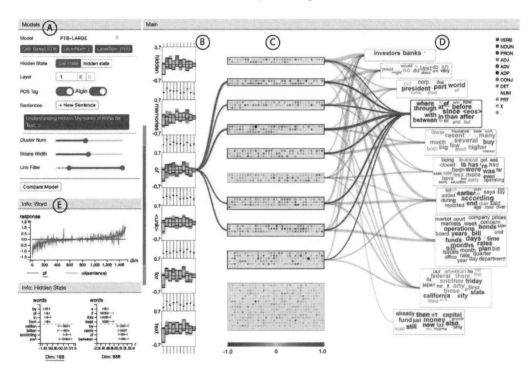

Figure 11.7 – Global explanation of the RNN model (using RNNVis) to understand the process as a whole (how hidden states, layers, and so on impact model outputs and predictive processes)

Source: https://blog.acolyer.org/2019/02/25/understanding-hidden-memories-of-recurrent-neural-networks/

Here, for example, the co-clustering visualization shows different word clouds for words with positive and negative sentiments. Using global explanations, we can simulate the model's predictive process and understand correlations with regards to parameters or the model's architecture (for example, hidden states and layers). Global explanations offer two perspectives of explainability: the high-level model process and the predictive explanations. On the other hand, local explanations give insights into single predictions. Both explanations are valuable if we wish to understand the model's performance and validate it comprehensively.

In the analyze component, we can analyze the model's performance using the techniques we have explored, such as data slicing, Bias and threat detection, and local and global explanations. In the next section, we will learn how to govern and control ML systems to efficiently guide it to achieve operational or business objectives.

Govern

The ML systems' efficacy is dependent on the way it is governed to achieve maximum business value. A great part of system governance involves quality assurance and control, as well as model auditing and reporting, to ensure it has end-to-end trackability and complies with regulations. Based on monitoring and analyzing the model's performance, we can control and govern ML systems. Governance is driven by smart alerts and actions to maximize business value. Let's look into how alerts and actions, model quality assurance and control, and model auditing and reports orchestrate the ML system's governance.

Alerts and actions

Governing a ML system involves monitoring and analyzing the ML application. Here, system developers can be alerted about when the system is showing anomalous behavior such as failed requests, slow server response times, server exceptions, errors, or high latency. Alerting the system developers or admin can ensure quality assurance and prevent system failures. There are two different types of alerts: alerts for system performance and model performance-based alerts. Here are some examples of alerts for system performance:

- Rule-based alerts for failed requests based on a threshold
- Rule-based alerts for server response time based on a threshold
- Rule-based alerts for server exceptions based on a threshold
- Rule-based alerts for availability based on a threshold

Model performance alerts are generated when the model experiences drift or anomalous feature distribution or bias. When such events are recorded, the system administrator or developers are alerted via email, SMS, push notifications, and voice alerting. These alert actions (automated or semi-automated) can be used to mitigate system performance deterioration. Depending on the situation and need, some possible actions can be evoked, such as the following:

- Deploying an alternative model upon experiencing high model drift

- Retraining a model

- Training a new model

- Restarting the ML system

- Redeploying the ML system

Model quality assurance and control

A model's quality assurance and control mechanism can be quite rewarding for those using an ML system, if we wish to prevent many possible mishaps and to ensure regular and healthy monitoring and functionality of the ML system. It is recommended to have a framework or mechanism for model quality assurance and control. For this, a quality assurance framework for ML systems, as shown in the following diagram, can enable the mechanism for your organization. It is a modular framework that's used to monitor three important aspects of ML systems:

Figure 11.8 – Model Quality Assurance Framework

Quality assurance experts can help your company or organization put a test mechanism into place to validate whether the data being used for training has been sanitized, ensure the data being used for model inference does not contain threats for that ML system, and to monitor data drift to understand and validate the changing environment. Monitoring and testing data can be achieved by quality assurance or test engineers, together with product managers, by doing the following:

- Understand and validate the data's statistical relations (for example, mean, median, mode, and so on) for training, testing, and inferring data.

- Develop tests to verify the aforementioned statistics and relationships (using scripts).

- Evaluate the distribution of characteristics using feature engineering techniques such as feature selection, dimensionality reduction, and so on.

- Retrain and review the performance of all models.

- Monitor the performance of all the models at regular intervals with new datasets.

- Raise an alert if another model (from the model inventory) performs with better accuracy than the existing model.

- Perform tests at regular intervals.

Model auditing and reports

Model auditing and reporting is essential if you want to have enough information for the regulators and for compliance with the law. Having end-to-end traceability for the model ensures great transparency and explainability, which can result in transparent governance mechanisms for an organization or company. The goal of model auditing and reporting is to assess the model's performance and based on that, enable ML system governance. In the following diagram, we can see a big-picture overview of the model transparency chart that's generated from auditing and reporting:

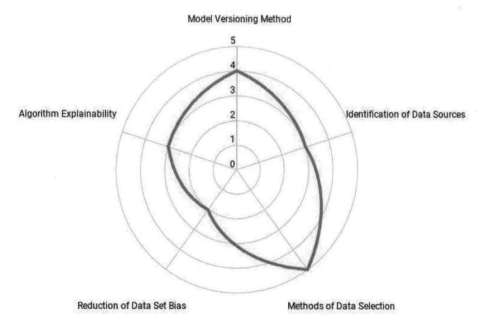

Figure 11.9 – Model Transparency chart

Model assessments based on auditing and reporting will ensure healthy, transparent, and robust governance mechanisms for organizations and enable them to have end-to-end traceability in order to comply with the regulators. Having such mechanisms will help save organizations a great amount of time and resources and enable efficiency in interactions with the regulators.

Enabling continuous monitoring for the service

The Explainable Monitoring Framework can be resourceful if we wish to monitor ML systems in production. In the next chapter, we will enable the Explainable Monitoring Framework for the business use case we worked on in the previous chapters. We will enable continuous monitoring for the system we have deployed. We will then monitor the ML application that's been deployed to production and analyze the incoming data and the model's performance to govern the ML system to produce maximum business value for the use case.

Summary

In this chapter, we learned about the key principles for monitoring an ML system. We explored some common monitoring methods and the Explainable Monitoring Framework (including the monitor, analyze, and govern stages). We then explored the concepts of Explainable Monitoring thoroughly.

In the next chapter, we will delve into a hands-on implementation of the Explainable Monitoring Framework. Using this, we will build a monitoring pipeline in order to continuously monitor the ML system in production for the business use case (predicting weather at the port of Turku).

The next chapter is quite hands-on, so buckle up and get ready!

12
Model Serving and Monitoring

In this chapter, we will reflect on the need to serve and monitor **machine learning** (ML) models in production and explore different means of serving ML models for users or consumers of the model. Then, we will revisit the **Explainable Monitoring framework** from *Chapter 11*, *Key Principles for Monitoring Your ML System*, and implement it for the business use case we have been solving using MLOps to predict the weather. The implementation of an Explainable Monitoring framework is hands-on. We will infer the deployed API and monitor and analyze the inference data using **drifts** (such as data drift, feature drift, and model drift) to measure the performance of an ML system. Finally, we will look at several concepts to govern ML systems for the robust performance of ML systems to drive continuous learning and delivery.

Let's start by reflecting on the need to monitor ML in production. Then, we will move on to explore the following topics in this chapter:

- Serving, monitoring, and maintaining models in production
- Exploring different modes of serving ML models
- Implementing the Explainable Monitoring framework
- Governing your ML system

Serving, monitoring, and maintaining models in production

There is no point in deploying a model or an ML system and not monitoring it. Monitoring performance is one of the most important aspects of an ML system. Monitoring enables us to analyze and map out the business impact an ML system offers to stakeholders in a qualitative and quantitative manner. In order to achieve maximum business impact, users of ML systems need to be served in the most convenient manner. After that, they can consume the ML system and generate value. In previous chapters, we developed and deployed an ML model to predict the weather conditions at a port as part of the business use case that we had been solving for practical implementation. In this chapter, we will revisit the Explainable Monitoring framework that we discussed in *Chapter 11*, *Key Principles for Monitoring Your ML System*, and implement it within our business use case. In *Figure 12.1*, we can see the **Explainable Monitoring** framework and some of its components, as highlighted in green:

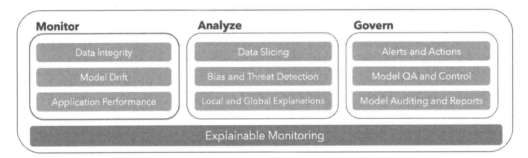

Figure 12.1 – Components of the Explainable Monitoring framework to be implemented

We will implement Explainable Monitoring for these areas: *Data Integrity*, *Model Drift*, *Application Performance*, *Bias and Threat Detection*, *Local and Global Explanations*, *Alerts and Actions*, *Model QA and Control*, and *Model Auditing and Reports*. These components are the most significant, in our use case, to understand the implementation of Explainable Monitoring. We will leave out *Data Slicing* because we do not have much variety in terms of the demographics or samples within the data (for example, sex, age groups, and more). By using information from other components, we can assess the model's performance and its fairness. In this chapter, we will implement components of the **Monitor** and **Analyze** modules: *Data Integrity*, *Model Drift*, *Application Performance*, *Bias and Threat Detection*, and *Local and Global Explanations*. The remaining component implementations will be covered in *Chapter 13*, *Governing the ML System for Continual Learning*. Before we move on to the implementation process, let's take a look at how models can be served for users to consume.

Exploring different modes of serving ML models

In this section, we will consider how a model can be served for users (both humans and machines) to consume the ML service efficiently. Model serving is a critical area, which an ML system needs to succeed at to fulfill its business impact, as any lag or bug in this area can be costly in terms of serving users. Robustness, availability, and convenience are key factors to keep in mind while serving ML models. Let's take a look at some ways in which ML models can be served: this can be via batch service or on-demand mode (for instance, when a query is made on demand in order to get a prediction). A model can be served to either a machine or a human user in on-demand mode. Here is an example of serving a model to a user:

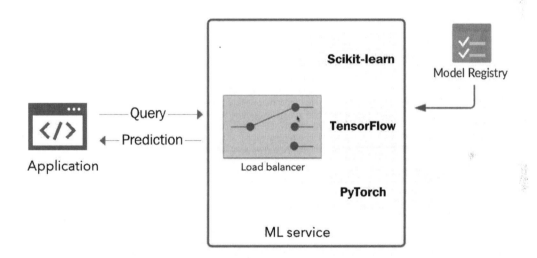

Figure 12.2 – Serving a model to users

In a typical scenario (in on-demand mode), a model is served as a service for users to consume, as shown in *Figure 12.2*. Then, an external application on a machine or a human makes a query to the prediction or ML service using their data. The ML service, upon receiving a request, uses a load balancer to route the request to an available resource (such as a container or an application) within the ML application. The load balancer also manages resources within the ML service to orchestrate and generate new containers or resources on demand. The load balance redirects the query from the user to the model running in a container within the ML application to get the prediction. On getting the prediction, the load balance reverts back to the external application on a machine, or to a human who is making the request, or to the query within the model prediction. In this way, the ML service is able to serve its users. The ML system orchestrates with the model store or registry to keep itself updated with either the latest or best-performing models in order to serve the users in the best manner. In comparison to this typical scenario where users make a query, there is another use case where the model is served as a batch service.

Serving the model as a batch service

Batch processing or serving is applied to large quantities or batches of input data (that is, not single observations but bunches of observations together). In cases where there is a large bunch of data to be inferred, a model is normally served in batch mode. One example of this is when the model is used to process the data of all consumers or users of a product or service in one go. Alternatively, a batch of data from a factory for a fixed timeline might need to be processed to detect anomalies in the machines. Compared to on-demand mode, batch mode is more resource-efficient and is usually employed when some latency can be afforded:

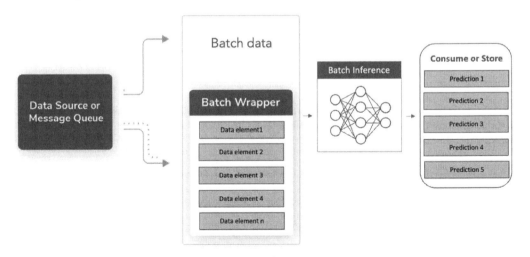

Figure 12.3 – Batch inference

One of the key advantages of batch processing is that unlike a REST API-based service, a batch service might require lighter or less infrastructure. Writing a batch job is easier for a data scientist compared to deploying an online REST service. This is because the data scientist just needs to train a model or deserialize a trained model on a machine and perform batch inference on a batch of data. The results of batch inference can be stored in a database as opposed to sending responses to users or consumers. However, one major disadvantage is the high latency and it not being in real time. Typically, a batch service can process hundreds or thousands of features at once. A series of tests can be used to determine the optimal batch size to arrive at an acceptable latency for the use case. Typical batch sizes can be 32, 64, 128, or 518 to the power of 2. Batch inference can be scheduled periodically and can serve many use cases where latency is not an issue. One such example is discussed next.

A real-world example

One real-world example is a bank extracting information from batches of text documents. A bank receives thousands of documents a day from its partner institutions. It is not possible for a human agent to read through all of them and highlight any red flags in the operations listed in the documents. Batch inferencing is used to extract name entities and red flags from all the documents received by the bank in one go. The results of the batch inference or serving are then stored in a database.

Serving the model to a human user

Before processing a request from human users, it is essential to check whether the user has adequate permissions to use the model. Additionally, in most cases, it is helpful to know the context in which the request was made. Gathering the context of the request will enable the model to produce better predictions. After gathering the context, we can transform it into model-readable input and infer the model to get a prediction.

In practice, here are the key steps in serving an on-demand model to human users:

1. Validate or authorize the request.

2. Analyze and gather contextual information (for example, historic data, user experience data, or any other personal data of the user).

3. Transform any contextual information into a model-readable input or schema.

4. Infer the model with input data (with the request and contextual information) to make a prediction or get an output.

5. Interpret the output as per the context.

6. Relay the output to the user.

> **A real-world example**
>
> Consider a chatbot serving human customers to book flight tickets. It performs contextual inference to serve human users.

Serving the model to a machine

We can serve a machine or an external application using a REST API or a streaming service based on the use case. Typically, machine inference data requirements are either predetermined or within a standard schema. A well-defined topology and data schema in the form of a REST API or streaming service will work. Serving on demand to a machine or human varies from case to case, as, in some scenarios, demand may vary (for example, at a particular time of day when the demand for serving the user might be high, such as in the afternoon). To handle a high demand from the service, autoscaling (on the cloud) can help spawn more resources on demand and kill any idle resources to free up more resources. However, autoscaling is not a one-stop solution for scaling, as it cannot handle sudden or peculiar spikes in demand on its own:

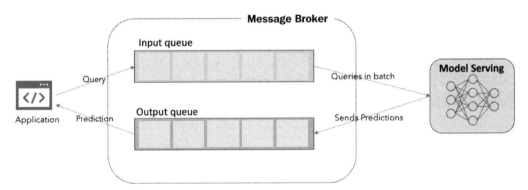

Figure 12.4 – Message broker for on-demand serving

The approach shown in *Figure 12.4* is resource-efficient to handle high volume demand spikes. To handle sudden spikes, message brokers such as Apache Kafka or Spark can be useful. A message broker runs processes to write and read to a queue: one process to write messages in a queue and another process to read from that queue. The served model is periodically connected to the message broker to process batches of input data from the queue to make predictions for each element in the batch. After processing the input data batches and generating predictions, the predictions are written to the output queue, which is then pushed to the users as per their requests.

A real-world example

Consider a social media company that has millions of users. The company uses a single or common ML model for the recommender system to recommend newsfeed articles or posts to users. As the volume of requests is high in order to serve many users, it cannot depend on a REST API-based ML system (as it is synchronous). A streaming solution is better as it provides asynchronous inference for the company to serve its users. When a user logs into their application or account hosted on a machine (such as a social media company server), the application running on their machine infers the ML model (that is, the recommender system) via a streaming service for recommendations for the user newsfeed. Likewise, thousands of other users log in at the same time. The streaming service can serve all of these users seamlessly. Note that this wouldn't have been possible with the REST API service. By using a streaming service for the recommender system model, the social media company is able to serve its high volume of users in real time, avoiding significant lags.

Implementing the Explainable Monitoring framework

To implement the Explainable Monitoring framework, it is worth doing a recap of what has been discussed so far, in terms of implementing hypothetical use cases. Here is a recap of what we did for our use case implementation, including the problem and solution:

- **Problem context**: You work as a data scientist in a small team with three other data scientists for a cargo shipping company based in the port of Turku in Finland. 90% of the goods imported into Finland arrive via cargo shipping at various ports across the country. For cargo shipping, weather conditions and logistics can be challenging at times. Rainy conditions can distort operations and logistics at the ports, which can affect supply chain operations. Forecasting rainy conditions in advance allows us to optimize resources such as human resources, logistics, and transport resources for efficient supply chain operations at ports. Business-wise, forecasting rainy conditions in advance enables ports to reduce their operational costs by up to approximately 20% by enabling the efficient planning and scheduling of human resources, logistics, and transport resources for supply chain operations.

- **Task or solution**: You, as a data scientist, are tasked to develop an ML-driven solution to forecast weather conditions 4 hours in advance at the port of Turku in Finland. This will enable the port to optimize its resources, thereby enabling cost savings of up to 20%. To get started, you are provided with a historic weather dataset with a 10-year-timeline from the port of Turku (the dataset can be accessed in the Git repository of this book). Your task is to build a continuous learning-driven ML solution to optimize operations at the port of Turku.

So far, we have developed ML models and deployed them as REST API endpoints inside a Kubernetes cluster at `http://20.82.202.164:80/api/v1/service/weather-prod-service/score` (the address of your endpoint will be different).

Next, we will replicate a real-life inference scenario for this endpoint. To do this, we will use the test dataset we had split and registered in *Chapter 4, Machine Learning Pipelines*, in the *Data ingestion and feature engineering* section. Go to your Azure ML workspace and download the `test_data.csv` dataset (which was registered as `test_dataset`) from the **Datasets** section or the Blob storage that is connected to your workspace, as shown in *Figure 12.5*:

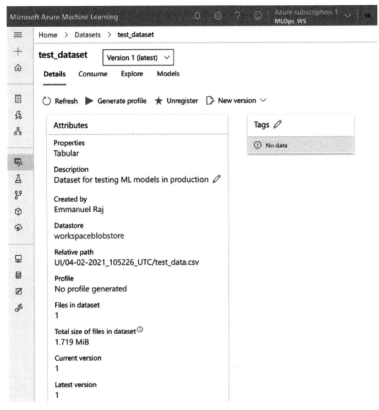

Figure 12.5 – Downloading the validation dataset (which was previously split and registered)

Get ready to infer the `test_data.csv` data with the REST API endpoint or ML service. Go to the `12_Model_Serving_Monitoring` folder and place the downloaded dataset (`test_data.csv`) inside the folder. Next, access the `inference. py` file:

```
import json
import requests
import pandas as pd

data = pd.read_csv('test_data.csv')
data = data.drop(columns=['Timestamp', 'Location', 'Future_
weather_condition'])

url = 'http://20.82.202.164:80/api/v1/service/weather-prod-
service/score'
headers = {'Content-Type':'application/json'}

for I in range(len(data)):
            inference_data = data.values[i].tolist()
            inference_data = json.dumps(""dat"": [inference_
data]})
            r = requests.post(url, data=inference_data,
headers=headers)
            print(str(i)+str(r.content))
```

In the preceding code, we perform the following steps:

1. In the `inference.py` file, begin by importing the necessary libraries, such as `json`, `requests`, and `pandas`.

2. Next, import the dataset (`test_data.csv`) to use to infer with the endpoint.

3. Drop the unnecessary columns for inference, such as `Timestamp`, `Location`, and `Future_weather_condition` (we will predict this final column by querying the endpoint).

4. Next, point to the URL of the endpoint (you can find this by navigating to **Azure ML Workspace | Endpoints | Weather-prod-service | Consume**). For simplicity, since we did not have authentication or keys set up for the service, we have the header application/JSON with no keys or authentication.

5. Finally, we will loop through the data array by inferring each element in the array with the endpoint. To run the script, simply replace `'url'` with your endpoint and run the following command in the Terminal (from the folder location) to execute the script:

```
>> python3 inference.py
```

The running script will take around 10–15 minutes to infer all of the elements of the inference data. After this, we can monitor the inference and analyze the results of the inferring data. Let's monitor and analyze this starting with data integrity.

Monitoring your ML system

The **Monitor** module is dedicated to monitoring the application in production (that is, serving the ML model). The action monitor module has the following three functionalities:

- Data integrity:

    -To register the target dataset

    -To create a data drift monitor

    -To perform data drift analysis

    -To perform feature drift analysis

- Model drift

- Application performance

Let's take a look at each of these functionalities in more detail next.

Data integrity

To monitor data integrity for inference data, we need to monitor data drift and feature drift to see whether there are any anomalous changes in the incoming data or any new patterns:

- **Data drift**: This is when the properties of the independent variables change. For example, data changes can occur due to seasonality or the addition of new products or changes in consumer desires or habits, as it did during the COVID-19 pandemic.

- **Feature drift**: This is when properties of the feature(s) change over time. For example, the temperature is changing due to changing seasons or seasonality, that is, in summer, the temperature is warmer compared to temperatures during winter or autumn.

To monitor drifts, we will measure the difference for the baseline dataset versus the target dataset. The first step is to define the baseline dataset and the target dataset. This depends on use case to use case; we will use the following datasets as the baseline and target datasets:

- **Baseline dataset**: This is the training dataset.

- **Target dataset**: This is the inference dataset.

We will use the training dataset that we previously used to train our models as the baseline dataset. This is because the model used in inference knows the patterns in the training dataset very well. The training dataset is ideal for comparing how inference data changes over time. We will compile all the inference data collected during inference into the inference dataset and compare these two datasets (that is, the baseline dataset and the target dataset) to gauge data and feature drifts for the target dataset.

Registering the target dataset

The training dataset was registered in *Chapter 4, Machine Learning Pipelines*, in the *Data ingestion and feature engineering* section. We need to register the inference dataset within the **Datasets** section of the Azure ML workspace.

Inference data is collected as a result of using the `azureml.monitoring` SDK (the `modelDataCollector` function). By enabling monitoring functions using the `modelDataCollector` function in your scoring file (in `score.py`, as we did in *Chapter 6*, *Key Principles of Deploying Your ML System*), we store inference data in the form of a time-series dataset in the Blob storage. In the Blob storage connected to your Azure ML workspace, inference data is stored in the `modeldata` container. In the `modeldata` container, the inference data (including both inputs and outputs) is stored the form of CSV files that are partitioned inside folders. These are structured as per year, per month, and per day (when the inference data was recorded in the production). Inside the partitioned folders, inference data is stored in CSV files that are named `inputs.csv` and `outputs.csv`. We need to register these `input.csv` files to monitor data drift and feature drift. Follow these steps to register the `input.csv` files:

1. Go to the **Datasets** section and click on **Create dataset**. Then, select the **From datastore** option, as shown in *Figure 12.6*:

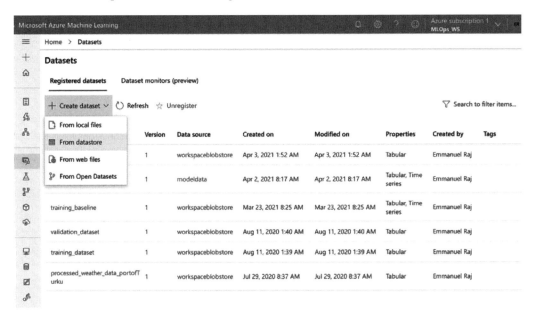

Figure 12.6 – Registering the inference dataset

2. Name the dataset (for example, `Inputs-Inference-Dataset`), select the dataset type as **Tabular**, and write an appropriate description in the **Description** field name by describing the purpose of your dataset. Click on **Next** to specify the datastore selection. Select the **modeldata** datastore, as shown in *Figure 12.7*:

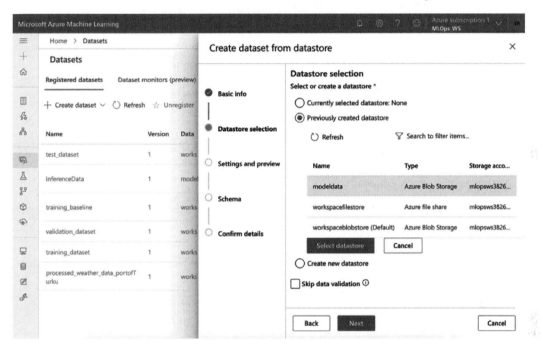

Figure 12.7 – Datastore selection (the Inputs-Inference-data registration)

3. After selecting the **modeldata** datastore, you will be prompted to mention the path of the file(s). Click on the **Browse** button to specify the path. You will be presented with a list of files in your **modeldata** datastore. Go to the location where you can spot an `input.csv` file. You can find this in the folder of your `support vectorclassifier model`, which is inside the folder with your service name (for example, `prod-webservice`). Then, go into the subfolders (the default, inputs, and folders structured with dates), and go to the folder of your current date to find the `input.csv` file. Select the **input.csv** file, as shown in *Figure 12.8*:

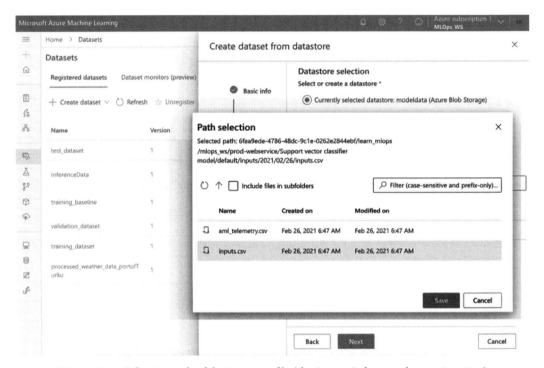

Figure 12.8 – Selecting path of the input.csv file (the Inputs-Inference-data registration)

4. After selecting the `input.csv` file, click on the **Save** button and change the last
    part to include `/**/inputs*.csv` (as shown in *Figure 12.9*). This is an important
    step that will refer to all of the `input.csv` files in the `inputs` folder dynamically.
    Without referencing all of the `input.csv` files, we will confine the path to only
    one `input.csv` file (which was selected previously in *Figure 12.8*). By referring to
    all of the `input.csv` files, we will compile all of the input data (the `inputs.csv`
    files) into the target dataset (for example, `Inputs-Inference-Data`):

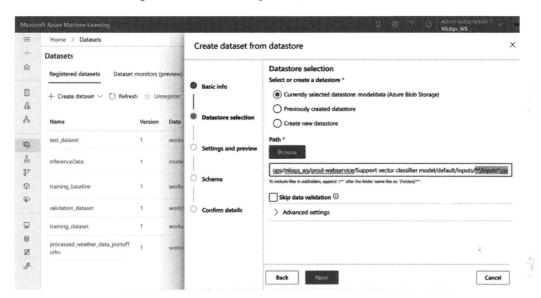

Figure 12.9 – Referencing the path to dynamically access all the input.csv files

5. Click on the **Next** button to advance to **Settings and preview**:

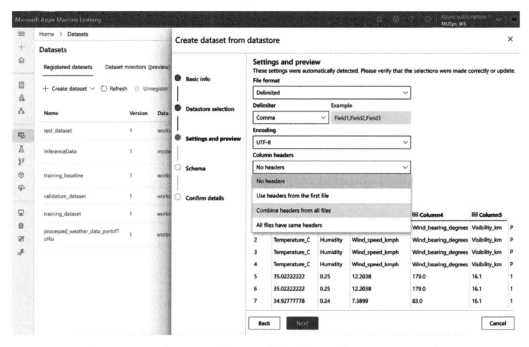

Figure 12.10 – Settings and preview (the inference dataset registration)

As shown in *Figure 12.10*, we can configure the settings and preview the dataset. Point to the correct column names by selecting the **Column headers** dropdown and then selecting **Combine headers from all files**. Check for the correct column names (for example, **Temperature_C** and **Humidity**). After selecting the appropriate column names, click on the **Next** button to advance to the next window. Select the right schema by selecting all the columns you would like to monitor, along with their data types, as shown in *Figure 12.11*:

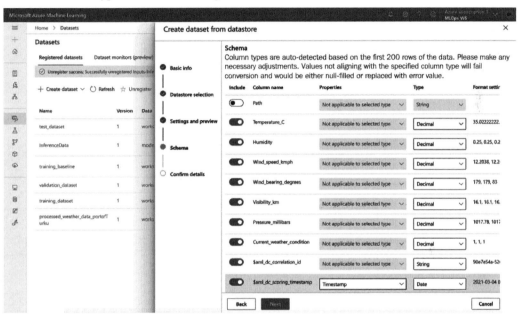

Figure 12.11 – Schema selection (the inference dataset registration)

Make sure that you select the **Timestamp** and **Date** properties in the **$aml_dc_scoring_timestamp** column as these contain the timestamps of the inference. This step is important. Only a time-series format dataset can be used to compute drift (by the Azure drift model); otherwise, we cannot compute drift. After selecting the right schema by selecting all of the columns, click on **Next** to confirm all of the necessary details (such as the name of the dataset, the dataset version, its path, and more).

6. Click on the **Create** button to create the dataset. When your dataset has been created successfully, you can view the dataset from the **Dataset** section in your Azure ML workspace. Go to the **Datasets** section to confirm your dataset has been created. Identify and click on your created dataset. Upon clicking, you will be able to view the details of your registered inference dataset, as shown in *Figure 12.12*:

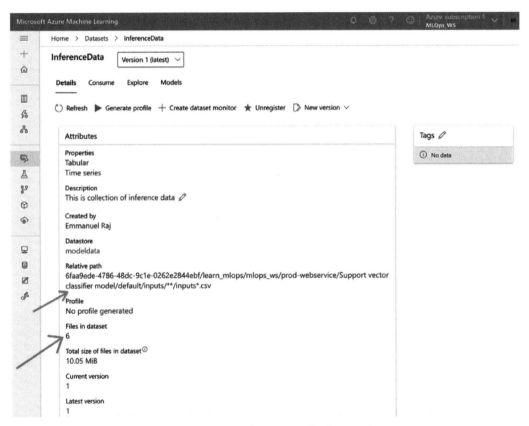

Figure 12.12 – Viewing the registered inference dataset

You can see all the essential attributes of your registered dataset in *Figure 12.12*. It is important to note that the relative path is dynamic and it points to the referencing all of the `input.csv` files. The result of referencing all of the input files is shown in **Files in dataset**. This will show multiple files in the long run (that is, it shows 6 files after 6 days of registering the dataset). It might be 1 file for you, as you have only just registered the dataset. With the passing of days or time, the number of `input.csv` files will keep increasing as a new `input.csv` file is created in the datastore in Blob storage each day. Congratulations on registering the inference data. Next, we will configure the data drift monitor.

Creating the data drift monitor

To monitor data drift and feature drift, we will use built-in drift monitoring features from the Azure ML workspace as part of the **Datasets** section. To monitor drifts, let's set up a `Data Drift Monitor` feature on our Azure ML workspace:

1. Go to your workspace and access the **Datasets** section. Then, select **Dataset Monitors** (it is in preview mode at the moment, as this feature is still being tested). Click on **Create**, as shown in *Figure 12.13*:

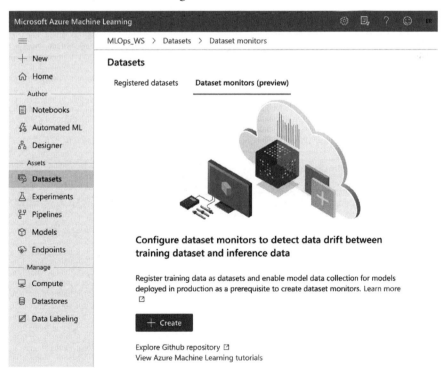

Figure 12.13 – Creating the data drift monitor

2. Upon selecting the **Create** button, you will be prompted to create a new data drift monitor. Select the target dataset of your choice.

3. In the *Registering the target dataset* section, we registered the `inputs.csv` files as `Input-InferenceData`. Select your inference dataset as the target dataset, as shown in *Figure 12.14*:

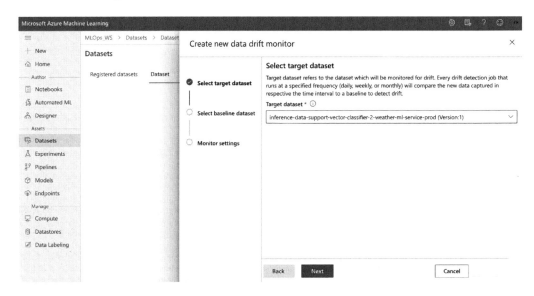

Figure 12.14 – Select target dataset

4. After selecting your target dataset, you will be prompted to point to your baseline dataset, which should be your training dataset (it was used to train your deployed ML model). Select your baseline dataset, as shown in *Figure 12.15*:

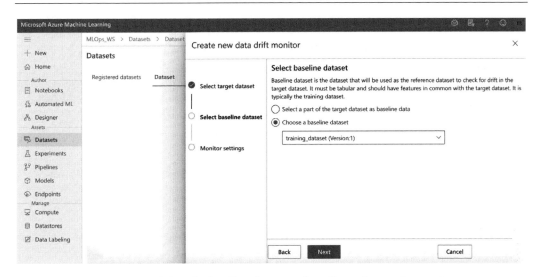

Figure 12.15 – Select the baseline dataset and configure the monitor settings

5.   After selecting the baseline dataset, you will be prompted to set up monitor settings, such as the name of data drift monitor (for example, `weather-Data-Drift`), the compute target to run data drift jobs, the frequency of data drift jobs (for example, once a day), and the threshold for monitoring drift (for example, 60). You will also be asked to give an email of your choice to receive notifications when the data drift surpasses a set threshold.

6.   After configuring the settings, create a data drift monitor. Go to your newly created data drift (in the **Datasets** section, click on **Dataset Monitors** to view your drift monitors), as shown in *Figure 12.16*:

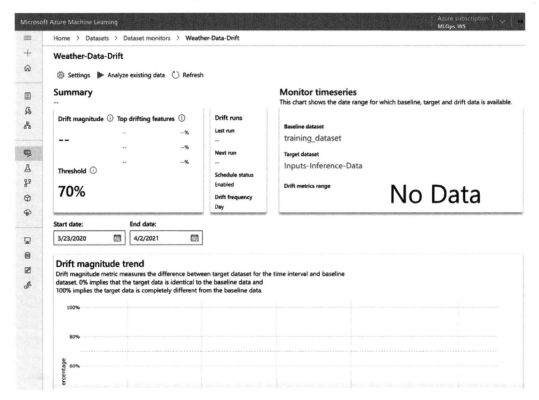

Figure 12.16 – Data drift overview (it is currently empty)

When you access your data drift monitor, you will see that there is no data. This is because we haven't computed any drift yet. In order to compute drift, we need a compute resource.

7. Go to the **Compute** section, access the **Compute clusters** tab, and create a new compute resource (for example, **drift-compute – Standard_DS_V2 machine**), as shown in *Figure 12.17*:

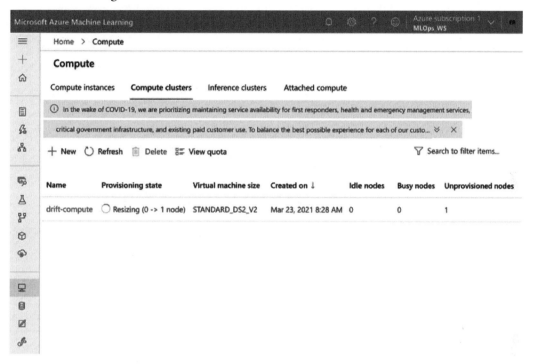

Figure 12.17 – Creating a compute cluster to compute data drift

8. After creating the compute cluster, go back to your data drift monitor (for example, **Weather-Data-Drift**). Next, we will compute the data drift.

9. Click on **Analyze existing data** and submit a run to analyze any existing inference data, as shown in *Figure 12.18*:

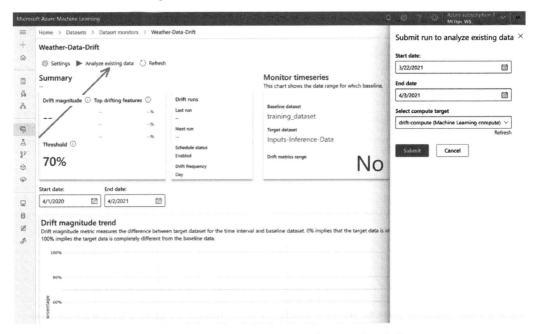

Figure 12.18 – Submitting run to analyze any data drift

10. Select the start and end dates and the compute target (which was created previously, that is, **drift-compute**). Then, click on **Submit** to run drift computation. It will usually take around 10 minutes to analyze and compute data drift. You can track the progress of your runs in the **Experiments** section of your Azure ML workspace.

    Data drift analysis: After successfully finishing the run, data drift has been computed. Using the drift overview, as shown in *Figure 12.19*, we can monitor and analyze your ML model performance in production. We can view the data drift magnitude and drift distribution by features:

Figure 12.19 – Data Drift magnitude trend

The way that model drift is measured by the Azure ML service is that it uses a separate drift model (maintained by Azure), which looks at the baseline and compares inference data. This comparison results in a simple statistical percentage or degree of change in data.

In *Figure 12.19*, the **Drift magnitude trend** suggests that we have had inferences made to the model on 3 days (that is, **03/23/21**, **04/03/21**, and **04/04/21**).

The analysis shows that the data drift on these three occasions is below the threshold of 70% (this is the red line, which indicates the threshold). The data drift on **03/23/21** is around 50%; on **04/03/21**, it is around 44%; and on **04/04/21**, it is 40%. This gives us an idea of the changing trend in the incoming inference data to the model. Likewise, we can monitor feature drift.

- **Feature drift analysis**: You can assess individual features and their drift by scrolling down to the **Feature details** section and selecting a feature of your choice. For example, we can see the **Temperature_C** distribution over time feature, as shown in *Figure 12.20*:

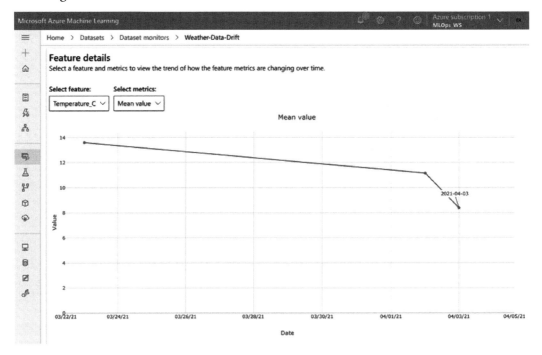

Figure 12.20 – Feature drift trend (Temperature_C)

To monitor the feature change over time, we can select some metrics of our choice for the feature. Metrics such as **Mean value**, **Min value**, **Max value**, **Euclidean distance**, or **Wasserstein distance** are available to analyze feature drift. Select a metric of your choice (for example, **Mean value**). We have selected the **Mean value** metric to assess the temperature drift, as shown in *Figure 12.20*. The **Mean value** metric has changed from 14 to 8 as time has progressed; this shows the change of drift in the **Temperature_C** feature. Such a change is expected as seasonal changes give rise to changes in temperature. We can also monitor feature distribution change, as shown in *Figure 12.21*:

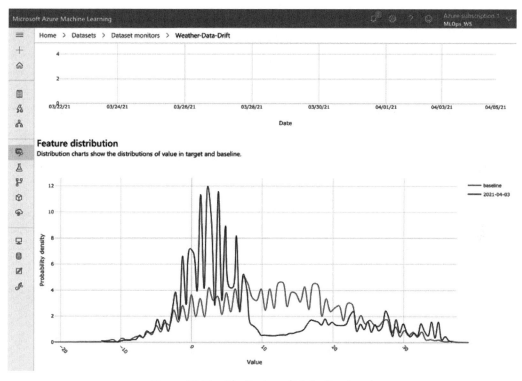

Figure 12.21 – The Feature distribution trend

If the drift is drastic or anomalous, we need to check for the quality of input data being inferred into the system. Insights into feature drift enable us to understand the changing data and world around us. Likewise, we can monitor model drift to understand the model performance in accordance with the changing data and world.

Model drift

Monitoring model drift enables us to keep a check on our model performance in production. Model drift is where the properties of dependent variables change. For example, in our case, this is the classification results of the weather (that is, rain or no rain). Just as we set up data drift in the *Creating the data drift monitor* section, we can also set up a model drift monitor to monitor model outputs. Here are the high-level steps to set up model drift:

1. Register a new dataset (for example, **Output-Inference-Data**) by referencing all of the `Outputs.csv` files. The **Outputs** dataset can be created from the **Datasets** section. When creating an outputs inference dataset, select the important columns (for example, **Future_Weather_Condition**) and change the dataset into tabular and time-series format (drift can only be computed in time-series data) by selecting a column with **Timestamp**.

2. Create a new monitor (for example, the model drift monitor) from the **Dataset** section, and click on **Dataset Monitor**. Select the feature to monitor (for example, **future weather condition**) and set a threshold that you want to monitor.

3. Analyze the model drift in the overview (as shown in *Figure 12.22*):

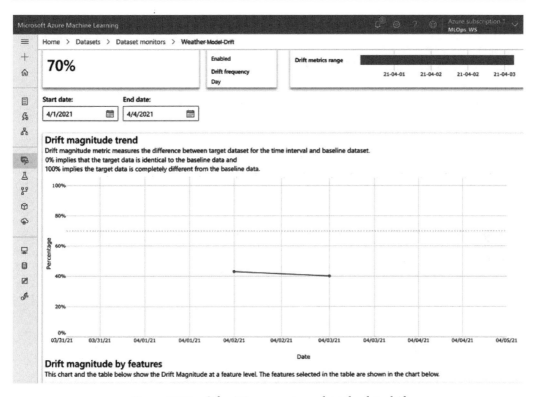

Figure 12.22 – Submitting a run to analyze the data drift

If your model drift has surpassed a set threshold, then that may be an indication that you should retrain or train your model comparison results in a simple statistical percentage or a degree of change in data. When the data drift has gone past the threshold (for example, 70%), we can notify the administrator or product owner via email or take actions such as deploying another model or retraining the existing model. Using smart actions, we can govern ML systems to produce maximum value. We will explore ways to govern ML systems in the next chapter (*Chapter 13, Governing the ML System for Continual Learning*). So far, we have implemented the setting up data drift, feature drift, and model drift. Next, let's monitor the ML system's application performance.

Application performance

You have deployed the ML service in the form of REST API endpoints, which can be consumed by users. We can monitor these endpoints using Azure Application Insights (enabled by Azure Monitor). To monitor our application performance, access the Application Insights dashboard, as shown in *Figure 12.23*. Go to the **Endpoints** section in your Azure ML service workspace and select the REST API endpoint your ML model is deployed on. Click on **Application Insights url** to access the Application Insights endpoint connected to your REST API endpoint:

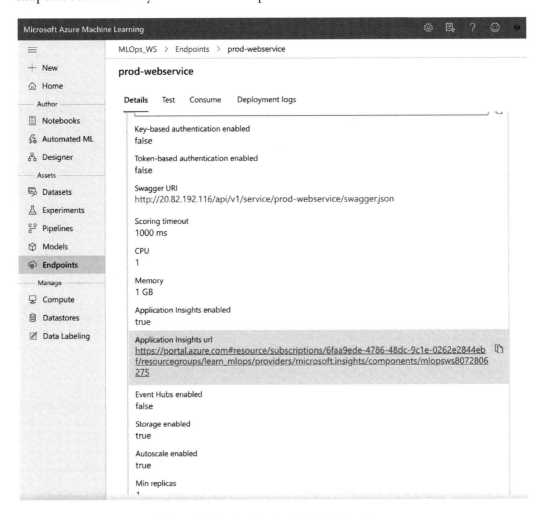

Figure 12.23 – Application Insights Overview

From the **Application Insights Overview** section, we can monitor and analyze critical application performance information for your ML service. Additionally, we can monitor information such as failed requests, server response time, server requests, and availability from the **Overview** section, as shown in *Figure 12.24*:

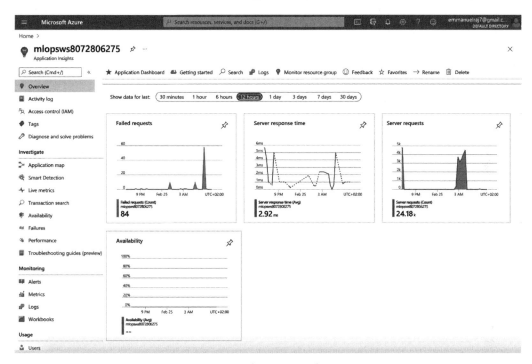

Figure 12.24 – Application Insights Overview

Based on these metrics and this information, we can monitor the application performance. Ideally, we should not have any failed requests or long server response times. To get deeper insights into the application performance, we can access the application dashboard (by clicking on the button at the top of the screen), as shown in *Figure 12.25*:

Figure 12.25 – Application dashboard with a more detailed performance assessment

From the application dashboard, we can monitor the application performance in more detail. For instance, we can monitor application usage, reliability, and other information. In terms of usage, **Unique sessions and users** is critical information to monitor the number of unique users the application is able to serve. Additionally, the **Average availability** information is useful to assess the availability of the service for our users. With this information, we can make scaling decisions if more resources are needed to serve users.

We can monitor application reliability by assessing information such as the number of failed requests, server exceptions, and dependency failures. We can monitor responsiveness using information such as the average server response time and CPU utilization. Ideally, the application should not have any failures, and if there are any failures, we can take a deeper look into the application logs, as shown in *Figure 12.26*, by accessing **Transaction search** or logs:

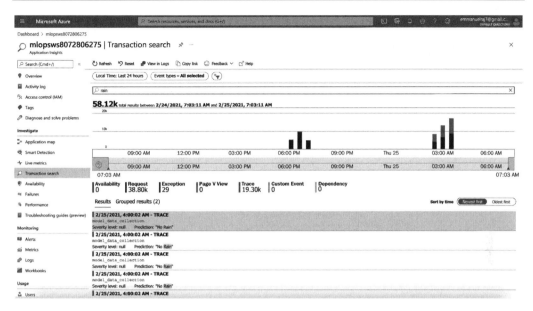

Figure 12.26 – Accessing the logs to understand any errors or failures

We can take a closer look into the logs of applications to understand any failures or errors in order to debug the application and maintain the healthy functioning of the application. A functional ML application results in satisfied users and maximum business impact. Therefore, monitoring applications can be rewarding to reveal potential failures and maintain the application in order to serve users in the most efficient way.

Analyzing your ML system

Monitoring and analyzing your ML system in production in real time is key to understanding the performance of your ML system and ensuring its robustness to produce maximized business value. Humans play a key role in analyzing model performance and detecting subtle anomalies and threats. We can analyze model performance to detect any biases or threats and to understand why the model makes decisions in a certain pattern. We can do this by applying advanced techniques, such as data slicing, adversarial attack prevention techniques, or by understanding local and global explanations.

Data slicing

For our use case, we will leave out data slicing as we do not have much variety in terms of demographics or samples within the data (for example, sex, age groups, and more). To measure the fairness of the model, we will focus on bias detection.

Bias and threat detection

To determine the model bias in production, we can use a bias-variance trade-off method. This makes it simple to monitor and analyze the model bias or any possible threat. It goes without saying that there might be better methods to monitor bias, but the idea here is to keep it simple, as, sometimes, simplicity is better and more efficient.

The disparity between our model's average prediction and the right value we are attempting to predict is the bias. Variance is the variability of the estimation of the model for a given data point or a value that informs us of our data spread. Analyzing bias and variance for inference data for the deployed model reveals the bias to be 20.1 and variance to be 1.23 (you can read more on analyzing bias and variance at `https://machinelearningmastery.com/calculate-the-bias-variance-trade-off/`). This means our model has high bias and low variance; therefore, it might be a good idea to train or retrain our model with inference data to balance the bias-variance.

Local and global explanations

Local and global explanations offer different perspectives on model performance. Local explanation offers a justification for model prediction for a specific or individual input, whereas global explanation provides insights into the model's predictive process, independent of any particular input. We previously looked at global explanations while exploring monitoring drifts in *Figure 12.19*. We can further investigate feature distribution, as shown in *Figure 12.21*, to understand local explanations in detail.

Analyzing your ML system for fairness, bias, and local and global explanations gives us key insights into model performance, and we can use this information to govern our ML system.

Governing your ML system

A great part of system governance involves quality assurance and control, model auditing, and reporting to have end-to-end trackability and compliance with regulations. The ML systems' efficacy (that is, its ability to produce a desired or intended result) is dependent on the way it is governed to achieve maximum business value. So far, we have monitored and analyzed our deployed model for inference data:

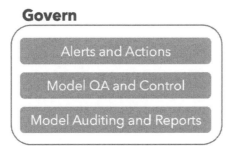

Figure 12.27 – Components of governing your ML system

The efficacy of an ML system can be determined by using smart actions that are taken based on monitoring and alerting. In the next chapter, we will explore ML system governance in terms of alerts and actions, model QA and control, and model auditing and reports.

Summary

In this chapter, we learned about the key principles of serving ML models to our users and monitoring them to achieve maximized business value. We explored the different means of serving ML models for users or consumers of the model and implemented the Explainable Monitoring framework for a hypothetical business use case and deployed a model. We carried out this hands-on implementation of an Explainable Monitoring framework to measure the performance of ML systems. Finally, we discussed the need for governing ML systems to ensure the robust performance of ML systems.

We will further explore the governance of ML systems and continual learning concepts in the next and final chapter!

13
Governing the ML System for Continual Learning

In this chapter, we will reflect on the need for continual learning in **machine learning (ML)** solutions. Adaptation is at the core of machine intelligence. The better the adaptation, the better the system. Continual learning focuses on the external environment and adapts to it. Enabling continual learning for an ML system can reap great benefits. We will look at what is needed to successfully govern an ML system as we explore continuous learning and study the governance component of the Explainable Monitoring Framework, which helps us control and govern ML systems to achieve maximum value.

We will delve into the hands-on implementation of governance by enabling alert and action features. Next, we will look into ways of assuring quality for models and controlling deployments, and we'll learn the best practices to generate model audits and reports. Lastly, we will learn about methods to enable model retraining and maintain CI/CD pipelines.

Let's start by reflecting on the need for continual learning and go on to explore the following topics in the chapter:

- Understanding the need for continual learning
- Governing an ML system using Explainable Monitoring
- Enabling model retraining
- Maintaining the CI/CD pipeline

Understanding the need for continual learning

When we got started in *Chapter 1, Fundamentals of MLOps Workflow*, we learned about the reasons AI adoption is stunted in organizations. One of the reasons was the lack of continual learning in ML systems. Yes, continual learning! We will address this challenge in this chapter and make sure we learn how to enable this capability by the end of this chapter. Now, let's look into continual learning.

Continual learning

Continual learning is built on the principle of continuously learning from data, human experts, and the external environment. Continual learning enables lifelong learning, with adaptation at its core. It enables ML systems to become intelligent over time to adapt to the task at hand. It does this by monitoring and learning from the environment and the human experts assisting the ML system. Continual learning can be a powerful add-on to an ML system. It can allow you to realize the maximum potential of an AI system over time. Continual learning is highly recommended. Let's have a look at an example:

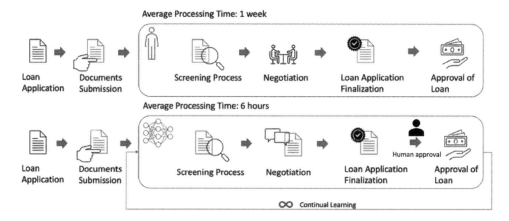

Figure 13.1 – A loan issuing scenario – a traditional system versus an ML system assisted by a human

There are several advantages to deploying a model (enabled by continual learning) compared to having a traditional process in an organization that is fully dependent on human employees. For example, in the preceding diagram, we can see the steps of a bank's loan approval process in two cases. The first scenario is driven by human experts (such as in a traditional bank setup) only. The second scenario is where the process is automated or augmented using an ML system to screen applications, negotiate, provide loan application finalization (where a human expert reviews the ML system's decision and approves or rejects it), and approve the loan. The processing time of the traditional setup is 1 week, while the processing time of the ML system (working together with human experts) is 6 hours.

The ML system is faster and more sustainable for the bank as it is continually learning and improving with a human assistant's help. Human employees have a fixed term of employment in a company or job. When they leave, their domain expertise is gone, and training a new employee or onboarding a new employee for the same task is costly. On the other hand, an ML model working together with or assisted by human experts that learns continually as time progresses manages to learn with time and retains that knowledge indefinitely (with regards to time). The continual learning that's acquired by the ML system (together with human experts) can be retained forever by the bank compared to the traditional approach, where human employees are constantly changing. Continual learning can unleash great value for an ML system and for the business in the long run.

The need for continual learning

The following diagram shows some of the reasons why continual learning is needed and how it will enhance your ML system to maximize your business value:

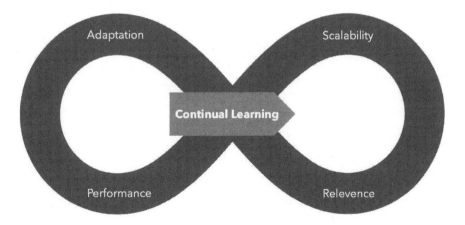

Figure 13.2 – Benefits of continual learning

Let's go through the benefits of continual learning in detail:

- **Adaptation**: In most straightforward applications, data drift might stay the same as data keeps coming in. However, many applications have dynamically changed data drifts, such as recommendation or anomaly detection systems, where data keeps flowing. In these cases, continually learning is important for adapting and being accurate with predictions. Hence, adapting to the changing nature of data and the environment is important.

- **Scalability**: A white paper published by IDC (`https://www.seagate.com/files/www-content/our-story/trends/files/idc-seagate-dataage-whitepaper.pdf`) suggests that by 2025, the rate of data generation will grow to 160 ZB/year, and that we will not be able to store all of it. The paper predicts that we will only be able to store between 3% and 12%. Data needs to be processed on the fly; otherwise, it will be lost since the storage infrastructure cannot keep up with the data that is produced. The main trick here is to process incoming data once, store only the essential information, and then get rid of the rest.

- **Relevance**: Predictions from ML systems need to be relevant and need to adapt to changing contexts. Continual learning is needed to keep the ML systems highly relevant to and valuable in the changing contexts and environments.

- **Performance**: Continual learning will enable high performance for the ML system, since it powers the ML system to be relevant by adapting to the changing data and environment. In other words, being more relevant will improve the performance of the ML system, for example, in terms of accuracy or other metrics, by providing more meaningful or valuable predictions.

For these reasons, continual learning is needed in an ML system, so without continual learning, we cannot reach the maximum value an ML system has to offer. In other words, projects are doomed to fail. Continual learning is the key to succeeding in AI projects. An efficient governance strategy as part of Explainable Monitoring can enable continual learning. An important part of continual learning is model retraining, so that we can cope with evolving data and make relevant decisions. To do this, we can fuse Explainable Monitoring and model retraining to enable continual learning:

Explainable Monitoring + Model Retraining = Continual Learning

Going ahead we will see continual learning in depth. Now, let's explore how we can bring efficient governance to ML systems.

Explainable monitoring – governance

In this section, we will implement the governance mechanisms that we learned about previously in *Chapter 11, Key Principles of Monitoring Your ML System*, for the business use case we have been working on. We will delve into three of the components of governing an ML system, as shown in the following diagram:

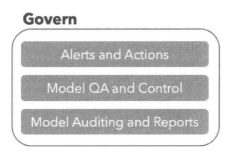

Figure 13.3 – Components of governing your ML system

The effectiveness of ML systems results from how they are governed to maximize business value. To have end-to-end trackability and comply with legislation, system governance requires quality assurance and monitoring, model auditing, and reporting. We can regulate and rule ML systems by monitoring and analyzing model outputs. Smart warnings and behavior guide governance to optimize business value. Let's look at how the ML system's governance is orchestrated by warnings and behavior, model quality assurance and control, model auditing, and reports.

Alerts and actions

Alerts are generated by performing scheduled checks to detect conditions. Upon meeting a condition, an alert is generated. Based on the alert that's generated, we can perform actions. In this section, we will learn about these elements and how they are orchestrated to govern an ML system.

What is an alert?

An alert is a scheduled task running in the background to monitor an application to check if specific conditions are being detected. An alert is driven by three things:

- **Schedule**: How often should we check for conditions?
- **Conditions**: What needs to be detected?
- **Actions**: What should we do when a condition is detected?

We can create alerts based on application performance to monitor aspects such as the following:

- Alerts for availability based on a threshold
- Alerts for failed requests based on a threshold
- Alerts for server response time based on a threshold
- Alerts for server exceptions based on a threshold
- Alerts based on a threshold for data drift
- Alerts based on a threshold for model drift
- Alerts based on errors or exceptions

An important area of governing ML systems is dealing with errors, so let's turn our attention to error handling.

Dealing with errors

Potential errors are always possible in an application. We can foresee them by addressing all the possible edge cases for our ML application. Using the framework shown in the following diagram, we can address these errors. The purpose of this framework is to identify edge cases and automated debugging methods to tackle possible errors. This will keep the ML service up and running:

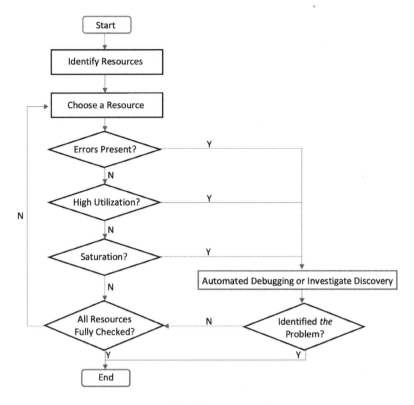

Figure 13.4 – Framework for debugging and investigating errors

As shown in the preceding diagram, we started by identifying resources where errors might be present and choosing a resource to address that error. Upon choosing a resource, we check for errors by checking for high utilization of resources and resource saturation (a resource is saturated when its capacity is fully utilized or its capacity is past a set threshold). In the case of either issue, we investigate the discovery by investigating logs and devising a solution to handle any errors. Eventually, we automate debugging by using premade scripts to handle any issues (blocking the system from functioning optimally), for example, by restarting the resource or reloading a function or file to get the resource up and running in a healthy state.

By addressing all the possible edge cases and devising automated error handling or debugging, we can make our applications failure-proof to serve our users. Having a failure-proof application enables robustness, making sure the users have a seamless experience and value from using the ML application. Once you have identified an error, address it by investigating or creating an automated debugging process and solving the error. After all, prevention is better than a cure. Hence, checking for all possible edge cases and addressing them beforehand can be rewarding.

We can handle potential errors by using exception handling functionalities. Exception handling is a programming technique that is used for dealing with rare situations that necessitate special care. Exception handling for a wide range of error types is easy to implement in Python. We can use the `try`, `except`, `else`, and `finally` functionalities to handle errors and exceptions, as shown in the following diagram:

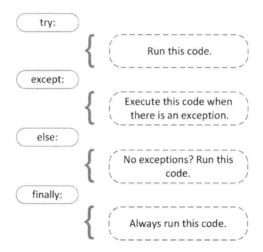

Figure 13.5 – Handling exceptions and edge cases

All the statements are executed before an exception is encountered in the `try` clause. The exception(s) that are found in the `try` clause are caught and treated with the `except` block. The `else` block allows you to write parts that can only run if there are no exceptions in the `try` clause. Using `finally`, with or without any previously experienced exceptions, you can run parts of code that should always run.

Here is a list of some possible common exceptions or errors to look out for:

S.no	Error Name	Cause
1	FileNotFound	When a file or artifact is not found in a mentioned location.
2	TimeoutError	Time to perform a process exceeds the default timeout of the executing function or process.
3	IndexError	The code is attempting to reach an invalid index outside the bounds of a list.
4	KeyError	The code is attempting to reach an invalid key in a dictionary.
5	TypeError	If you try to call a function or use an operator on anything of the wrong type. This typically happens when a value is not of the expected type.
6	RuntimeError	When the program cannot execute your code.

These edge cases or errors are common and can be addressed in the application by using `try` and `exception` techniques. The strategy is to mitigate situations where your ML system will look very basic or naive for the user; for example, a chatbot that sends error messages in the chats. In such cases, the cost of errors is high, and the users will lose trust in the ML system.

We will implement some custom exception and error handling for the business use case we have been implementing and implement actions based on the alerts that are generated. Let's get started:

1. In your Azure DevOps project, go to our **book repository (previously cloned in your Azure DevOps project)** and go to the folder named 13_ Govenance_Continual_Learning. From there, access the score.py file. We will begin by importing the required libraries. This time, we will use the applicationinsights library to track custom events or exceptions of Application Insights that are connected to the endpoint:

```
import json
import numpy as np
import os
import pickle
import joblib
import onnxruntime
import logging
import time
from azureml.core.model import Model
from applicationinsights import TelemetryClient
from azureml.monitoring import ModelDataCollector
from inference_schema.schema_decorators import input_
schema, output_schema
from inference_schema.parameter_types.numpy_parameter_
type import NumpyParameterType
```

As shown in the preceding code, we have imported the TelemetryClient function from the applicationinsights library. We will use the TelemetryClient function to access the Application Insights that are connected to our endpoint. Provide your instrumentation key from Application Insights to the TelemetryClient function.

2. This **Instrumentation Key** can be accessed from your Application Insights, which should be connected to the ML application, as shown in the following screenshot:

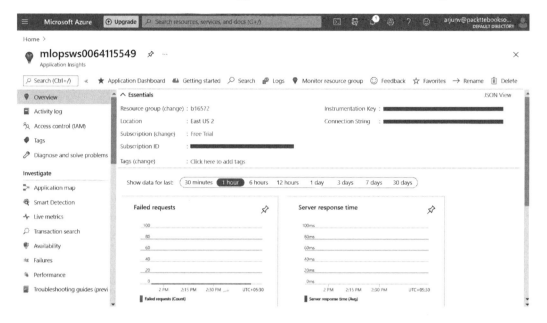

Figure 13.6 – Fetching an instrumentation key from Application Insights

3. After fetching your **Instrumentation Key**, provide the `TelemetryClient` function, as shown in the following code. Here, we create a `TelemetryClient` object in the `tc` variable, which is used to track custom events:

```
def init():
    global model, scaler, input_name, label_name, inputs_
dc, prediction_dc, tc
    tc = TelemetryClient('xxxxxxxx-xxxx-xxxx-xxxx-
xxxxxxxxxxxx')
    scaler_path = os.path.join(os.getenv('AZUREML_MODEL_
DIR'),
'model-scaler/1/model-scaler.pkl')
    # deserialize the model file back into a sklearn
model
    try:
        scaler = joblib.load(scaler_path)
    except Exception as e:
        tc.track_event('FileNotFound', {'error_message':
```

```
    str(e)},

                                        {'ErrorCode': 101})
    model_onnx = os.path.join(os.getenv('AZUREML_MODEL_
DIR'),
'support-vector-classifier/2/svc.onnx')


        try:
        model = onnxruntime.InferenceSession(model_onnx,
None)
    except Exception as e:
        tc.track_event('FileNotFound', {'error_message':
str(e)},

{'ErrorCode': 101})
    input_name = model.get_inputs()[0].name
    label_name = model.get_outputs()[0].name
    # variables to monitor model input and output data
    inputs_dc = ModelDataCollector("Support vector
classifier model", designation="inputs", feature_
names=["Temperature_C", "Humidity", "Wind_speed_kmph",
"Wind_bearing_degrees", "Visibility_km", "Pressure_
millibars", "Current_weather_condition"])
    prediction_dc = ModelDataCollector("Support vector
classifier model", designation="predictions", feature_
names=["Future_weather_condition"])
```

Two custom events are tracked in the init function to monitor whether a
FileNotFound error occurs when we load the scaler and model artifacts. If
a file is not found, the tc.track_events() function will log the error message
that's generated by the exception and tag the custom code 101.

4. Likewise, we will implement some other custom events – that is, ValueNotFound,
    OutofBoundsException, and InferenceError – in the run function:

```
@input_schema('data', NumpyParameterType(np.
array([[34.927778, 0.24, 7.3899, 83, 16.1000, 1016.51,
1]])))
@output_schema(NumpyParameterType(np.array([0])))
def run(data):


        try:
```

```
            inputs_dc.collect(data)
        except Exception as e:
            tc.track_event('ValueNotFound', {'error_
message': str(e)},
    {'ErrorCode': 201})
```

We use `try` and `except` to collect incoming data using the model data collector function. This collects the incoming data and stores it in the `blob` storage connected to the Azure ML service. If the incoming data contains some anomalous data or a missing value, an exception is raised. We will raise a `ValueNotFound` error using the `track_event` function so that we can log the exception message and custom code (in this case, a random or custom number of 201 is given to track the error). After collecting the incoming data, we will attempt to scale the data before inference:

```
        try:
            # scale incoming data
            data = scaler.transform(data)
        except Exception as e:
            tc.track_event('ScalingException',
    {'ScalingError': str(e)},
    {'ErrorCode': 301})
```

Scaling data is an important pre-inference step. We need to make sure it is done right, without any errors. `try` and `except` can be handy in this case, since we are trying to scale the data using a `scaler` file that's been loaded in the `init` function.

If scaling the data is not successful, then an exception is raised. Here, we use the `track_event` function to track the exception on Application Insights. We generate a custom event named `ScalingError` in case an exception is generated. An exception message and an error code of `301` is logged on Application Insights. Likewise, the most important step of dealing with the scoring file – inferencing the model – needs to be done meticulously.

Now, we will use `try` and `except` again to make sure the inference is successful without any exceptions. Let's see how we can handle exceptions in this case. Note that we are accessing element number 2 for the `model.run` function. This causes an error in the model's inference as we are referring to an incorrect or nonexistent element of the list:

```
try:
        # model inference
        result = model.run([label_name], {input_
name:
data.astype(np.float32)})[2]

# this call is saving model output data into Azure Blob
        prediction_dc.collect(result)
        if result == 0:
            output = "Rain"
        else:
            output = "No Rain"
        return output
    except Exception as e:
            tc.track_event('InferenceException',
{'error_message':
str(e)}, {'InferenceError': 401})

        output = 'error'
        return output
```

In case an exception occurs when the model is being inferenced, we can use the `track_event()` function to generate a custom event called `InferenceError`. This will be logged on Application Insights with an error message and a custom error code of `401`. This way, we can log custom errors and exceptions on Application Insights and generate actions based on these errors and exceptions.

Now, let's look at how to investigate these errors in Application Insights using the error logs and generate actions for it.

Setting up actions

We can set up alerts and actions based on the exception events that we created previously (in the *Dealing with errors* section). In this section, we will set up an action in the form of an email notification based on an alert that we've generated. Whenever an exception or alert is generated in Application Insights, we will be notified via an email. Then, we can investigate and solve it.

Let's set up an action (email) upon receiving an alert by going to Application Insights, which should be connected to your ML system endpoint. You can access Application Insights via your Azure ML workspace. Let's get started:

1. Go to **Endpoints** and check for Application Insights. Once you've accessed the Application Insights dashboard, click on **Transaction search**, as shown in the following screenshot, to check for your custom event logs (for example, inference exception):

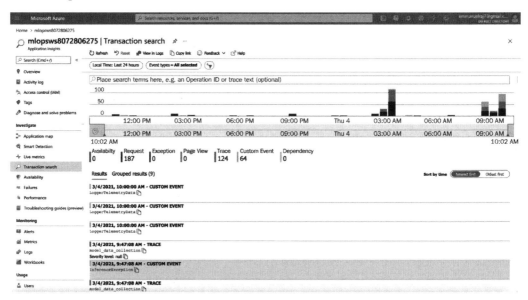

Figure 13.7 – Checking the custom event logs

2. You can check for custom events that have been generated upon exceptions and errors occurs via the logs, and then set up alerts and actions for these custom events. To set up an alert and action, go to the **Monitoring** > **Alerts** section and click on **New alert rule**, as shown in the following screenshot:

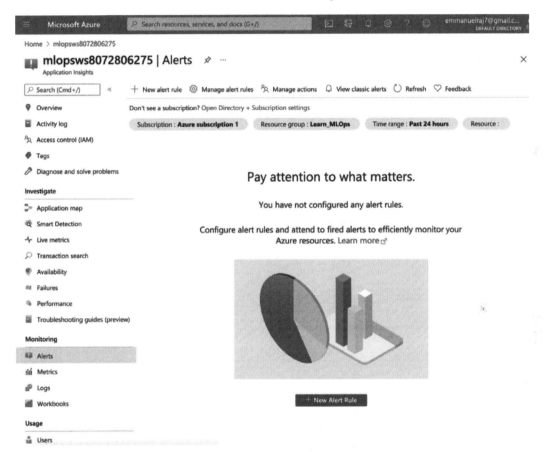

Figure 13.8 – Setting up a new alert rule

3. Here, you can create conditions for actions based on alerting. To set up a condition, click on **Add condition**. You will be presented with a list of signals or log events you can use to make conditions. Select **InferenceError**, as shown in the following screenshot:

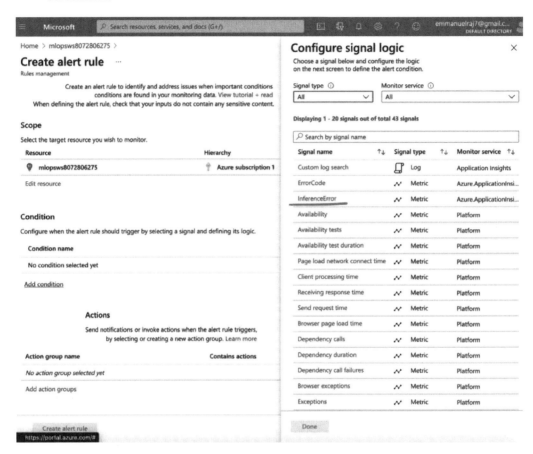

Figure 13.9 – Configuring a condition

4. After selecting the signal or event of your choice, you will get to configure its condition logic, as shown in the following screenshot. Configure the condition by setting up a threshold for it. In this case, we will provide a threshold of 400 as the error raises a value of 401 (since we had provided a custom value of 401 for the `InferenceError` event). When an inference exception occurs, it raises an `InferenceError` with a value above 400 (401, to be precise):

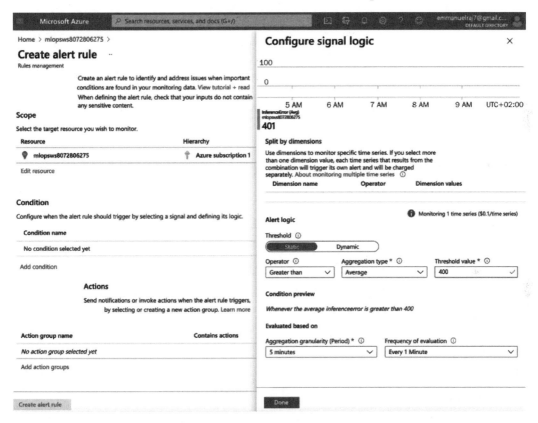

Figure 13.10 – Configuring the condition logic and threshold

5. After setting up the threshold, you will be asked to configure other actions, such as running an **Automation Runbook**, **Azure Function**, **Logic App,** or **Secure Webhook**, as shown in the following screenshot. For now, we will not prompt these actions, but it is good to know that we have them since we can run some scripts or applications as a backup mechanism to automate error debugging:

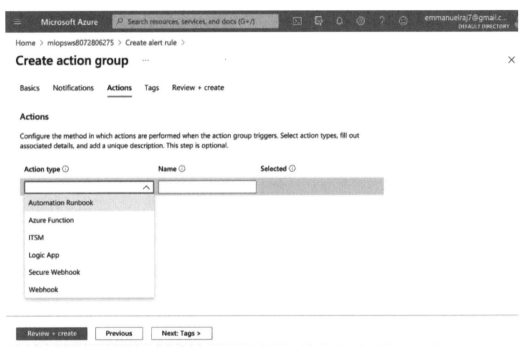

Figure 13.11 – Actions to automate debugging (optional)

This way, we can automate debugging by having pre-configured scripts or applications set up in case an error occurs or to prevent errors. Prevention is better than a cure, after all!

6. Finally, we will create a condition. Click **Review and create** to create the condition, as shown in the preceding screenshot. Once you have created this condition, you will see it in the **Create alert rule** panel, as shown in the following screenshot. Next, set up an action by clicking on **Add action groups** and then **Create action group**:

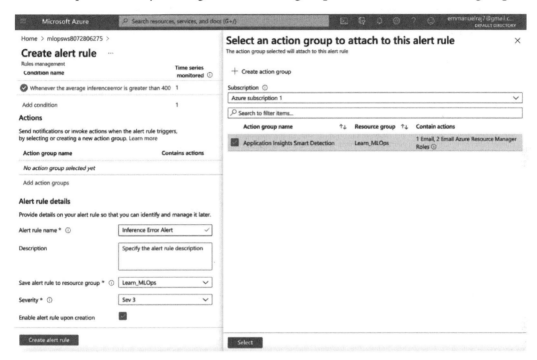

Figure 13.12 – Creating an action group

7. Provide an email address so that you can receive notifications, as shown in the following screenshot. Here, you can name your notification (in the **Alert rule name** field) and provide the necessary information to set up an email alert action:

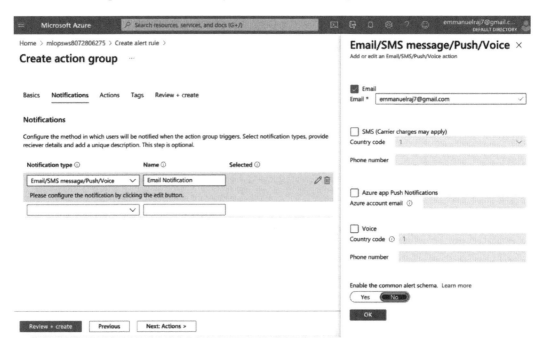

Figure 13.13 – Configuring email notifications

After providing all the necessary information, including an email, click on the **Review + Create** button to configure the action (an email based on an error). Finally, provide alert rule details such as **Alert rule name**, **Description**, and **Severity**, as shown in the following screenshot:

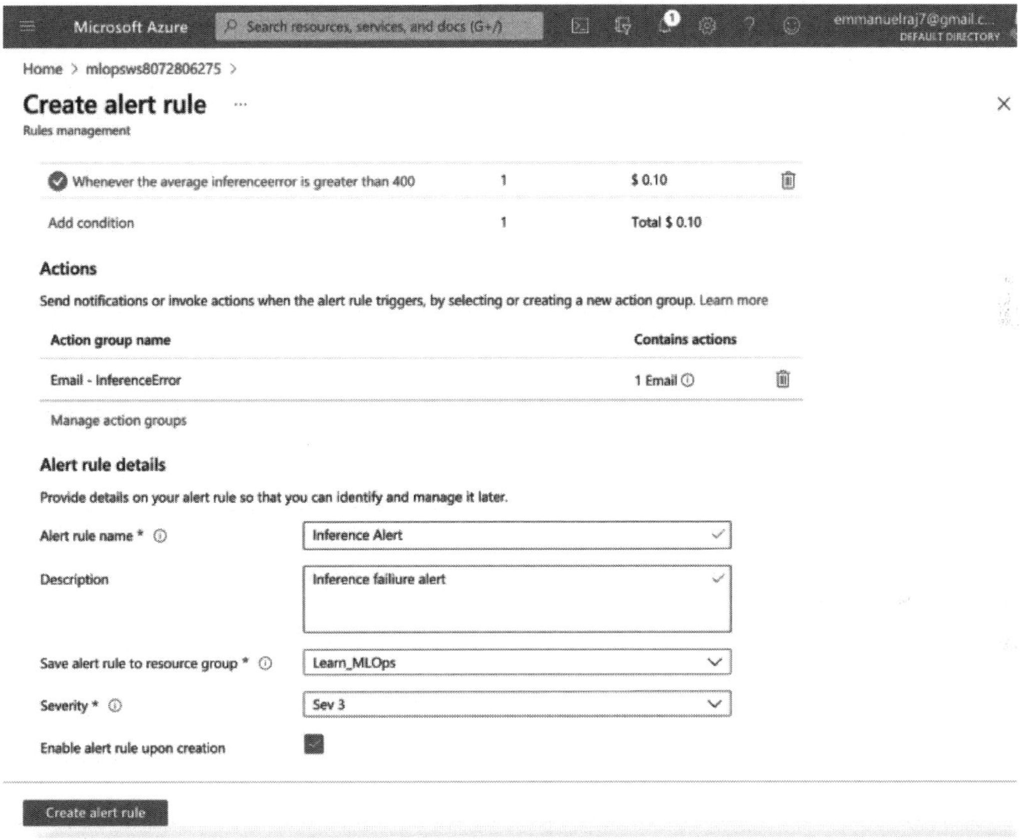

Figure 13.14 – Configuring email notifications

8. Click on **Create alert rule** to create an email alert based on the error (for example, `InferenceError`). With that, you have created an alert, so now it's time to test it. Go to the `13_Govenance_Continual_Learning` folder and access the `test_inference.py` script (replace the URL with your endpoint link). Then, run the script by running the following command:

```
python3 test_inference.py
```

9. Running the script will output an error. Stop the script after performing some inferences. Within 5-10 minutes of the error, you will be notified of the error via email, as shown in the following screenshot:

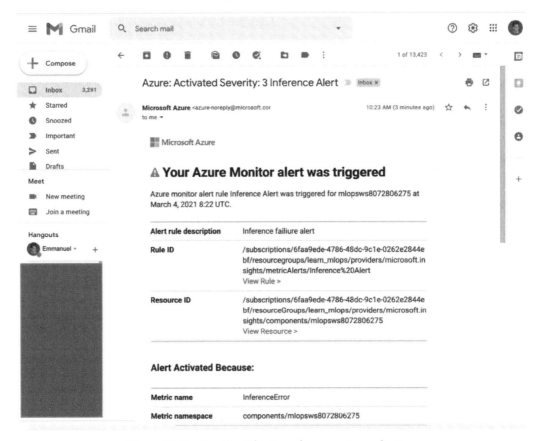

Figure 13.15 – Email notification of an error in production

Congratulations – you have successfully set up an email action alert for an error! This way, you can investigate when an error has been discovered in order to resolve it and get the system up and running.

Next, let's look at how to ensure we have quality assurance for models and can control them in order to maximize business value.

Model QA and control

Evolving or dynamically changing data leads to increased prediction error rates. This may result from data drift as the business and external environment change, or it may be due to data poisoning attacks. This increase in prediction error rates results in having to re-evaluate ML models as they are retrained (manually or automatically), leading to the discovery of new algorithms that are more accurate than the previous ones. Here are some guidelines for testing ML models with new data:

- Enable continual learning by retraining your models and evaluating their performance.

- Evaluate the performance of all the models on a new dataset at periodic intervals.

- Raise an alert when an alternative model starts giving better performance or greater accuracy than the existing model.

- Maintain a registry of models containing their latest performance details and reports.

- Maintain end-to-end lineages of all the models to reproduce them or explain their performance to stakeholders.

Model auditing and reports

Establishing a periodic auditing and reporting system for MLOps is a healthy practice as it enables an organization to track its operations end to end, as well as comply with the law and enable them to explain its operations to stakeholders upon request. We can ensure that the ML system conforms to the conventions that have been established and deliberated at the societal and governmental levels. To audit and report MLOps, it is recommended for auditors to inspect the fundamentals of an audit, shown in the following image:

Figure 13.16 – Fundamentals of an audit report for ML Operations

Data audit

Data is what drives many of the decisions made by ML systems. Due to this, the auditors need to consider data for auditing and reporting, inspecting the training data, testing the data, inferring the data, and monitoring the data. This is essential and having end-to-end traceability to track the use of data (for example, which dataset was used to train which model) is needed for MLOps. Having a *Git for Data* type of mechanism that versions data can enable auditors to reference, examine, and document the data.

Model audit (fairness and performance)

Auditors of ML systems need to have a hacker's mindset to identify the different ways in which a model could fail and not give fair predictions. First, the training data is inspected and compared to the inference data using Explainable AI techniques. This can help auditors make fair judgments about each model and each of its predictions on an individual level. To make fairness and performance assessments for each model, we can use data slicing techniques, which can reveal valuable information for making an assessment. Due to this, it is valuable for auditors to request the results of data slicing for the required demographics and slices of data. To make a collective assessment, we can compare models and assess their performance. This can reveal another angle of information for making fairness and performance assessments.

If a model audit were to proceed, it would assess the model's inputs (training data), the model itself, and its outputs. Data consistency and possible biases in the training data will need to be assessed. For example, if a resume screening model had been trained on previous or historic decisions where candidates had received job offers and workers were promoted, we'd want to make sure that the training data hasn't been influenced by past recruiters' and managers' implicit biases. Benchmarking against competing models, performing statistical tests to ensure that the model generalizes from training to unknown results, and using state-of-the-art techniques to allow model interpretability are all parts of the model evaluation process.

Project and governance audit

Is it necessary to have a deep understanding of AI models to audit algorithms? Certainly not. An audit of an AI system's progress is like a project management audit. Is there a clear target for the desired achievement? This is a good and straightforward question to ask if a government entity has implemented AI in a particular environment. Furthermore, is there a viable framework to manage the model after the developers leave, if external developers have been applied to the AI system? To reduce the need for specialist expertise, the company must have extensive documentation of concept creation and the staff who are familiar with the model. Hence, auditing the development and governance practices can be rewarding in the long run.

Auditing data considerations, model fairness and performance, and project management and governance of ML systems can provide a comprehensive view of MLOps. Using error alerts and actions, we can perform timely investigations into errors to get the system up and running and in some cases, we can even do automated debugging to automate error resolution and MLOps. Finally, by undertaking model quality assurance, control, and auditing, we can ensure efficient governance of our MLOps. Next, we will look at how to enable model retraining so that we have continual learning capabilities for our ML system.

Enabling model retraining

So far, we've talked about what model drift is and how to recognize it. So, the question is, what should we do about it? If a model's predictive performance has deteriorated due to changes in the environment, the solution is to retrain the model using a new training set that represents the current situation. How much should your model be retrained by? And how can you choose your new workout routine? The following diagram shows the **Model retrain** function triggering the **Build** module based on the results of the **Monitor** module. There are two ways to trigger the model retrain function. One is manually and the other is by automating the model retraining function. Let's see how we can enable both:

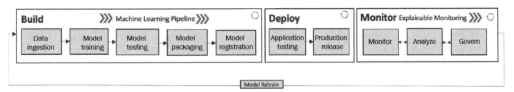

Figure 13.17 – Model retraining enabled in an MLOps workflow

Manual model retraining

The product owner or quality assurance manager has the responsibility of ensuring manual model retraining is successful. The manual model triggering step involves evaluating model drift and if it goes above a threshold (you need to determine a threshold for drift that will trigger model retraining), then they must trigger the model training process by training the model using a new dataset (this can be the previous training dataset and the latest inference data). This way, the product owner or quality assurance manager has full control over the process, and also knows when and how to trigger model retraining to deliver maximized value from the ML system.

Automated model retraining

If you want to fully automate the MLOps pipeline, automating model drift management can be an ideal approach to retraining the production model. Automating model drift management is done by configuring batch jobs that monitor application diagnostics and model performance. Then, you must activate model retraining. A key part of automating model drift management is setting the threshold that will automatically trigger the retraining model function. If the drift monitoring threshold is set too low, you run the risk of having to retrain too often, which will result in high compute costs. If the threshold is set too high, you risk not retraining often enough, resulting in suboptimal production models. Figuring out the right threshold is trickier than it seems because you have to figure out how much additional training data you'll need to reflect this new reality. Even if the environment has changed, replacing an existing model with one that has a very small training set is pointless. Once you have the threshold figured out, you could have jobs (for example, as part of the CI/CD pipeline) that compare the feature distributions of live datasets to those of training data on a regular basis (as we did in *Chapter 12, Model Serving and Monitoring*). When a large deviation is detected (or above the defined threshold), the system can schedule model retraining and deploy a new model automatically. This can be done using a work scheduler such as Jenkins or Kubernetes Jobs or CI/CD pipeline cron jobs. This way, you can fully automate the MLOps pipeline and the model retraining part.

Note that it doesn't make sense to retrain the model in cases where there is low new data coming in or if you are doing batch inference once in a blue moon (for example, every 6 months). You can train the model before inference or periodically whenever you need to.

Maintaining the CI/CD pipeline

As you may recall, in *Chapter 10, Essentials of Production Release*, we mentioned that *a model is not the product; the pipeline is the product*. Hence, after setting up automated or semi-automated CI/CD pipelines, it is critical to monitor the performance of our pipeline. We can do that by inspecting the releases in Azure DevOps, as shown in the following screenshot:

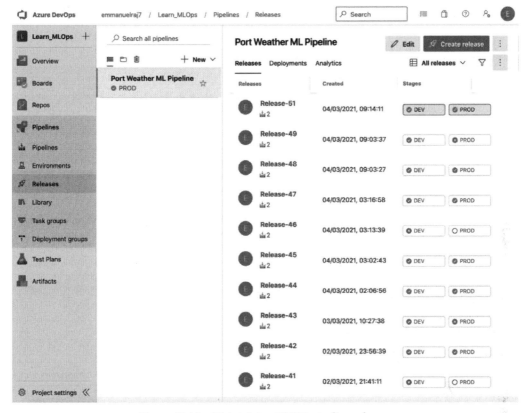

Figure 13.18 – Maintaining CI/CD pipeline releases

The goal of an inspection is to keep the CI/CD pipeline in a healthy and robust state. Here are some guidelines for keeping the CI/CD pipeline healthy and robust:

- If a build is broken, a **fix it asap** policy from the team should be implemented.

- Integrate automated acceptance tests.

- Require pull requests.

- Peer code review each story or feature.

- Audit system logs and events periodically (recommended).

- Regularly report metrics visibly to all the team members (for example, slackbot or email notifications).

By implementing these practices, we can avoid high failure rates and make the CI/CD pipeline robust, scalable, and transparent for all the team members.

Summary

In this chapter, we learned about the key principles of continual learning in ML solutions. We learned about Explainable Monitoring (the governance component) by implementing hands-on error handling and configuring actions to alert developers of ML systems using email notifications. Lastly, we looked at ways to enable model retraining and how to maintain the CI/CD pipeline. With this, you have been equipped with the critical skills to automate and govern MLOps for your use cases.

Congratulations on finishing this book! The world of MLOps is constantly evolving for the better. You are now equipped to help your business thrive using MLOps. I hope you enjoyed reading and learning by completing the hands-on MLOps implementations. Go out there and be the change you wish to see. All the best with your MLOps endeavors!

Other Books You May Enjoy

If you enjoyed this book, you may be interested in these other books by Packt:

Interpretable Machine Learning with Python

Serg Masís

ISBN: 978-1-80020-390-7

- Recognize the importance of interpretability in business
- Study models that are intrinsically interpretable such as linear models, decision trees, and Naïve Bayes
- Become well-versed in interpreting models with model-agnostic methods
- Visualize how an image classifier works and what it learns
- Understand how to mitigate the influence of bias in datasets
- Discover how to make models more reliable with adversarial robustness
- Use monotonic constraints to make fairer and safer models

Mastering Azure Machine Learning

Christoph Körner , Kaijisse Waaijer

ISBN: 978-1-78980-755-4

- Setup your Azure Machine Learning workspace for data experimentation and visualization
- Perform ETL, data preparation, and feature extraction using Azure best practices
- Implement advanced feature extraction using NLP and word embeddings
- Train gradient boosted tree-ensembles, recommendation engines and deep neural networks on Azure Machine Learning
- Use hyperparameter tuning and Azure Automated Machine Learning to optimize your ML models
- Deploy, operate and manage your ML models at scale

Packt is searching for authors like you

If you're interested in becoming an author for Packt, please visit `authors.packtpub.com` and apply today. We have worked with thousands of developers and tech professionals, just like you, to help them share their insight with the global tech community. You can make a general application, apply for a specific hot topic that we are recruiting an author for, or submit your own idea.

Leave a review - let other readers know what you think

Please share your thoughts on this book with others by leaving a review on the site that you bought it from. If you purchased the book from Amazon, please leave us an honest review on this book's Amazon page. This is vital so that other potential readers can see and use your unbiased opinion to make purchasing decisions, we can understand what our customers think about our products, and our authors can see your feedback on the title that they have worked with Packt to create. It will only take a few minutes of your time, but is valuable to other potential customers, our authors, and Packt. Thank you!

Index

Printed in Great Britain
by Amazon